SAGE was founded in 1965 by Sara Miller McCune to support the dissemination of usable knowledge by publishing innovative and high-quality research and teaching content. Today, we publish over 900 journals, including those of more than 400 learned societies, more than 800 new books per year, and a growing range of library products including archives, data, case studies, reports, and video. SAGE remains majority-owned by our founder, and after Sara's lifetime will become owned by a charitable trust that secures our continued independence.

Los Angeles | London | New Delhi | Singapore | Washington DC | Melbourne

Advance Praise

'In *Enterprise-wide Coaching: The Ten Commandments,* John Hoover continues to advocate applying the craft of coaching through an organizational lens to maximize the value and benefits of coaching for both Your client leaders being coached and the entire enterprise. Dr Hoover advocates and explains how taking a strategic approach to coaching executives requires a systems perspective. John's book will prepare executive coaches and those who manage coaching functions in organizations to use the 11 Core Competencies of the International Coach Federation (ICF) to align what individual leaders do best with what their organizations need most—all in a cultural context that will ensure coaching consistency and continuity wherever in the world the coaching takes place'.

—Damian Goldvarg PhD, Master Certified Coach (MCC),
Certified Speaker Professional (CSP)
President, The Goldvarg Consulting Group, Inc.
Former Global President (2013 and 2014), International
Coach Federation

'John Hoover and *Enterprise-wide Coaching: The Ten Commandments* are planting a flag in the ground for taking a systems approach to coaching across global enterprises to strengthen the fabric of their leadership tapestries'.

—Paulette Rao, MCC, Board Certified Coach (BCC)
Author of *Transformational Coaching: Shifting Mindsets for Sustainable Change* and *Conscious Marketing: Marketing from the Inside Out*

'Implementing leadership coaching interventions in corporations requires large investment in terms of money and time for planning, execution and monitoring. However, the desired outcome from such coaching engagements often does not translate into results at the desired level since the organization could not derive significant benefits from its large investment. The reasons could be many, and hence it cannot be generalized in defining critical success factors for such engagements for different types of organizations. However, Dr John Hoover's latest book *Enterprise-wide Coaching: The Ten Commandments* rightly identifies the missing link. On the basis of his vast experience in organizational transformation through executive coaching, along with a strong academic background in behavioural science and experience of cutting-edge practices in human resource functions, Dr Hoover strongly advocates making the organization a co-client in coaching engagements to ensure the voices of both the leader and the organization are heard and honoured in coaching engagements. This book is a great resource for organizations with a strong belief that leadership coaching is not a one-off event but needs to be conducted enterprise-wide. I am confident that the reader of this book will gain new insights on how to effectively deploy coaching throughout the enterprise as well as challenge some of the dysfunctional processes'.

—**Dr Sraban Mukherjee, Certified Professional Co-Active Coach (CPCC), Professional Certified Coach (PCC)**
Author of *Corporate Coaching: The Essential Guide* and *Competency Mapping for Superior Results: Getting Maximum from Your Talent*

'Innovation is both essential and messy. Disruptive professional coaching for leaders inside organizational systems is innovation. Dr Hoover's book cogently describes the reason coaching is hard to be explicitly clear about as a standalone professional practice. A focus on the nature of human development for leaders means we must consider the systemic influences upon an individual leader and his or her teams. The organization is the first client, the individual leader candidate for coaching is the second client and the system-wide relationships for that leader are the third client. The discipline of coaching is rigorous and sustaining the role of a coach requires tenacity rather than presuming to know more than the leader of the organizational system about what serves the strategy and performance outcomes best. This book provides clarity about the purpose, the scope and the process of coaching partnerships when effective, as well as a direct pathway for organizational leaders to create a generative partnership with dedicated and professional practitioners'.

—Janet Harvey, MA, MCC, Accredited
Coaching Supervisor (ACS)
Former Global President of International Coach
Federation and Founder of Invite Change

'Contextual coaching clearly positions the organization and the individual as co-clients with equal responsibilities as well as potential gains. In an increasingly complex world, this collaborative approach most efficiently maximizes the benefits of a coaching engagement and provides a framework for an ethical partnership with the coaching provider. Dr Hoover's model offers his substantive, well-grounded and systemic approach in straightforward language with clear reasoning and specific tools'.

—Francine Campone, EdD, MCC
Director, Evidence-Based Coaching, Fielding Graduate
University and Principal, F. Campone Coaching & Consulting

ENTERPRISE-WIDE
COACHING

Thank you for choosing a SAGE product!
If you have any comment, observation or feedback,
I would like to personally hear from you.

Please write to me at **contactceo@sagepub.in**

Vivek Mehra, Managing Director and CEO, SAGE India.

Bulk Sales

SAGE India offers special discounts
for purchase of books in bulk.
We also make available special imprints
and excerpts from our books on demand.

For orders and enquiries, write to us at

Marketing Department
SAGE Publications India Pvt Ltd
B1/I-1, Mohan Cooperative Industrial Area
Mathura Road, Post Bag 7
New Delhi 110044, India

E-mail us at **marketing@sagepub.in**

Get to know more about SAGE

Be invited to SAGE events, get on our mailing list.
Write today to **marketing@sagepub.in**

This book is also available as an e-book.

ENTERPRISE-WIDE
COACHING

THE TEN
COMMANDMENTS

JOHN HOOVER

Los Angeles | London | New Delhi
Singapore | Washington DC | Melbourne

First published in 2018 by

SAGE Publications India Pvt Ltd
B1/I-1 Mohan Cooperative Industrial Area
Mathura Road, New Delhi 110 044, India
www.sagepub.in

SAGE Publications Inc
2455 Teller Road
Thousand Oaks, California 91320, USA

SAGE Publications Ltd
1 Oliver's Yard, 55 City Road
London EC1Y 1SP, United Kingdom

SAGE Publications Asia-Pacific Pte Ltd
3 Church Street
#10-04 Samsung Hub
Singapore 049483

Published by Vivek Mehra for SAGE Publications India Pvt Ltd, typeset in 11/14 Californian FB by Fidus Design Pvt. Ltd., Chandigarh and printed at Saurabh Printers Pvt Ltd, Greater Noida.

Library of Congress Cataloging-in-Publication Data
Name: Hoover, John, author.
Title: Enterprise-wide coaching: the ten commandments / John Hoover.
Description: Thousand Oaks, California: SAGE, 2018.
Identifiers: LCCN 2017057818 (print) | LCCN 2017059183 (ebook) | ISBN 9789352806447 (E-Book) |
    ISBN 9789352806430 (pbk: alk. paper)
Subjects: LCSH: Executive coaching. | Organizational behavior. | Leadership.
Classification: LCC HD30.4 (ebook) | LCC HD30.4 .H665 2018 (print) | DDC 658.4/07124—dc23
LC record available at https://lccn.loc.gov/2017057818

ISBN: 978-93-528-0643-0 (PB)

SAGE Team: Manisha Mathews, Sandhya Gola, Ashmita Ahuja and Ritu Chopra

Contents

Prologue

For more than two decades, I have been in the challenging and exciting space of building my own enterprise, while at the same time providing Fortune 500 enterprises with subject-matter experts in leadership development and coaching, human capital consulting and career transition coaching and consulting. The same organizational issues that face my client organizations are challenges to me and my team at Partners International. For more than 20 years, as the Founder and CEO of Partners International, I have been battling inertia, entropy and other challenges that impede the forward motion and growth of my organization in a parallel effort with helping client enterprises battle similar impediments and accomplish similar goals.

What has become immutably apparent through study, reflection and palpable experience in the field is that organizations are systems and prove out the principles of systems theory over and over again. Small, simple systems and large, complex systems are alike, and the same rules apply to them along a scalable continuum. Agility and, ultimately, sustainable profitability are products of leadership transparency and trust in organizational leadership. Without enterprise-wide consistency and continuity in leadership behaviour, the long-term success of any organization is at risk. For this reason, we have labelled the framework and the process we use to coach leaders and teams around the world through Partners International as 'contextual coaching'.

Dr John Hoover has played a pre-eminent role for more than 10 years at Partners International, identifying and refining how to coach leaders and teams with a systemic approach that simultaneously and symbiotically produces benefits for the individual leader being coached and the organization sponsoring the coaching. As Andrea Chester, Dr Michael Valentine and David Saias continue to champion organization-focused coaching for Partners International, increasing numbers of organizational leadership development policymakers around the world are seeking to achieve better alignment between their investments in leadership development and their global strategic agendas.

My hope is that Dr Hoover's book will help you better understand and finally achieve what the aforementioned leadership development policymakers are experiencing as they establish and maintain internal and external coaching structures and practices that generate impressive returns on their leadership coaching investments on both individual leaders and entire organizations.

Amy Friedman
CEO and Founder
Partners in Human Resources International

Foreword
Global Standards and Global Partners

Foreword to the Foreword by John Hoover, PhD, Professional Certified Coach (PCC)

The CEO and Executive Director of the International Coach Federation (ICF), Magdalena Mook, has been gracious in expanding on the concept of credentialing and the importance of global standards in the coaching industry and contributing those thoughts to this book. Coaching is a field where life and business coaching practitioners can, and often do, proclaim themselves to be masters of the craft without corroboration of an external, independent, non-profit credentialing body such as ICF. In the quest for defining what professionalism, or at least adherence to rigorous standards, truly looks like, Magdalena, on behalf of ICF, is leading the charge to bring such rigour to the coaching industry. While there are other external, independent, non-profit credentialing bodies out there, ICF has the largest and most far-reaching membership around the world, as well as perhaps the most rigorous threshold for credentialing coaches.

Although ICF currently credentials coaches without distinction between life, business or executive coaches, the Federation is well-positioned to be the standard bearer for owning the space around business or executive coaching as well as beginning to identify and define nuances and/or specialized areas of focus in preparing coaches as business and executive coaching practitioners. That being said, the case for standards is an important conversation and one I am grateful Magdalena was willing to articulate as part of this book.

Enterprise-wide Coaching is not specifically about standards and practices in coaching as much as it is about framing executive coaching in the cultural and organizational context of the organization sponsoring the coaching engagements. As far as Magdalena weighing in on standards, it is important to put a stake in the ground and commit ourselves as an industry to becoming increasingly responsible and accountable in the years ahead. Even as we push back boundaries and creatively deepen awareness more than ever before, coaching must not go backwards when it comes to rigour and pursuit of excellence.

The number of organizations that require ICF credentials for both their internal and external coaches has grown significantly in the past decade, but not evenly. The number of for-profit and anti-profit corporations in the public and private sectors requiring ICF certification is now growing at a rate that eclipses previous years. The wisdom of having standards, especially around ethics in coaching, is spreading as organizational decision-makers demand more of a return on their coaching spends and appreciably improved leadership and organizational performance *across the entire enterprise.* Having rigour, consistency and continuity across the field of coaching and across simple and complex organizations is a move forward. Not having them is a step backwards. Having standards at all is forward motion. Having *unified* standards is a leap forward. ICF's mission is to enhance the practice of coaching no matter where it takes place around the world. The promise of this book is to enhance the practice of coaching and bring rigour, consistency among internal and external coaches, and continuity to coaching across all corporate systems, no matter where the coaching is taking place—in the local organization, in the world or in both. As Magdalena and her ICF colleagues as well as contemporaries from other credentialing bodies and academic institutions work to make coaching a more consistent value worldwide, the quality of practitioners will elevate and the results of their coaching will become increasingly powerful.

Author's note: In Magdalena's defence, or perhaps for her protection, this book (outside of her contribution) can be decidedly edgy (at times approaching snarkiness) when describing the self-appointed and self-anointed masters of the coaching universe with accountability to no one. Magdalena is a gracious leader who can be edgy in a progressive way when appropriate, but never in a snarky sort of way. So, please understand that any rapier wit concerning stoic, Freudian-appearing, beard-stroking coaches does not necessarily reflect Magdalena's opinion. Those opinions belong to the edgy author. And with that proviso, Magdalena writes the following.

GLOBAL STANDARDS AND GLOBAL PARTNERS: WHY THEY MATTER?

The coaching field has been developing and evolving rapidly over the last several decades. The number of professional coaches continues to increase steadily, as does awareness of coaching. Increased awareness has led to expanded use of coaching by individuals and organizations alike. This is good news.

The bad news is that the marketplace is becoming increasingly crowded to the point that organizational sponsors of coaching and prospective coaching clients may get confused when making their purchasing decisions. There are so many practitioners that claim to provide the highest quality of service and best outcomes, how does one evaluate competing—and sometimes contradictory—statements and determine which claims are accurate, which are examples of creative marketing and which are downright untrue? Minus regulation, how can consumers evaluate quality, make an educated decision and end up with the right coach for themselves and/or their organizations?

CREDENTIALS AND ACCREDITATION

This is where standards and quality assurance come into play. Recognized standard-setting organizations provide value on a global basis. Perhaps the best-known example is the International Organization for Standardization (ISO), an independent, non-governmental body composed of representatives from more than 160 national standards organizations around the globe.

In the field of higher education, universities are accredited by regional accreditation organizations to ensure consistency and quality. Individual colleges within a university can also be accredited by discipline-specific bodies. For example, in the United States, medical schools and osteopathic schools are accredited by the Liaison Committee on Medical Education and the Commission on Osteopathic College Accreditation, respectively, while business colleges may pursue accreditation from the Association to Advance Collegiate Schools of Business.

In the field of coaching, ICF endeavours to fill the need for training and education standards as well as individual knowledge and skills benchmarks. Utilizing the ICF definition of coaching, Code of Ethics and Core Competencies as a basis, ICF has created standards to ensure consistency in training, education and learning outcomes on a global basis. The development of this body of knowledge, as verified by job analysis, allowed for creation of a credentialing process for individual coach practitioners and accreditation for coach-training programmes.

Coaching is becoming the primary instrument for aligning individual executive strengths with strategic organizational needs in the cultural context of organizations. Therefore, the coaches must come to the engagements sharing a consistent foundation in training, standards and ethics. Layer on top of that an alignment framework that connects individual coaching engagements and the corporate strategic agenda, and coaching, as a leadership development power tool, grows from a leadership *suggestion* or a *fix* to an enterprise-wide leadership *solution.*

It all begins with coaching competence. Personnel certification/credentialing has become an important element of verifying the competence of an increasingly mobile, global and virtual workforce, underscoring the value of industry-recognized credentials that can be carried across national borders and organizational brands. Credentials are necessary in part because they establish boundaries and criteria that contribute to a common understanding of a product or service, defining what it does and what it stands for. The aforementioned foundation is a concrete mixture of coaching competence and credentials, solid and strong to support leaders through their most challenging transitions.

WHY ICF?

As an independent, not-for-profit credentialing and accreditation body, ICF exists in service to the coaching industry and to consumers of coaching. This means that the organization's policies and processes around credentialing and accreditation are governed by a single question: 'Will this enhance the quality of services and integrity of the coaching profession?' The mission of the ICF's credentialing programme is to:

1. Protect and serve consumers of coaching services
2. Measure and certify competence of individual practitioners
3. Inspire pursuit of continuous development

To this end, the ICF focuses on ensuring that coaches holding an ICF credential are professionally trained practitioners who have met stringent education and client experience requirements and demonstrated a thorough understanding and application of the coaching competencies that set the standard in the profession.

As of October 2017, more than 23,000 individuals in 130 countries held an ICF credential, demonstrating the designation's truly global reach. This number will only continue to grow, with more than 5,000 individuals choosing to begin the application process for an ICF credential in the past 12 months.

To ensure quality and consistency in coaching education, ICF has accredited more than 500 programmes offering coach-specific training. These programmes have submitted their curriculums for review, and they were found in alignment with ICF's Code of Ethics, definition of coaching and Core Competencies for coaches. These programmes and their leaders are also obliged to follow ICF's stringent Code of Conduct for training. For a credential to be a true measure of knowledge and skills, it must be independent of any specific course or of any specific provider and said course or provider's agenda. This is part of what sets ICF's credentialing programme apart—in addition to being truly global, it is truly independent.

COACHING ETHICS

As the field of professional coaching evolves, one must pay attention to all the facets of the system. Arguably, one of the crucial elements of ICF standards is its Code of Ethics, which functions in conjunction with the organization's Ethical Conduct Review and Program Complaint processes. The Code's purpose is to promote professional and ethical coaching practices and to raise awareness of ethical coaching practices outside the industry as well as raise *accountability* inside the coaching industry.

The ICF Code of Ethics is a living and evolving document. It is reviewed every three years to ensure that it truly reflects the reality of the coaching marketplace for coach practitioners and the clients alike. The increasing popularity of coaching in organizations brought about many changes to the ICF Code of Ethics in July 2015. These changes included adding the definition of a sponsor, specific references to internal and external coaches and expanded language around coaching agreements and confidentiality. The Ethical Conduct Review process provides a venue where individuals can bring complaints about alleged breaches of the Code by ICF members and credential holders. ICF provides for the review, investigation and response to alleged unethical practices or behaviour deviating from the established ICF Code for practitioners and ICF-accredited training programmes. The 2013 ICF Organizational Coaching Study by PwC revealed that confidentiality remains top-of-mind for organizations using coaching and ethical standards and are of the utmost importance for external and internal coach selection.

RECOGNIZING EXCELLENCE

Since 2005, ICF's International Prism Award programme (originally an ICF Chapter initiative developed by ICF Toronto) has celebrated the achievements of organizations around the globe that use coaching to achieve extraordinary results. Dozens of ICF Chapters also offer local Prism Award programmes to celebrate organizations in their communities that have built strong coaching cultures.

The Prism Award criteria and selection process have been refined for more than a decade to better position the International Prism Award as the gold standard for organizations that coach their leaders. Rigorous professional standards are the hallmark of ICF Prism Awards, addressing and accounting for key strategic goals, organizational culture and discernible and measurable positive impacts.

Every year a growing number of companies apply for Prism Award recognition, indicating broader appreciation and application of coaching in organizations as well as increased willingness of organizational coaching sponsors and champions to share their success stories.

Recent ICF Prism Awards recognized the following organizations:

AFCC (Automotive Fuel Cell Cooperation) (2017 Global Winner)

EY (Ernst & Young) (2017 Honorable Mention)

GlaxoSmithKline (2016 Global Winner)

Beyond Emancipation (2016 Honorable Mention)

Coca-Cola HBC Russia (2016 Honorable Mention)

Previous Prism Award honourees included Rogers Communications, Banner Health, Roche Turkey, United Nations Secretariat, NASA and the University of Texas at Dallas—to mention just a few. Prism reflects ICF's expanding commitment to the same cultural and organizational focus that *contextual coaching* is committed to: recognizing and enhancing people, performance and profitability in organizations as cooperative, collegial and collaborative collectives of individuals.

CONCLUDING THOUGHTS TO LAUNCH THE BOOK

Now more than ever, it is crucial for leaders in organizations to have access to tools and information that allow them to make informed and sound decisions around coaching engagements. As the standard-setting organization for the coaching profession, ICF provides organizations with valuable tools for establishing strong coaching cultures, a clear definition of coaching, Core Competencies, a Code of Ethics and a system for accreditation and credentialing that empowers organizational decision-makers to confidently make informed and strategic purchasing decisions. ICF has also invested significant resources in research and thought leadership around coaching in organizations. This book is an evidence of that.

With ICF members in more than 130 countries, the organization has access to data and input concerning coaching from every corner of the world. The research conducted with individuals and organizations allows us to observe the evolution of and anticipate trends in application of coaching best practices. Partnering with other organizations and academic institutions provides insight into the role coaching plays in their long-term, strategic visions. An independent partner, such as ICF, provides a place not only for gathering of information and gaining knowledge, but also for constructive and innovative creation of new solutions and new thinking about the future of coaching and its impact in the world and across any enterprise.

Magdalena N. Mook
CEO and Executive Director, ICF

Acknowledgements

There are many people to thank for their tireless work to bring executive coaching into focus through an organization development lens. Amy Friedman, of course, the Founder and current CEO of Partners in Human Resources International[1] has been pursuing a true balance in individual and organizational growth and development for more than a decade. She explains her role in this campaign in the Prologue (given earlier). Suffice to say that none of this would be happening were it not for Amy's leadership. Working closely with Amy are Andrea Chester, who now leads the global contextual coaching practice at Partners International, and her boss, Partners International Managing Director, David Saias. Partners International Thought Leader, Dr Michael Valentine, carries the torch and improves on past successes and best practices when coaching leaders all the while developing teams is taking a systems approach.

I was introduced to SAGE by my colleague and friend Dr Sraban Mukherjee, author of *Corporate Coaching: The Essential Guide*, and numerous other publications. I have been encouraged and inspired by leaders in the coaching industry too numerous to mention. My short gratitude list must include Dr Damian Goldvarg and Janet Harvey, former Global Chairs of International Coach Federation, and my classmates at the Coaching Supervision Academy. Magdalena Mook, Executive Director and Global CEO

---

[1] See www.partners-international.com

of International Coach Federation, wrote the Foreword to this book. I am a huge fan of Magda and owe a great deal to her for her support and encouragement.

Finally, as I skip over the names of numerous notable people there simply isn't room to mention, I would be negligent not to mention Dr Paul Gorrell who was the seminal thinker behind what is now called contextual coaching. Meryl Moritz, MCC (Master Certified Coach), Paulette Rao, MCC (who brought me in to teach coaching in the Advanced Diploma in Coaching programme at New York University [NYU]) and Dr Anna Tavis (who brought me in to teach coaching in the Human Resource Leadership Masters programme at NYU). All are heroes to me. Leni Wildflower, who originally introduced me to the Evidence-Based Coaching programme at Fielding Graduate University, Francine Campone, who now leads this highly successful programme at Fielding, Dr Katrina Rogers, President of Fielding Graduate University, and Dr Judy Stevens-Long and Dr Marcella Benson-Quaziena, who hired me to teach for the master's degree in organizational development and leadership at Fielding, are all life changers.

My colleague, Laurie Kelley, who made the introduction that got me hired to coach MBA candidates at Yale School of Management, continues to be a great friend and colleague. To supportive friends like Gayle Kennedy-Hill, John Shalhoub, Bill Schubert, Chris Cooper, Alan Morlend, Paul Keenan, Howard and Beezie Davis: thank you. To new friends such as Ron Moser, Francis and Heidi Benjamin, and Steve Stone; doing what I do is much more enjoyable knowing the likes of you.

In closing, editorial staff makes the world go around and my Editor from SAGE truly made this book happen. Also, the Production Editor kept me accountable and accurate in the final stages of production. Thanks beyond measure to the SAGE team.

Part I

ENTERPRISE-WIDE COACHING
The Ten Commandments

> Stop wasting money on executive coaching!
> Shocked to hear that said aloud?
> Good.

It seems like a strange thing for an ICF certified coach and Coaching Supervision Academy graduate who actively supervises a network of over 250 executive coaches around the globe to say when executive coaching can potentially produce enormous value and a sizable return on an organization's coaching spend. However, the latter is true only if the coaching is conducted in a well-orchestrated, deliberate and systematic manner that mindfully aligns what individual leaders do best with what organizations need most. The guiding principles are clear:

1. Executive coaching must produce a benefit for the sponsoring organization that is consistently equal to the benefit for the leader(s) being coached.
2. The leader being coached (coaching client) and the organization must be considered co-clients to ensure that the voices of both the individual leader and the organization are heard and honoured in coaching engagements.
3. In order to gain enterprise-wide value from coaching, data from all coaching engagements throughout the organization must be gathered, compiled and analysed to expose patterns, trends, gaps and opportunities in leadership development— all without compromising coaching client confidentiality.

Executive coaching is one of the (if not the) most expensive singular investments organizations make in leadership development. To conduct executive coaching without programmes, processes and protocols in place to rigorously coach through an organizational lens makes as much sense as buying a Mercedes SUV, parking it in your driveway and only using it to store lawn fertilizer.

Hauling gardening supplies is one use for a high-end SUV. But to only use the SUV to store supplies after transporting them from the Home Depot and never to perform any of the other functions an expensive motor vehicle is designed and engineered to perform is wasting money on the SUV. If 'wasting money' seems too harsh, soften it to 'partial return on investment (ROI)'.

Yet conducting executive coaching engagements as individual, disassociated, unrelated and non-aligned, one-off assignments with nothing to guarantee alignment, continuity and cultural consistency is the most common way organizations currently conduct their coaching operations. Let us hope by the time the copyright on this book is five years old, the prior statement will no longer be true.

Enterprise-wide coaching is a blueprint for coaching in the full context of complex for-profit, not-for-profit and governmental organizations. It is also a roadmap for moving from an organization's current state of executive coaching to an advanced and enhanced state of organization development with coaching as the catalytic engine for transformation.

Hopefully, coaching in your organization is enterprise wide. But is it also enterprise-*wise*? Is there truly knowledge, experience and even passion around aligning what leaders do best with what organizations need most and, moreover, creating systems of accountability for coaching practitioners and the emerging or established leaders they coach.

Compared to US practices of law, psychology, medicine, accounting, selling insurance, financial advising and a host of other professions, coaching of any type remains officially unregulated with no state, federal or mandatory oversight in sight. Although we use the term loosely, coaching is not technically a 'profession' because, by definition, a profession requires special education or training, has a governing body to regulate practitioners, has a licensure that declares practitioners competent to practise and/or has a universal set of standards for practitioners to comply with and credentials to maintain through continuing education. In short, in an industry where no licences are issued, licences cannot be revoked. More credentials are required of a 5th grade teacher in US public schools than of someone being paid an obscene amount of money to coach the CEO of a powerful, global corporation.

Organizations need a way to create rigour, consistency and continuity, and enact standards for the coaching of their emerging and established leaders. Coaching certificate programmes the world over are graduating a steady stream of life coaches; although there is generally no distinction between life and executive coaches. Research commissioned by Magdalena's ICF and conducted by PricewaterhouseCoopers LLP places the number of coach practitioners worldwide at approximately 53,300. These coaches are responsible for an industry that totals approximately US$2.3 billion in annual revenue. Globally, active coach practitioners report average annual income from coaching of US$51,000; it's notable that both globally and within each world region, these annual revenues can vary considerably. More likely, by invoking turn of the (twentieth) century economist, Vilfredo Pareto, 20 per cent of practicing coaches earn 80 per cent of the US$2.3 billion and vice versa.

Regardless of how it is sliced and diced, coaching has reached critical mass as at least a micro industry yet cannot legitimately call itself a profession. Likewise, academic training or regulatory preparation has only recently begun through institutions of higher learning such as New York University (NYU) and Fielding Graduate University for those on the corporate side who hire coaches and manage coaching engagements in a way that deliberately aligns the growth and development needs of individual coaching clients with the strategic agendas of their organizations. *Enterprise-wide Coaching* will be required reading.

Enterprise-wide Coaching introduces organizational coaching function managers and the coaches they hire and manage to theories, methods and techniques enabling them to design and structure organizational coaching functions through an organization development lens, thus ensuring that coaching engagements, which are sponsored and paid for by an organization for the purpose of developing, correcting or enhancing management and/ or leadership skills and behaviours in individuals and groups, will be contextually aligned with the sponsoring organization's talent, leadership and global business strategy and will produce maximum and mutual ROI for individuals or groups receiving coaching in addition to the sponsoring organization.

As Magdalena Mook pointed out in the Foreword, even in this day and age, many people (even on the corporate side) think they are buying coaching and are instead receiving consulting, mentoring, counselling or all-of-the-above and do not know the difference. Our coaching industry is on a steep learning curve and the educators and corporate consumers of coaching need to be running, not strolling, towards advanced knowledge of the craft of coaching as well as coaching's proper place in leadership development.

Contextual Coaching Commandment

Coach in the Context of the Organization

C ontextual coaching means coaching in the context of the organization or, if you prefer, coaching through an organizational lens. As mentioned in the introduction, it means aligning what leaders do best with what the organization needs most. Enterprise-wide alignment between leadership development, of which executive coaching is the purest form, and corporate strategy is critical to successful executive development, not to mention optimal execution of the organization's most pressing organizational needs.

Without compromising any of the confidentiality, craft and reflective practice that help make executive coaching the most powerful (and expensive) individual leadership development intervention available, elevating the voice and presence of the organization in coaching engagements is essential to maximizing the value of the organization's coaching investment.

If the goal of executive coaching is to build leaders who will build businesses, the approach to developing leaders, whatever it is, must be framed in the context of the organization so that the cultural, corporate and contextual needs of the business are never excluded from executive coaching conversations. The symbiotic relationship between individual leaders and the organizations that employ them must be defined and documented in the context of the collective. If organizations that sponsor executive coaching engagements hope to maximize enterprise-wide value and benefits from developing their leaders, the leadership development processes, protocols and guiding principles must align with, and thereby advance, the strategic agenda of the organization. In short, the coaching must be enterprise-*wide* and enterprise-*wise*.

Traditional, ad hoc executive coaching engagements that are not contextually aligned with the strategic agenda of the organization are inherently myopic. In other words, they are inherently enterprise-*blind*. The leader being coached might become a better person or a better leader, but to what end and in what context? The odds are poor that a broader organizational agenda will be well served by executive coaching, strategic team alignment or any leadership development activity when executive coaches' or group process facilitators' peripheral visions are too narrow to see the full organizational spectrum. Chances are slight and mostly coincidental that detached and isolated leadership development activities—especially executive coaching—will add significant enterprise-wide value. There is no reason they shouldn't add value across the organization. In fact, coaching that does not add enterprise-wide value equal to the individual value to the leader being coached is, at best, a partially wasted investment and opportunity.

TEN ORGANIZATIONAL LENSES

Each of the ten commandments of contextual coaching describes a dimension of coaching through an organizational lens. To establish the organizational context within which the contextually aligned coaching will take place, talent strategy designers must establish:

1. Criteria for selecting, training and supervising executive coaches
2. Enterprise frameworks within which coaching engagements take place

3. Reporting and data analysis processes and procedures to ensure coaching consistency, alignment with the sponsoring organization's strategic agenda and data mining opportunities

CRITERIA FOR COACHES: WAGGING THE DOG

Historically—you will hear that word a lot throughout this book to calibrate how executive coaching got to be much of what it is today—organizations historically began employing coaches to improve sales performance, management and leadership performance, and a variety of other functions. This mostly dates back to the 1990s, although it was happening to a lesser degree long before that. Perhaps as many as 50 years before according to some. Coaching did not really catch fire until the 1990s and then accelerated into the millennium. The great Wall Street house-of-cards collapse of 2008 nearly did to executive coaching what Mrs O'Leary's cow did to Chicago in 1871. Executive coaching was growing like a forest fire in high winds and dry timber before the backfire of 2008 nearly extinguished it.

Some of those other functions coaches were hired to address involved conflict resolution, transforming mean bosses into nice bosses and helping high-performing subordinates remain high-performing despite their mean bosses. Helping geeky executives transform into slick and polished executives was another biggie—exposing a shortage of coaches who could speak Geek. Coaching to improve communication skills, develop executive presence, round off sharp elbows, stop inappropriately touching and leering at employees ... the list was and continues to be long.

From the perspective of someone with more than 25 years' experience in executive coaching under his belt and over 10 years' experience supervising hundreds of executive coaches and strategic team alignment facilitators worldwide as a premium provider of coaching services to nearly half of the Fortune 500, the landscape does not look much different for coaching than it did a decade ago—except that there are exponentially more coaches in the marketplace. We are seeing an increase in demand for coaching emerging leaders as well as established leaders, but the coaching budgets favour the established leaders and, even then, especially when there is a desire to correct behaviour—as in executives behaving badly.

There are basically two types of executive coaching: (a) developmental, in which the desire is to truly get an emerging or established leader better prepared for enhanced and expanded leadership responsibilities and (b) corrective, in which something about someone has come off the rails and the organization has a vested interest in getting the executive back on track. This is particularly popular when the executive is a high producer and the organization needs the revenue train back up to speed as soon as possible. Most organizations are willing to pay a boatload of money to get a senior executive's behaviour modified, especially when the current behaviour has become noisy, abusive or a contact sport. Coaches are also tasked, albeit not that often, to keep the firm out of court or mitigate any settlement.

Stipulating that, except for the immediate preceding, the aforementioned is for the most part true of coaching in the vast majority of organizations and the use of coaches as adult supervision for executives behaving badly (some a little badly/some legally actionable) or as a charm school for geeks is as common today as it was in the 1990s—when the likes of Thomas Leonard and Janet Harvey were founding the ICF—and even years before that.

The earlier historical reference is more of a reminder that coaches are still selected and vetted by many organizations to coach their executives much in the same way they were selected and vetted 20 years ago. When middle-level human resource (HR) managers were, and often still are, in charge of recruiting and hiring coaches for top-of-the-house executives, they only want to be convinced that a coach will provide trustworthy and reliable adult supervision for misbehaving executives or provide adequate, hopefully competent, support for emerging and established leaders who need special developmental attention. Since there is no governance over the coaching industry, like there is over mental health practitioners, lawyers, accountants, financial advisors, doctors, dentists and even puppy day care providers, it was up to the corporate coaching head to somehow be convinced of the coach's competence.

Where a coach went to school, what degrees a coach earned, the type of real P&L business experience a coach had, if there had been some sort of formal coach training (more common now than 10 years ago), if the coach dressed appropriately and had clean fingernails—were part of the criteria used to determine if someone *should* be able to coach an executive, or at least keep the executive out of trouble. References always helped and still do. Case studies are common requests in coach interviews (although they are self-created by the coaches and as Benjamin Franklin said, 'One is never nearer perfection than on a job application'—or words to that effect). People hiring coaches for corporate executive coaching, even if they were high-level executives themselves, went mostly with their gut reactions. Why not? Considering the statistical probabilities that a newly hired executive will last somewhere around three years, most hiring decisions appear indeed to be made somewhere in the intestinal region.

While a growing number of organizations are developing well-thought-out, sophisticated and structured criteria, processes and procedures to ensure that the external and internal coaches they employ are highly competent practitioners, the vast majority of organizational policymakers do not include contextual alignment in that vetting. Contextual alignment means ensuring that the executive coaches will be naturally inclined, hopefully, trained and educated in the craft of contextual alignment between leaders and organizations. A great global business strategy begins with a great global talent strategy. A great coaching strategy is at the core of that reactor.

Contrast to the growing sophistication of coach selection and vetting with old-school HR managers, inexperienced in the ways of coaching, doing what many rational people would do if they do not know what constitutes a good coach or good coaching, it is easy to see how the tail came to wag the dog. Remember to this day there is no universal governance on coaching. So anybody who wants to be a coach can call themselves a coach, hang out a shingle, put up a website and charge what the market will bear. Unless something is said in a coaching conversation that leads someone to sue for actionable damages in a court of law, there are few boundaries.

Imagine a world where mental health practitioners, lawyers, accountants, financial advisors, doctors, dentists and even puppy day care providers are not required by law to carry liability insurance to indemnify themselves against legal accusations (real or imagined) from their clients. It will never happen. Coaches, unlike licensed mental health professionals, are not required to carry indemnification insurance at all except from time-to-time by deep-pocket corporations who hire coaches and want somebody else sitting beside them behind the defendants' table if anything involved with executive coaching should land in court.

And so, the people placed in charge of hiring coaches and running the coaching programmes in organizations of all sizes, wanting to learn the best criteria for hiring coaches, asked the ones they thought would know best, the coaches, how coaching works and how coaching engagements should be conducted. That is not unlike asking a pirate where the best place is to hide your jewellery so the pirate won't be able to find and steal it from you. I am taking some licence with my portrayal of coaches because I am one and thereby have some latitude. More importantly, the essence of this story is true.

Imagine a gaggle of overstarched and overimpressed (with themselves) master coaches (no reference to ICF, which actually have rigorous standards in place before awarding the designation of Master Certified Coach) stroking their beards and nodding their heads in contemplation. 'First of all, you turn your executives over to us, at which point they become coachees. The executives' power and rank mean nothing to us, they are now little people whom we will help to become radically transformed into the image we have created for them'.

Sidebar moment here: The term 'coachee' came from who knows where. But it clearly implies a disparity of power, knowledge, wisdom or all of these. Think of other word pairs. A trainer has a distinct knowledge advantage over a trainee. A mentor has a distinct experience advantage over a mentee. An employer has a distinct power advantage over an employee. A helper must have something the helpee needs. It would follow then that a coach has an advantage of some sort over a coachee. Indeed, that advantage might and should be knowledge, skill and awareness of how the craft of coaching is intended to help the executive coaching client become more self-aware and organizationally aware en route to becoming a better, more self-aware and organizationally aware, savvy and effective leader.

But executive coaching is a heuristic, emergent process of becoming increasingly self-aware and organizationally aware. And, through it, the coaching client becomes increasingly empowered to make better decisions, present himself or herself better and more appropriately as an executive, and a host of other improvements—none of which play out as a disparity of power. Coaching clients are empowered from day one to fire their coaches. ICF and a host of other organizations who play in the coaching space or are consumers of executive coaching have long since abandoned the derogatory term 'coachee' in favour of 'coaching client', 'client', 'participant', 'leader (being coached)', 'learner' and other more empowered monikers. Organizations of no less stature than Hogan have officially abandoned the term 'coachee' in favour of 'coaching candidate'.

'Coachee' implies some sort of disparity, no matter how you slice it. Organizations and skilled coaching practitioners are recognizing it, and the term is fading into history where it belongs along with flogging and bloodletting. End of sidebar.

And so, the overstarched coaches told their eager-to-learn HR managers how they take their coachees away to some remote location, draw a cloak of secrecy around them, lower a cone of confidentiality to cover them and work a mysterious, almost magical prestidigitational process with their little people, bringing the coachees back to the organization in, say, two or three years, as radically transformed human beings. Radically transformed into what exactly, who knew? The self-proclaimed master coaches' self-designed jobs were to mess with people's little heads and collect a lot of cheques.

You would be surprised how many heads of corporate coaching practices nod and nod and nod when that (tongue-only-slightly-in-cheek) story is told in workshops or at conferences. Why such a brutal portrayal? Because the one-client approach to executive coaching is like making a Stepford Wife. The way to derive the greatest value from executive coaching, which is being paid for by the organization, is to treat the organization and the leader being coached as co-clients and not the creation of a Stepford executive in search of a place to be productive.

A whole chapter awaits on treating the leader being coached and the organization paying for the coaching as co-clients. For now, be aware that there are still overstarched and over-(self)-rated coaches who do not care about, have no interest in and have no background or orientation to appreciate the essential symbiotic relationship between the leader being coached and his or her organizational mothership. As every systems-based marriage and family counsellor knows, the client in relationship counselling (as it is in relationship coaching) is not Partner #1 nor is it Partners #1's significant other. The client is the *relationship* between the two that determines each one's success in the context of their organization environment. The leader being coached and the organization sponsoring the coaching are most assuredly co-clients.

It was a great experience recently to sit in a meeting room listening to Hogan representatives discuss reputational scars with dozens of our New York ICF members. Many coaches today are youthful, smart, sharp, knowledgeable, well-trained and full of enthusiasm to help their clients—unlike the old-school, over-starched types I have been describing as an (extreme) example.

Even so, the notion of coaching through an organizational lens as opposed to a strictly individual lens is in its early stages of adoption.

Once a coach becomes aware and accepting, not to mention skilled and effective at coaching the relationships between coaching clients and the organizations that employ them, they lose their starch, restore proper perspective on who they are and the purpose they serve, and devote themselves to the craft of coaching executives. In short, the tail stops wagging the dog. This book is about exactly that: helping all types and levels of managers, directors, vice presidents (VPs) and above understand and appropriately, efficiently and effectively execute their responsibilities to serve the growth and development of executives and their organizations. It is up to internal heads of coaching practices, not the independent or even internal coaches they hire and manage, to ensure the coaching assignments they oversee are contextually aligned, enterprise-*wide* and enterprise-*wise*.

All this work, including nuanced sub-processes, must be based upon and aligned with the sponsoring organization's established leadership development principles, values or competencies. Because any competent global business strategy conversation must begin with competent talent and leadership development strategy conversation, coaching in the context of the organization requires knowing the organization and continuously asking, 'How is this helping the leader being coached and the organization paying for the coaching?' It is not so much that the tail wags the dog or the dog wags the tail, but that the wagging must be a valuable experience for the whole animal.

Enterprise Frameworks Within Which Coaching Engagements Take Place

There is an African proverb that says, 'If you want to run fast, run alone. If you want to run far, run with others'. Speed needs to be light and unencumbered. Covering long distances would seem to require the same qualities. But even without extra weight or encumberment, just the fact that extra distance is required suggests that extra support and encouragement will help. In a corporate environment where there is a symbiotic relationship among individuals and between individuals and the entire organizational population, the mutual support generated can help sustain individual and organization for the long haul and help them successfully struggle through difficult passages.

Shortly, you will see 10 dimensions of organization that can be used as a baseline for establishing an enterprise-wide framework for executive coaching in organizations. The unique and specific growth and development (even corrective) desired outcomes of coaching engagements are the micro focus of an engagement and keep the engagement highly personalized. That is the level at which coaching engagements that are not aligned to the strategic agenda of the organization get stuck. And that isolated, individual work tends to be the complete depth and breadth of their organizational value.

When an organization-wide perspective is introduced, the context changes. Better said, a context is established that deepens and broadens the engagement and delivers exponentially more value to the individual being coached as well as to the organization as a whole. Individual awareness is joined with organizational awareness. The dimensions of organization provide structure as they frame the engagement.

Contextual coaching is not a particular methodology or approach to the craft of coaching such as David Rock's Neuroleadership approach, James Flaherty's Integral Coaching, Adlerian Coaching, Gestalt Coaching, Somatic Coaching or any other specific methodology or technique. Specific techniques or coaching methodologies can all operate inside the contextual framework, thus giving organizational macro context to the micro issues inside the framework of coaching engagements.

When legendary musician Count Basie was asked what the best kind of music is (classical, jazz, contemporary, etc.), he reportedly answered, 'If it sounds good, it is good'. So the coaching methodologies and techniques inside the contextual coaching framework are good if they produce the positive, affirmative and appreciative transformational impact on the leader being coached. What extends that value to the entire organization is the framework that contextually aligns individual gains with enterprise-wide needs.

The 10 generic dimensions of contextual coaching you will find ahead are just that: a generic framework. If your organization has established a set of leadership competencies, then those obviously become the contextual framework for all the coaching across the organization, which, in many cases, means around the world. One of the underlying assumptions here is that the leadership competencies are aligned with the organization's global strategic agenda.

Hopefully so. Otherwise, what is the point of pointing the bow of a leader's ship into a direction that leads him or her away from the organization's global strategic agenda? Is there something to be gained by pointing leaders south when the strategic direction of the organization is north? To use the most clinically sophisticated language: That is just silly.

Some organizations call their leadership competencies leadership values, leadership priorities, leadership disciplines, leadership characteristics or whatever. The point is they have taken the time and effort to accomplish two things: (a) identify what leadership excellence looks like in the context of their organizations and (b) align those leadership competencies, values, priorities, disciplines or characteristics with the organizations' over-arching strategic agenda. This is how the context in contextual coaching is derived and ensures, among other things, consistency and continuity in the coaching across the enterprise and around the world.

REPORTING AND DATA ANALYSIS TO ENSURE COACHING CONSISTENCY, ALIGNMENT WITH THE ORGANIZATION'S STRATEGIC AGENDA AND DATA MINING OPPORTUNITIES

Before looking at the 10 generic dimensions of organization, Commandment 10 is 'No Data Left Behind' and explores the enormous amount of organizational data that is discussed during coaching conversations. Data collection and analysis is briefly mentioned here in Commandment 1 to connect the dots between individual data and organizational data. Better said, to point out how individual data collected in the course of coaching conversations can be rolled up into organizational data with farther-reaching meaning and value.

If the point of contextual coaching is to significantly widen and deepen the impact of executive coaching across the enterprise, the broader value of an individual coaching engagement must be considered. In perhaps a crudely bovine analogy, when an animal is butchered (some say harvested) to prepare the meat for human and non-human consumption, virtually every part of the animal is used in one manner or another so nothing is wasted. The person wearing a leather jacket and shoes made from the hide of the animal might have eaten other parts of the beast for breakfast, lunch or dinner.

In contextual coaching, there are enormous amounts of data discussed in a variety of coaching conversations. With consistent and strategic reporting protocols in place, these individual observations and organizational perspectives are captured in action plans and updates to action plans. All of this without compromising confidentiality since action plans only reveal information that the coaching client (who owns the data) has elected to release. Even so, data from action plans as well as 360-degree-structured interview reports can be parsed to produce overarching themes and patterns that emerge from the data pool without revealing sources or subjects of the interviews or coaching dialogues.

Organizations routinely pay consulting firms obscene amounts of money to conduct selected interviews and focus groups, distribute questionnaires, surveys and fill in boilerplate forms that spit out thick three-ringed binders filled with generic organizational observations. There is no big problem with this approach to organizational analysis, mostly conducted by recent MBA graduates—except for the obscene money thing.

Most organizational decision-makers do not realize that they are already gathering far more intimate, revealing and reliable information about their organizations during coaching conversations. Emphasizing again that, without compromising confidentiality, it is possible to aggregate that data and subject it to analysis in its aggregated form. Unless there is some sort of fee imposed for conducting the analysis and composing a document, this more intimate, revealing and reliable information about organizations is made available for the price the organization is already paying for the coaching. Save the $5,000,000 on your ginormous consulting firm.

The micro data is compiled and combined with macro data, and an organization-wide story emerges from the individual stories that compose individual coaching engagements. As Commandment 10 will deal with it in greater detail, without an enterprise-wide coaching strategy that includes deliberate reporting processes and protocols to capture invaluable data, that data and all it reveals about the health, well-being and competitive potential of the organization, evaporates into the ether. That is when organizational decision-makers retain the services of major consulting firms in an attempt to recreate the lost data. Sorry colossal consulting firms, I believe organizations have better things to do with their millions. Like coaching in organizational context.

At best, the consulting firms produce a poor imitation of the real content captured in coaching engagements. Meanwhile, the contextual coaching reports themselves are strategically designed and deployed to align the micro issues in coaching engagements to the context-defining macro organizational issues ensure continuity and consistency from coaching engagement, to coaching engagement across the organization. Quality control and consistent supervision of coaches in their craft and techniques all fall into the bucket that begins with reporting. If you have never considered the potential enterprise-wide value of a single coaching report, it is time to broaden your thinking—for the sake of the parts and the sake of the whole.

TEN ORGANIZATIONAL LENSES

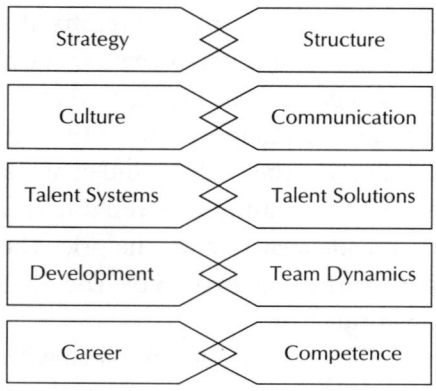

In the absence of specific organizational leadership competencies, values, priorities, disciplines or characteristics like the ones you might have created for your organization, the 10 dimensions of organization listed previously constitute the framework of the contextual coaching engagements discussed throughout this book. In Appendix A at the end of the book, you will see a reference guide of questions and issues to be addressed through contextual coaching and framed in underutilized, overutilized and optimally utilized leadership behaviours.

Strategy

Strategic awareness is essential to success within an organization. Individuals responsible for the performance of others have strategic imperatives that are critical to their positions, just as strategic awareness among managers and executives is essential to individual and organizational success. Without an understanding of and appreciation for the larger organizational, future-focused picture, it is difficult to measure whether or not the ways in which individual goals and strengths are being coached are in the best interests of the organization. We assume they are, but how can we be sure?

The assumption is that any personal growth and development of individuals within organizations is good for the organization. But, as mentioned earlier, that is not always the case, especially if the leader being coached lacks organizational sensitivities and sensibilities.

Coaching that emphasizes the strategic context of the individual's and organization's work life pays exponentially greater dividends than coaching that focuses too narrowly on the individual. The strategic component of contextual coaching increases awareness and sharpens skills around those issues that affect the internal organizational population as well as all outside stakeholders.

Strategy is a concern for individuals at all levels of the organization. For those who operate at the CEO level, setting the overall corporate direction is a key responsibility and an obvious marker of long-term success or failure. C-level individuals need to be visionary and custodial at the same time. They need to look into the future and understand where the organization needs to go in light of trends, market forces and stakeholder aspirations while, at the same time, assuring the preservation of their companies' operational excellence, integrity and preferred position in a volatile market.

Other individuals in the organization also need to fully understand what the overall corporate strategy is and become deft at explaining it to others. They need to develop the ability to represent the vision to other employees and to persuasively articulate its value proposition to win over their fellow team members and gain buy-in. There are undoubtedly localized strategic agendas connected to individual business units or divisions that must also be reconciled while executing aspects of the larger strategy. These sub-strategies help to define the goals for the business units as well as to drive individuals towards organization-wide performance and business results.

If the coaching client is newly hired to the organization, the coaching process can be uniquely helpful. Newly hired individuals have particular challenges in moving into strategic responsibilities and often require assimilation coaching. They might have less experience in determining corporate direction for themselves or their teams. By assisting emerging leaders with strategic planning along with the process of tying their coaching plan to the larger corporate and business unit strategies, the coach further prepares the individual for future roles and helps the emerging leader to effectively integrate the corporate vision at different levels.

Moving from strategy to action, however, can be a challenge for many individuals who are more visionary than transactional in orientation. The contextual coach may therefore assist the coaching client in mapping specific tactics as a means to manage the effective execution of strategic initiatives.

Structure

Depending on the coaching client's level within the organization, the strategy of his or her area of responsibility must roll up and integrate with larger business units and/or the overarching corporate strategy. This invokes the need for enhanced awareness of intentional design and structure. It is critical for the individual coaching process to relate to the structure of the organization to both illustrate and understand how the coaching client's efforts will be blended with (and enhance) the work of others. It must also roll down to the strategic concerns of those who report into the coaching client's area of the business. In pursuit of flawless execution, the organizational structure must be synchronized with the goals and expectations set forth in its strategic plan.

As the contextual coach or the individual responsible for organizational coaching outcomes, you help keep the coaching process organizationally focused by identifying the position of your coaching client within the corporate structure and promote understanding of all the strategies at play. By knowing the reporting relationships, expectations for your coaching client and the team members, and how structural strategies can best be integrated and communicated, you will be able to provide a powerful service to your coaching client and the larger corporate constituencies being served.

When considering the structure of the organization, place emphasis on your coaching client's relationship with the appropriate managing executive as well as critical alliances. Key to your coaching client's success is the relationship to his or her manager(s). Therefore, the manager is a fundamental constituent in this process and will be included in the communication process that surrounds your coaching engagement. The coaching coalition will be discussed further in Commandment 4. Meanwhile, the effective management of this important relationship in your coaching client's work life should deliberately be discussed and monitored throughout the coaching engagement.

Focusing on the organizational structure will also help you to identify the lines of authority and span of control that exist inside your coaching client's organization. The use of appropriate authority is crucial for your client in managing the leadership role as the coach or the individual responsible for organizational coaching outcomes helps your coaching client focus on structural issues. It will also be important to identify ways through which your coaching client can improve his or her line-of-sight and gain positive exposure to different levels in the organization.

Culture

The culture of any organization is constantly affecting the success of any individual or team operating within that system. Culture is the way in which an organization behaves and how its values are realized through its collective aspirations and day-to-day actions. Human beings create culture whenever and wherever they organize themselves, and culture is influenced by individuals at all levels of an organization. It is not simply a top-down phenomenon. It is human and organizational systems in motion.

The markers of any culture can be both simple and complex. Some can be as obvious as the paint on the walls, the way a lobby is designed or the way people in the organization dress. Other markers are more difficult to grasp and can require a great deal of investigation to identify, much less interpret, their meaning and level of profundity. These more nuanced aspects of an organization's culture can be easily overlooked when people remain at the surface level or in a myopic coaching experience. If culture is ignored or taken for granted, it can create potential future problems for anyone who works inside the organization or relies on the organization's performance in any way. Individuals can derail and create negative impact when they demonstrate behaviours that are unacceptable and run counter to the cultural expectations of an institution. Because of the conflict these kinds of mistakes create, they are not easily forgotten or forgiven. Crossing beams with the organizational culture, even if through sheer ignorance, can leave what Hogan calls reputational scars.

Managing the culture is a political process. While it can sometimes cause moral conflict within a person, managing the culture does not require an individual to go against his or her core values or to be a manipulative person. Obviously, it is best if an employee is able to do some cultural analysis before joining a firm to ensure that personal moral convictions are not in conflict with organizational culture in a way that challenges personal authenticity and integrity. Yet no matter how well an employee interprets a culture before joining a firm, new and undisclosed aspects of the system will reveal themselves over time and present new challenges.

Coaching clients will benefit when you, as the coach or the individual responsible for organizational coaching outcomes, consider and pay attention to how different aspects of the organizational culture will enable success or create obstacles. This is especially true if the coaching client has joined a new team or is beginning a new position in the firm where risk is involved. This process requires you as the coach or the individual responsible for organizational coaching outcomes to do cultural analysis early on in the engagement in order to gain awareness of the cultural factors that might be at play and impact the progress of the coaching engagement. Coaching clients, like anyone else in the system, are culture carriers who communicate the culture to others by words and deeds.

Communication

Communication is serious business when it comes to individual and organizational success. Perhaps more than anything else, an organization expresses its culture by the way it communicates. Communication skills and practices affect every aspect of a leader or team player's effectiveness. When dealing in the context of culture, you must supervise your contextual coaches to carefully study and consider how communication is managed within the organization. The way individuals communicate within the organization reveals telling information about how the company operates and how its people are treated.

For example, if information is disseminated on a strict 'need to know' basis, communication is being used as a command and control tool to exert authority. Does that ring true of your organization? Are emerging and established leaders, victims of command and control tactics when it comes to communication? Do the people above, below and beside them on the organization chart communicate openly and give access to ample data and information?

Do your coaching clients share information openly or on a 'need to know' basis with others above, below and/or beside them on the organization chart? How open or closed coaching clients choose to be regarding communication says much about their personalities and the cultural communication style of the organization. Are they driving the communication style of the organization or being victimized by it?

If your coaching clients and/or the organization are open about sharing information, and even make a priority out of keeping people informed, that also speaks volumes about the cultural context of their workplace. When it comes to communication, individuals (like organizations) range from 'open' to 'closed' and everywhere in between. 360-degree feedback will help to sort out where coaching clients fall on that continuum. As the coach or the individual responsible for organizational coaching outcomes, you should help coaching clients to process and make good use of that information.

More than anything else, coaching clients need to find an authentic voice—a voice that will serve both the individual and the constituents well—especially if the coaching client's communication style is in conflict with the communication style of the organization. The challenge for your coaching client is to balance personal and leadership communication styles with the larger imperatives of communication found in the everyday life of the organization. Unreliable or absent communication is typically at the heart of most workplace conflicts and frequently results in negative employee engagement. As emerging or established leaders, coaching clients must compensate, within their relevant spheres of influence, for whatever the organization lacks in the way of good communication practices.

As the coach or the individual responsible for organizational coaching outcomes, you will also need to help your coaching client learn how to communicate effectively with individuals and groups at different levels in a way that compliments and even compensates for the organization's style of communication. You should advise your client when it is appropriate to stretch past the standard communication style of the organization and when stretching might be problematic. Understanding and mastering how organizations communicate internally and externally will help coaching clients create communication plans for their team members and/or customers at key times during the execution of coaching strategies.

Talent Systems

Individuals are evaluated for the ways in which they fulfill the expectations associated with their jobs. Meeting performance goals is a major aspect to future advancement and will almost always

matter more to the manager than any individual development improvement. Many expectations are measured with business
results that are determined in advance as evaluative metrics.
Organizational tools that are used for this process are called
Performance Management Systems and typically involve processes
for defining job specifications, key result areas, key performance
indicators and business metrics. Performance Management
Systems are centralized and designed by HR and talent development
organizations to enable managers to monitor the individual
performance of team members and entire teams.

As the coach or the individual responsible for organizational
coaching outcomes, you will need to pay attention to the ways
your organization sets expectations, manages performance and
measures results in order to provide practical guidance that has
immediate impact. Most Performance Management Systems allow
for development planning, especially in responding to performance
gaps. This helps to make the system 'forward looking' instead of
simply evaluating the past. You can utilize the process of development planning as a powerful personal awareness and goal setting
exercise for coaching clients.

Other talent systems used by companies are important for the
coaching process. How coaching clients utilize hiring systems to
assist with team building is an example. The focus on talent is a
central role of leadership and hiring the right people is a first step
towards success. Many organizations use succession planning as
a key aspect of talent management, strategically focusing on the
future needs of the organization and installing a system for selecting
high potential individuals who can fill key roles in the future.
Typically, the talent planning process involves a partnership
between human resources, managers of the business and specialists
in talent and/or organization development.

Talent Solutions

In order to maximize the potential of employees, companies allocate
budgets towards specific kinds of learning and development

programmes that help to develop individuals and teams. These talent solutions are best designed to help meet strategic needs of the organization and to fill real gaps in employee performance and/or potential. The laser-accurate organizational analysis that contextual coaching makes possible is the best way to identify developmental needs and opportunities for individuals and teams.

It is best to have multiple ways to develop individuals and teams. This includes training in both individual and group settings. Many development programmes focus on how high-potential individuals are seen as key to the future based on their current success and the likelihood of future success related to their competencies or behavioural styles. When individuals are invited into the high-potential pool for future roles, they are often placed within accelerated leadership programmes. These programmes are multifaceted aspects of adult learning and are meant to increase an individual's adaptive capacity for expanding responsibilities within an organization. Accelerated programmes and other learning and development opportunities are available as talent solutions within an organization. Coaching strategies must reflect these and consider them through an organizational lens.

For coaching to become a true organizational process and derive enterprise-wide benefit, it must be mapped to the talent solutions made available to the emerging or established leader being coached. For instance, if a coaching client needs to learn to be more strategic and the organization sends individuals for advanced seminars in strategic planning, you as the coach or the individual responsible for organizational coaching outcomes might pave the way for your clients' enrolment in such programmes. The coaching process does not provide all the elements that coaching clients need in closing talent gaps. Therefore, create more opportunities for success for coaching clients as you connect the one-on-one work with other talent solutions provided internally or externally to the organization. This enables coaching clients to tap into a broad spectrum of organizational learning opportunities that will help them grow and develop.

As the coach or the individual responsible for organizational coaching outcomes, you need to work with coaching clients to find solutions outside of the coaching process that will help promote growth as a leader. You should also keep in mind that you will also need to work with coaching clients to find similar solutions for their direct reports who will benefit from tapping into company-wide learning and development opportunities.

Development

Companies employ contextual coaches to work with individuals for many reasons. With this investment, organizations demonstrate a sign of their commitment to their human capital. This is a strategic choice in light of the pressures and competition related to the talent war. The contextual coaching process does not erase the individual development work that can be achieved through a rich and focused coaching experience. The individual development process found in traditional executive coaching is still essential in this process and is not meant to be erased by sharing the coaching focus with the organization.

Individual development creates the opportunity for heightened self-awareness through the coaching process. When coaching clients become more aware of their modes of behaviour, they are better able to understand how to engage, empower and energize others. All individuals are blind to certain aspects of their behaviour and have some patterns of behaviour that may fail to motivate other members of their teams. Deepening self-awareness helps the individual to better anticipate the perceptions and reactions of others and to avoid falling into patterns that have a negative impact on others.

As Hogan assessment proponents would say, quality coaching can help coaching clients avoid creating reputational scars. Managing personal behavioural tendencies and coping with individual personality styles in ways that maximize human potential requires deep personal, introspective work. It is not easy to adjust behaviours rooted in the deepest dimensions of personality. With our histories, each of us can see evidence of repeated behaviours that get us in trouble. Identifying those behaviours and creating strategies to self-manage them is still a key aspect of developmental coaching.

As the coach or the individual responsible for organizational coaching outcomes, you will lead coaching clients through this process by helping them discover systems and strategies that repeat the developmental mode of addressing issues instead of the destructive mode of repeatedly reacting poorly to the same emotional triggers. Fundamentally, you will have the opportunity to open up new worlds to coaching clients by enabling the insight and understanding that personal changes are necessary for unlocking potential. Once achieved, your client will be able to more effectively and more consistently captivate the hearts and minds of others.

Dynamics of a Team

Team dynamics are elements of a team's style and relate directly to both innate personality traits and exhibited behavioural styles. Change within the individual can affect the relationships within a team and impact the way individuals work together. There is also the additional challenge of intolerance in teams not allowing individuals to change positively and create new futures for all involved.

With this in mind, development of the individual needs to be balanced with the intricacies and issues related to the dynamics of the team that surround him or her. The person is a social animal and our mode of behaviour or lack of behaviour is consistently interacting with other individual modes of behaviour. This interaction can stimulate great team synergy and group success. It can also lead to infighting, stress, lack of engagement and distrust—ultimately disabling the possibility of high team performance.

The coaching process for the individual should involve those with whom the individual works. Whether the team acts as a working group, cross-functional task force or clan of direct reports, its dynamics must be considered for the coaching work to have a sustainable impact. It also ensures that the coaching engagement is an organizational development process.

As the coach or the individual responsible for organizational coaching outcomes, you will become involved in understanding the dynamics of the many teams that coaching clients interact with, especially the one that he or she manages. Your understanding of the dynamics of the various teams will help your coaching client to see how changes in the individual's own behaviour may affect others and change the team dynamics as any systems analyst would predict.

Career

In light of the talent war and its increasing complexities, many companies have learned to partner career planning with talent management and employee development. Clearly, this is a retention strategy. This partnership means that companies are not simply providing career services at the point of exit for an employee (traditionally known as outplacement). Instead, they are providing processes for internal mobility and career planning where individuals can identify open roles inside the company, create career plans against organizational templates and identify company mentors to assist them in charting a course for the future.

In the past, career planning was seen as the responsibility of the individual employee and a 'secretive' process that demonstrated signs of disloyalty if the employee stuck his or her head up and looked around. Today, with the dynamics of a tight labour market, career planning has become a joint responsibility of the company in managing its assets of human capital and the employee who is seeking to maximize his or her options. The implications to emerging and established leaders being coached are obvious. The company wants to be an employer of choice to attract people. The individual wants to be an employee of choice and attract opportunity. The companies with retention strategies—coaching among them—merge these motivations and deepen their reputations as employers of choice by offering more opportunities for employees of choice.

The coaching process benefits from aligning the career goals of the individual with the organizational definitions of leadership discussed earlier and the overall talent strategy for the organization. It is important to work with coaching clients in determining how to envision possible career opportunities and how the coaching process can be helpful to move forward with a plan that aligns the interests of the individual and the organization. It may be about building a deeper network of relationships. It may be about closing some experience gaps in your coaching client's resume. But the work is done in the context of the organization helping coaching clients to see the potential to progress in the organization's unique cultural environment.

Competence

The clarity around competency and its associated behaviours is often found within organizational development systems that articulate enduring competencies by level, experience and/or role. Meanwhile, an organization may also use a specific and unique success model for the top of the organization and cascade that model through the talent planning process with high potentials. These are often described as emerging competencies because they can be aligned with the strategic future direction of the firm as it meets its business challenges.

For coaching, competence is a helpful way to frame and define the career potential of a coaching client. Aspirations need to be realistic. By noting gaps in competencies, individuals can build more attainable career paths. Without this sense, coaching clients may have objectives that are impossible to meet and may wind up frustrated by their inability to attain them. Of course, this kind of frustration affects job performance and employee engagement in the here and now. By noting the gaps that can be managed, especially if their organization provides them with tools, employees have the opportunity to maximize their potential and minimize their liabilities.

In contextual coaching, the coach not only addresses the coaching client's career goals but also helps to design future markers of personal success. The coach attempts to align these with the ways in which the organization understands them at various levels. This helps the coaching client to chart an organizational roadmap for career progress. Identifying how coaching clients line up against current leadership competencies can be beneficial for real-time performance as well as serve as a platform for preparing coaching clients for future performance demands.

CONTEXTUAL COACHING COMMANDMENT 1: CONCLUSION

Investments of time, money and other resources in executive coaching are too precious to leave the organizational benefits of coaching to chance. It is not enough to make a major spend on executive coaching and cross your fingers and hope to die if the benefits of the coaching do not somehow echo throughout the canyons of your organization. Micro focus and macro focus when the individual and the organization are truly co-clients (see Commandment 8) means that focusing only on the individual void in the organizational context in which that emerging or established leader is being coached is myopic.

As mentioned at the top of the chapter, if the goal of executive coaching is to *build leaders who will build businesses*, the approach to developing leaders, whatever it is, must be framed in the context of the organization so the cultural, corporate and contextual needs of the business are never excluded from executive coaching conversations.

Coaching in the context of the organization will ensure that you are not wasting money on executive coaching.

Contextual Coaching Commandment

*Coach with the
Art of Alignment*

There is a real estate broker in Boothbay Harbour, Maine. He tells the story of a woman who wanted to see a house on the back bay. It was a beautiful specimen with a wrap-around porch. She fell in love instantly and put earnest money down practically on the spot. She brought her husband to Boothbay Harbour the next weekend to show him their beautiful new summer house. The broker had barely unlocked the front door and ushered the husband inside when the woman, who had run around the wrap-around porch to the back, let out a terrifying scream.

'Where's the water?', she shrieked. 'When I bought this house, there was water here. Now there are only puddles, wet rocks and mud'.

Her husband nodded his head in a lovingly condescending way, wrapped his arm around her shoulder and consoled her.

'It will be back, Honey', he reassured her. 'Tides come in and go out several times a day. It's just how the ocean is'. He then turned to the real estate broker. 'I have a question for you', he said.

'How do they get the boats at anchor to all point the same direction?'

'Excuse me?', the broker replied.

'You know. They are always pointed in the same direction. Does the Chamber of Commerce send somebody out in a dingy every couple of hours to turn them?'

Needless to say, the broker was speechless that the man so knowledgeable one moment about tides was so clueless the next moment about wind. That is what alignment is in organizations: everybody's bow pointed into the wind. More importantly, whether your organizational population needs to be pointed uniformly into the prevailing marketplace winds or you need everyone to beat a tack towards a marker somewhere other than a close haul run into the wind, you need them to trim their sails uniformly and with precision. That is alignment.

Drilling deeper into the different dimensions of coaching in the context of the organization, the concept of alignment is ever present. Alignment in executive coaching, and leadership development in general, is more than the absence of chaos, although order is a positive outcome if it is not bolted down too tightly. Alignment is the intentional and deliberate establishment of purposeful relationships between people, processes, ideas and resources to initiate, accelerate and sustain desired outcomes. That sounds like a good way to spend a day at the office. As described extensively in Commandment 1, the most effective form of executive coaching in organizations must jointly focus on the growth and development of the emerging or established leader being coached and the organization he or she serves.

Echoing the mantra yet again, if executive coaching is intended to align what leaders do best with what organizations need most, the strengths and interests of individuals must be aligned with the vision, purpose and strategy that the organization has defined, and navigational beacons must be established and kept illuminated to keep the organization on course. Alignment between leadership strengths within an organization and the organization's strategic purpose is more an art than a science because it is not absolutely, infinitely and precisely replicable. The strengths and interests of leaders shift and drift from season to season, with stages of life, changes in faces, changes in roles and responsibilities and the ever-changing state of the industry—any industry.

THE FOUR LEVELS OF COACHING MOTIVATION

The four levels of coaching motivation will be explained more thoroughly in Chapter 9. For now, it is important to establish that not everyone who experiences coaching in organizations approaches the opportunity with the same level of motivation. Are the coaching clients (participants, candidates, leaders or however you refer to them) involved (a) voluntarily because they raised their self-selected hands seeking help as they prepare for expanded responsibilities or new roles and/or some other workplace challenge? Are the coaching clients (b) enthusiastic and willing participants in action-learning, strategic team alignment or other group leadership development activities that offer coaching as an enhancement and additional layer of support for the growth and development of the leaders involved? Option (b) simply stated, 'I wouldn't have a coach except that coaching is part of this programme. But since I'm in the programme, I really don't mind the coaching. It's sort of cool and there is no big agenda behind it'.

Are the leaders participating in executive coaching because (c) it is a requirement for participation in a mandated action learning, strategic team development or other group leadership development programme or, as is the case in some organizations, because participation in individual leadership coaching is required of every leader above a specified level? In the case of example (c), the motivation for participation in coaching activities runs more to compliance than to enthusiastic engagement. 'I know this coaching is part of an innocuous leadership development programme and not targeting me individually for anything they think I've done wrong, but it feels weird and I think it's a waste of time'. Although begrudging compliance might be the entry point motivation at level (c), coaching clients, participants and/or leaders being coached can still conceivably, and sometimes do, become converts and fans of the coaching process, the concept of coaching in general and coaching relationships.

At the fourth (d) level of motivation for coaching, the coaching client, participant, leader being coached or coachee[1] is involuntary, has no interest in receiving coaching, might even feel that coaching is pejorative and/or punitive and is involved because he or she is compelled to participate by company policy or threat of pending disciplinary action. The four levels of motivation for executive coaching in a couple of words:

1. Voluntary and enthusiastic
2. Compliant-but-likeable
3. Compliant-but-disagreeable
4. Involuntary and coerced

As a provider of executive coaching services for a great many Global Fortune 500 firms, let it go on record that requests come in to our offices for individual, top-of-the-rate-card engagements approximately 60 per cent of the time for category four engagements. There are actually category five situations, but we are legally bound not to disclose under threat of litigation with a capital L.

Out of the more than 250 or so coaches on the ground around the world for our firm, 30 per cent work in categories two and three because of the extensive work we do in strategic team alignment,

---

[1] One of the reasons that the term 'coachee' is falling into disfavour is because it sounds disempowering. As mentioned in Commandment 1, to be a 'coachee' makes it sound as if something is being done to the poor, powerless, disadvantaged individual rather than the individual being a fully empowered partner in the process. Terms like 'coaching client', 'participant', 'candidate' and 'leader' are used with increasing regularity about the individual being coached. You will not read the term 'coachee' in this book after this unless it is tongue-in-cheek.

which is never exactly the same twice and always uses coaches to give participants a safe space to deconstruct what happened during real-time, real-life working sessions. We only see about 10 per cent of our work in category one because; well, there are not that many category one requests anywhere from anyone. Unfortunately, executive coaching is still too stigmatized, in general, to see that much glee around it. Organizations often report very different numbers more in favour of voluntary coaching and that is where we all are working to move the percentages. Our direct experience as a coaching provider suggests that numbers have not moved that far in the aspirational direction as organizations are reporting.

So, to put the numbers to the four levels of coaching client motivation:

1. Voluntary and enthusiastic, 10 per cent
2. Compliant-but-likeable, 15 per cent
3. Compliant-but-disagreeable, 15 per cent
4. Involuntary and coerced, 60 per cent

A disclaimer is called for here. There are a number of organizations that provide coaching for all leaders (sometimes partners) at or above a certain level. These are the true coaching cultures. Generally speaking, because everyone gets coached in peer groups, the coaching is well received and the leaders/partners being coached are, again generally speaking, compliant and participative.

Just because you are not being coached because you are in trouble does not mean you have much appetite for it, if for no other reason your plate is full. Others in these coaching environments can be extremely enthusiastic and look to the coaching to help them get ahead. All coaching of this nature is, by definition, acceptable and even likeable, because it is truly not voluntary. One cannot opt out of it. One can ignore it. But why not take advantage of the opportunity—especially if coaching will grease the tracks to your next promotion?

The coaching that takes place in these coaching cultures is free to the coaching client, not coerced, and has no reason to be considered disagreeable unless one simply feels it is a waste of precious executive time. It can also be, despite any other original reason for coaching, a spectacular experience. The question remains: Is the mandatory coaching in coaching cultures aligning the strengths of the leaders being coached to the overarching strategic needs of the organization? Inquiring from the people managing the coaching functions in these coaching cultures, the answer is often, 'not exactly'.

It is still often about the executives finding their true selves and then somehow bringing that better, more aware and actualized self to work. That, according to one manager of the coaching function, 'improves our organization "one leader at a time"'. Considering that major organizations conducting this kind of executive coaching spend millions on major consulting firms to take employee temperatures and provide guidance on strategic direction; to not align the two functions is a head scratcher. The good news is that some major, marquee-name organizations are just starting to do that now (after much cajoling).

ALIGNMENT THROUGHOUT

Regardless of the level of motivation for participating in coaching activities or the specific structure, length or design of the

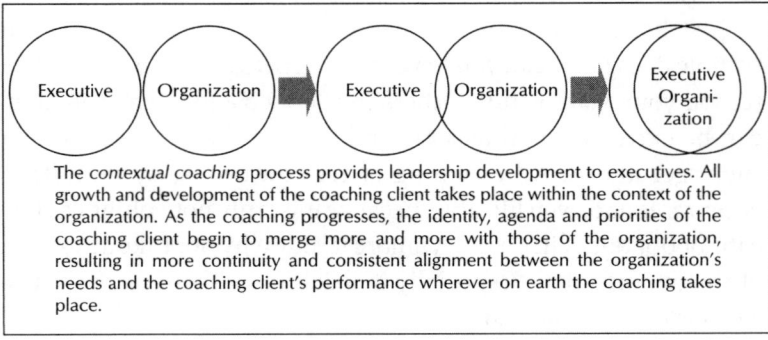

The *contextual coaching* process provides leadership development to executives. All growth and development of the coaching client takes place within the context of the organization. As the coaching progresses, the identity, agenda and priorities of the coaching client begin to merge more and more with those of the organization, resulting in more continuity and consistent alignment between the organization's needs and the coaching client's performance wherever on earth the coaching takes place.

Figure 2.1 Contextual coaching process.

coaching engagement, the work the coach and coaching client conduct together must be aligned with the organization's leadership development principles, priorities, values or competencies (see Figure 2.1). In turn, the leadership development agenda must be aligned with the organization's overarching global business strategy. 'Must be aligned', that is, if the strategic needs of the organization sponsoring (read: paying for) the engagement are to be served. There must also be alignment if the individual's success through coaching is to be defined in the *context* of the sponsoring organization's culture and global strategic agenda.

The presenting issues for the coaching engagement, regardless of what they are exactly or where they fall in the four levels of coaching client motivation, become the specific, targeted outcomes of the coaching engagement. With contextual coaching, the coaching engagement itself and all coaching engagements across the enterprise are framed in the context of the organization's cultural construct and strategic business agenda. This is the alignment of the individual micro-agenda with the organizational macro-agenda.

For coaches, individuals responsible for managing the coaching function in organizations, even coaching clients and other interested stakeholders, the essential question that points back to the need for contextual alignment is, 'How is this coaching engagement helping the individual *and* the organization?' That is, in fact, the essential question, which should be posed regarding any investment in learning and development—especially super-expensive leadership development interventions like executive coaching.

How and why is the participation of each person involved in executive coaching helping the individual and the firm? How and why is the coaching process itself helping the individual and the firm? How and why is this leadership development investment increasing the profitability and/or financial stability and success of the firm?

Organizations perform better and become more profitable and financially viable as soon as employees perform better. Employees perform better when their leaders perform better. Leaders perform better when their best thinking and productivity is enhanced and elevated by well-aligned coaching and leadership development.

ALIGNMENT IN ACTION

While contextual coaches work individually with their coaching clients, the contextual coaching model is a true organizational alignment process that will draw the strengths of the leader being coached closer to the performance needs of the organization. Contextual coaching was developed to be a comprehensive means to expand traditional executive coaching into an organization development process based on alignment.

Using a systems approach, contextual coaching produces simultaneous growth and development opportunities for the executive and the organization—not in opposite or tangential directions—but in the same direction—such as the racing or resting sailboats. The context of the executive remains a fundamental aspect of the coaching engagement and drives the developmental process for the individual emerging or established leader while, at the same time, enhancing and perhaps expanding the executive's role in the broader growth and development of the organization.

This dual focus means that you as a coach or the person responsible for the coaching function in your organization will address multiple contexts that affect the situation of coaching clients as well as will align the coaching process with the strategies, cultural imperatives, talent management systems and competency requirements of the entire organization. As the contextual coach or the person responsible for the coaching function in your organization, you will map the process to a changing organizational landscape, complete with enterprise-wide strategic agendas and individual issues, revealing how each compliments the other.

The ROI from this process is best identified when both the coaching client and the organization are seen as co-clients in the process (see Commandment 9). Because of this, the coaching process will satisfy both customers and achieve overall success within the engagement. Contextual coaches and those in charge of coaching functions in organizations learn to balance the needs of the individual with the requirements of the key constituents (i.e., the coaching client's manager, learning and development groups and HR departments) in each assignment. Those responsible for coaching functions in organizations need to operationalize all of this by designing a coaching strategy that aligns with the organization's overarching global business strategy.

Conceive It

The first step to designing a contextually aligned coaching strategy is to wrap a concept around how coaching executives could help align what they think, say and do with what the organization needs them to think, say and do to best achieve the organization's loftiest goals and aspirations. In essence, that simply means that you need to participate in or avail yourself of your organization's established leadership competencies, values, principles, priorities or whatever way your organization has defined leadership excellence and begin thinking about how coaching executives can make that definition of leadership excellence come alive in your organization.

Design It

The design function is essentially about mapping the process you will use to make a contextually aligned coaching function in your organization a reality. How will you set up coaching engagements to uniformly reflect your desired enterprise-wide alignment? How will you set up your stakeholder or coaching coalitions to keep the voice of the organization alive and active in all coaching engagements (see Commandment 4)? How will you select the correct coaches to support organizationally aligned coaching practices? Most independent coaches want no part of writing reports and being accountable for coaching through an organizational lens. How will your coaching reports and action plans be structured, distributed and processed to protect client confidentiality but provide valuable data back to the organization (see Commandment 10)? These and other questions that are answered in other commandments need to be well-thought-out as they become the building blocks of your organizationally focused coaching strategy. Answering these questions helps make your organizational coaching functions healthy, wealthy, enterprise-*wide* and enterprise-*wise*.

Launch It

How will you make coaching through an organizational lens the dominant way of thinking about and executing the executive coaching function in your organization? The launch is usually the make-or-break point for new ideas and concepts. An organizationally aligned, enterprise-*wide*/enterprise-*wise* coaching function in your organization is about as innovative an idea as you are going to find. Creativity, as Walt Disney defined it, is doing something completely unique that has never been done before. Taking an existing function like coaching and doing something different with it, specifically expanding on the concept and broadening its impact, is true innovation according to the Disney definition. That means it is something that people can get excited about. Launching a newly revamped contextual coaching initiative in your organization should energize people because it is about driving the company's success, not about correcting behaviour. Even though some behaviour might need to be corrected in the process. Talk to business-side people and they will say it makes more logical business sense than any description of coaching they have ever heard.

Execute It

The design comes to life with recruiting and vetting the right coaches who 'get it' about coaching through an organizational lens. Preferably, coaches who have real business-side experience and/or training and education in systems theory or organization development. These coaches will understand why it is so important for an organization to have an enterprise-wide and enterprise-*wise* programme of consistent quality that brings continuity and alignment to executive development and the attainment of strategic business objectives. The coaching management system and reporting protocols need to be consistent and reliable as well. For any contextual coaching framework to provide sustainable results, it must make sense to everyone and have a supportive infrastructure and platform to carry it forward. As with any successful initiative, no matter how brilliantly conceived, the ultimate success is in the execution. Coaching can no longer be an afterthought, but a mainstay of the executive talent development strategy that matches perfectly to the organizational strategic agenda.

CONTEXTUAL COACHING COMMANDMENT 2: CONCLUSION

You know why the boats anchored in Boothbay Harbour, Maine, all point in the same direction. That is because they are only passive and reactive when at anchor. Sometimes the organization needs to create its own wind and sail off into directions that amaze their own people as well as the global marketplace. When an organization does create its own wind, what possible sense does it make to not coach its executives in a framework designed specifically to align what its leaders do best with what the organization needs most? In organizations, always coach with an eye towards the art of alignment, aligning every function, at every level, all the time.

Contextual Coaching Commandment

Keep the Voice of the Organization Present and Alive in All Coaching Engagements

If you work late at night when the office corridors are quiet, you might hear a faint voice. It is usually difficult to discern where exactly the voice is coming from or what it is saying. But it seems to be coming from the walls, maybe, the ceilings and the floors, too. The voice is so faint that it only makes you look up from your computer screen and dart your eyes to the right and then to the left when there is no other sound.

During business hours or when night custodial vacuums are making loud sucking sounds, the voice is undetectable. The next time it is quiet and you are able to hear the voice, listen to it closely. It is the voice of your organization. It is not an 'official' pronouncement from the C-Suite. It is not the company line published in the newsletter or the annual report. Those are all well and good as far as they go or do not go. That faint, small voice is the actual voice of the real collective values, beliefs, hopes and fears of the organizational population. It is the organization asking:

'What about me?'

You lean forward and listen closer.

'What about me?'

That is what you thought you heard.

If your ears are sufficiently attenuated to hear the actual voice of the organic organization and to recognize what it is you are hearing, you might respond by asking, 'What *about* you?'

The voice of the organization might respond in any number of ways. It might quote Audrey II from *Little Shop of Horrors* and say, 'Feed me'.

It might do a Bill Murray imitation from *What About Bob?* and say, 'Give me, give me, give me. I need, I need, I need'.

It might just say, 'Please, don't forget about me. I don't want the payroll cheques to bounce'.

Like any other complex organism, an organization made up of carbon-based life forms must have its essential needs met in order to survive, much less thrive. Most free-economy organizations must also fulfil the desires and expectations of their customers/constituents. That includes meeting the life-sustaining needs of their internal populations.

Broken down even further, for-profit organizations need to generate sufficient revenues to cover payroll and all manner of expenses to keep the doors open. Anti-profit organizations also need to cover payroll and expenses to keep the doors open. Regardless of how organizations meet their needs or serve their missions, they in turn meet the needs of those who depend on them.

The real needs of an organization and/or the people who depend on it can be very different from the perceived needs of an organization and/or the people who depend on it. One of the greatest benefits of coaching people in organizations is the opportunity for individuals to reflect upon their personal and professional circumstances, challenges and opportunities, and to distinguish between things that are good for them and things less desirable. Organizations, as aggregates of individuals that need to function as a whole, need to do the same thing.

Most human beings have audible voices and language that can be used to clearly articulate wants, needs and desires, oftentimes with the help of a coach. Organizations need help to verbalize wants, needs and desires, as often if not more often with the help of a coach and a coaching coalition. In order to express themselves, organizations borrow vocal cords and the ability to write from the members of their organizational populations. In an organizational coaching engagement, the primary voices include the members of the coaching (or stakeholder) coalition (see Commandment 4).

The organization must be given a voice through the willingness and ability of the coalition members and other stakeholders to pay attention and articulate what is needed to help the organization survive and thrive. The feedback captured in multi-rater assessments and other coaching conversations (see Commandment 10) is one way that the organization's voice can be heard—even if the collective voice of the organization is blended with the wants, needs and desires of individuals, which, of course, it always is to some degree.

A simple way to create a distinction between the needs of the leader being coached and the needs of the organization sponsoring (read again: paying for) the coaching engagement is to ask a simple question: 'How is this helping the organization?'

Answering that question is one way to ensure the organization's vocal chords are well exercised throughout coaching engagements. It is easy to identify what the individual coaching client needs to survive and thrive. But what about the organization? What is the cultural context in which the individual coaching engagement takes place and against which its success will be measured?

Skilled contextual coaches and often HR professionals who manage the coaching function in organizations (often referred to as organizational sponsors) know that they must establish an enterprise-wide contextual framework for coaching engagements (see Commandments 1 and 2), and then coach to the specific growth and development needs of the individual coaching client within that contextual framework. When the organization asks, 'What about me?', the answer is in the contextual framework as established by the organization's leadership strategists. The answer, as always, must align what individual leaders do best with what organizations need most. In order to keep Commandment 3 of

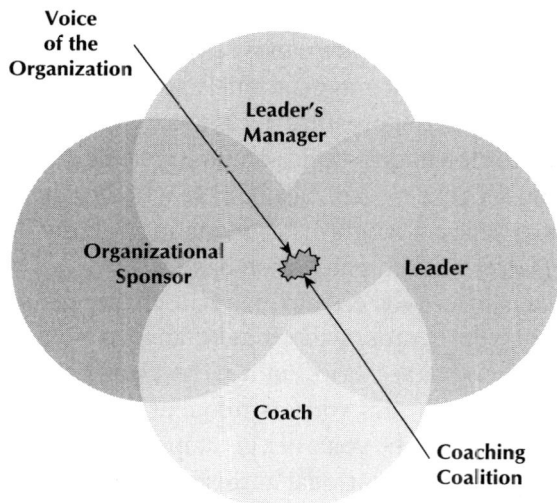

Figure 3.1 The voice of the organization comes alive in the coaching coalition.

Contextual Coaching, *keep the voice of the organization present and alive,* make sure the organization has vocal cords and/or an ability to write so it can cry out when individual interests pull value away from the good of the whole.

As you can see in Figure 3.1, the voice of the organization gains insight, clarity and volume where the members of the coaching coalition (that you are about to read in Commandment 4) converge. In the meantime, it is important that the organizational sponsor, the leader being coached, the leader's manager, the coach and as many people as possible in the organization all understand how to recognize the organization's voice when they hear it.

THE ORGANIZATION'S VOICE

The organization's voice always tells a story. Just as all data tells a story, everything that happens in an organizational system is the spine of a rich narrative that is complex, layered and meaningful to different constituencies in different ways. As you attempt to find the voice of your organization and bring it into every dimension of leadership development, most of all coaching, you need to understand the nature of organizational expression. Besides being loaded with jargon, the organization's voice in its most raw and unrefined condition might sound somewhat crude. Like organizational *culture*, which all organizations have whether they want one or not (James Belasco taught us as much in his book *Teaching the Elephant to Dance*), every organization has a *voice*.

The organization's voice, if not given the chance to exercise and condition the vocal cords, will often be almost indiscernible, as in the late-night office scenario. But it is there nonetheless. Because the organization's natural voice is frequently soft and scratchy. It does not sound like the voice of a great man or woman in a position of tremendous institutional authority speaking in sweeping platitudes or booming with bravado. As such, if it is heard at all, it sounds insignificant and unimportant.

The Truth and Nothing but the Truth

The true voice of the organization speaks the truth. It cannot lie or meander through mendacity, creating circuitous pathways to divert the internal and external populations' attention away from the facts. The true voice of the organization is all about facts and meaning. The manufactured voice of the organization is about lip syncing. The puppet moves its mouth while the ventriloquist puts words in it to craft a message to promote a profit- and/or power-driven purpose.

Speaking the truth is only occasionally inspirational, whereas inspiring messages can be scripted and delivered in powerful ways that indeed inspire and/or manipulate. The true voice of the organization, as accurate as it is, really only says, 'It is what it is. Nothing more nothing less'. Hopefully, 'what it is' is very good. Sometimes, it is very bad or somewhere in between. Whatever it is, that is all it will be. The scripted, manufactured voice of the organization can describe and embellish a drainage ditch to appear as grand as the English Channel or describe the pile of rubble that once was a manufacturing plant as the Freedom Tower in New York. Well-crafted and delivered messages can convince millions of people that what they are being led to believe is exponentially greater than whatever is the actual subject of the conversation.

All those who work for—or are otherwise intimately acquainted with—an organization have at least a faint echo of the organization's true voice somewhere in their heads. The rub comes when the true voice of the organization is dissonant with or downright antithetical to the company line. The fastest way to discredit the company line is to float a false description of something people know to be otherwise. Laying off hundreds of people in an 'unfortunate-but-inescapable need to reduce labour costs' is believable until the CEO of the company publicly exercises US$195 million in stock options that same week. That is when the stench starts.

An expectation can be a resentment waiting to happen. If people expect the organizations they work for or depend on to play a significant role in their lives, there is an emotional as well as a practical investment. When expectations (promises) are not kept, resentment begins. People do not walk around with 'resentment' tattooed on their foreheads or necessarily talk about it aloud. They might just slump a little at the shoulders, cast their eyes downward and secretly seethe inside.

Whether people in the organization are talking or publicly displaying their resentment, it can't be hidden because resentment has an odour. It seeps out of the pores of human epidermis. People might not be able to detect what exactly it is about or what is causing it, but they know something is not right and someone is not happy, regardless of a happy face or stiff upper lip they attempt to portray.

When small and vulnerable investors the world over lose everything (savings, retirement accounts, etc.) in market collapses requiring tax dollars from those same small and vulnerable investors to prop up the banks who bundled properties they knew were worthless—and the CEO of one of the most propped up banks spends over $1.5 million to redecorate his office a month later—it stinks. Does anything change because the odour? Not really. Is any guilty party terminated from his or her job to make the stinking stop? Rarely, if at all. Does anyone go to jail? A few perhaps. But justice is never fully served and the odour of resentment fills the air.

The reason these incongruities and flat out misrepresentations land on people so negatively and cause such resentment is because people know the truth is out there somewhere and what they are hearing is not it. Call it the elephant in the room or the skeleton in the closet. Misleading people who have a vested interest in the success of whatever is claiming success but not producing it is one of the fastest ways to marginalize, demoralize and disgust a working population.

Most inconsistencies between the audio-animatronic Stepford voice of the organization and real voice of the organization are not as glaring and dramatic as the ones described earlier. In most cases, even when people know that the company line is a little skewed, they might cut some slack because it is only a little off. Trust between the organization and the individuals that comprise it is at risk when the truth and the platitudes are not aligned. This is one reason that systems-based cultural and strategic contextual alignment between individual expectations and organizational performance and vice versa is so important when it comes to the voice of the organization.

Rivers in Harmony

Coaching in organizational context or through an organizational lens, which is what constitutes contextual coaching, can make an enormous contribution to aligning what the organization says and what it means. Think of it as two rivers. One is a river of truth and the other is a river of confusion at best and deceit at worst. If and when the rivers converge, the confluence will no doubt be turbulent and fraught with perilous currents, whirlpools, eddies, vortexes and holes in the riverbed.

Not far beyond the confluence, however, the whirling and swirling lessens and the water smooths out. Now that the waters of the two rivers have blended, they begin mitigating one another. It is similar to where major rivers like the Hudson in New York or the Mississippi in Louisiana flow into the sea. Fresh water mixes with salt water to form brackish water that can run for dozens of miles upstream. The farther upstream you travel, the greater the volume of fresh water versus salt water until the water is finally all fresh.

Similarly, moving farther out to sea, the saltier the water will become. The more mendacity there is in the converging rivers—that is the organization's potentially contrived and manipulative voice versus its true and authentic voice—the more likely the river water will remain mostly stinky as it flows downstream. In the reverse, the more refreshingly authentic water there is in the channel, the more likely the river might flow with clean, mendacity-free water.

The true and tainted voices of the organization can converge like mighty rivers, but it might be necessary to deliberately dig a deep channel to get the organization's true voice merged in sufficient quantities with the inauthentic voice. At the confluence of the organization's true voice and manipulative voice, enormous amounts of hydroelectric power can be generated by transforming the kinetic energy within the truth into a story of overcoming.

That simply means the merging of the stories in such a way that the company line can become truly aspirational in the context of the true story. In the same way that the tail and the dog can have a mutually enjoyable experience.

Coaching Is the Deep Channel

In Commandment 10, when the concept of 'No Data Left Behind' is elaborated upon, watch for how the truth about the organization can be captured and used for meaningful, strategic planning. For now, the question is: 'How does the truth (or the true story) of the organization emerge?' Many organizational designers, organization development specialists and talent developers think they have a handle on this. And major consulting firms like them to think that way.

Organizations in both the for-profit and anti-profit worlds, in the public and private sectors, are quick to spend millions upon millions of dollars on major consulting firms to conduct focus groups, interviews with critical stakeholders and distribute surveys to take their organizations' pulse and temperature. Although these marquee-name consulting firms employ state-of-the-art data-gathering devices and techniques, there is no real accounting for the veracity of those providing the information.

As sophisticated and 'scientific' as the data-gathering processes are, how is the fear factor factored in? In organizations where there is a reasonable expectation that truth telling will bring the wrath of the big kahunas upon your head (which is most organizations of any substantial size), who is going to sit in a room with other employees and trash the company? Not that trashing the company is necessarily speaking truth, but if it is the truth, who is going to say it aloud in front of colleagues, no matter how skilled the consulting facilitator is?

When the interviewer in private inquiry sessions is part of the firm the CEO retained to squirrel up information about what is right and what is wrong about the company, how deep is the trust that would allow one to truly articulate what is wrong with the company? How close to the truth will the interviewer actually get? Anonymous surveys might be the closest thing to getting at the truth. But the more generic the questions, the more limited and even contrived the data collected. The more the survey calls for long-form narrative, the greater the danger that, in the writing, the identity of the author might be revealed.

In the final analysis, major consulting firms who are generating millions of dollars in fees from deep-pocket organizations, don't want to be the bearers of bad tidings. Leaders in large, deep-pocket organizations are famous for killing messengers, even if the messengers take them on spectacular golf weekends. The result is that the mostly boilerplate reports and recommendations that the major consulting firms deliver to the big kahunas is about organizational design, talent development focus, increasing politically correct policies, etc.

Very little of such a report will describe how deeply an organizational population is bleeding and from how many cuts and lacerations, large and small. But lacerations, large and small, are what emerging and established leaders cannot seem to help but talk about when being interviewed privately about a colleague who is receiving executive coaching. When given the opportunity to participate in a structured interview 360-degree feedback session about a colleague, any competent external executive coach will tell you that the conversations immediately range beyond feedback on the individual and begin to encompass the micro-system issues as well as macro-system issues that comprise the context of the organizational working environment.

As Commandment 10 will describe in further detail, most if not practically all of this invaluable, authentic, intimate and honest feedback—such that no major consulting firm could ever hope to capture—is lost into the atmosphere. The words, the passion behind them, the ideas and confessions that men and women in leadership are bursting at the seams to speak aloud to somebody—they will most often speak to coaches, their coaches and the coaches who interview them as part of 360-degree-structured interviews.

The unvarnished truth about organizations is discussed in coaching conversations every day across the enterprise. When and where is it captured? When and where is it analysed (without compromising confidentiality, of course)? The voice of the organization is alive and well in executive coaching engagements, if the engagement is designed and delivered through an organizational lens. Data that is more trustworthy and true than anything a major consulting form can uncover flows freely in coaching conversations—all for the price that the organization is already paying for the coaching.

CONTEXTUAL COACHING
COMMANDMENT 3: CONCLUSION

If you work late at night when the office corridors are quiet, and you hear that faint voice ask, 'What about me?' Do not whip around, pull a big, fat three-ringed binder off the shelf and slam it on your desks saying,

> *This is the report we paid XYZ Consulting Group US$3 million to prepare for us. We know everything we need to know about you. Now go away because I have work to do. The only thing I want to see when I look up from this desk late at night is the Chick-fil-A cow.*

I am not sure exactly what you are working on so hard, but it might not be guided by the most accurate data available. Your strategic plan might be based on unreliable information that the big kahunas wanted XYZ Consulting Group to write up. But you buy into it because it was expensive, extensive (a mile wide and an inch deep) and commissioned by the highest institutional authority in the organization.

Nobody ever got fired for hiring XYZ Consulting and nobody ever enhanced his or her career by challenging XYZ Consulting's conclusions. Why question even a portion of XYZ Consulting's voracity? If the emperor is paying you handsomely to dress him well, which consulting firm is going to step forward and tell him he is still buck naked?

Which major consulting firm with huge advertisements in major airports is going to tell you that the true and authentic voice of the organization is speaking regularly in every executive coaching engagement? All you need to do is pay attention and listen.

Contextual Coaching Commandment

Coach Through an Organizational Lens by Establishing a Coaching Coalition

Keeping the voice of the organization alive in every coaching conversation and aligned with the context of the global enterprise requires the establishment of a four-cornered coaching coalition (see Figure 4.1); a group of interested, invested and involved stakeholders that usually includes (at the very least) the coach, the coaching client, the coaching client's manager and an organizational sponsor—usually an HR, talent or organization development (OD) partner. This coalition not only gives voice to the organization (as you saw illustrated in Figure 3.1), but it also constitutes the organizational lens and keeps all enterprise-*wide* organizational coaching engagements enterprise-*wise*. Your organization might prefer to call the coaching coalition a stakeholder coalition. What matters most is that a true support and encouragement team be established that will learn from the coaching engagement and carry those lessons forward once the coach is out of the picture to support the ongoing growth and development of the leader being coached.

Unless coaches are naturally inclined to coach through an organizational lens—and thankfully many coaches are—the need for a formally sanctioned coaching coalition is lost on them. Our experience with solo coaches attempting to authentically coach through an organizational lens is that many who try fail. They will put in an honest effort, but they wind up resenting the fact that the coaching career they signed on for—you know, the one where you give people advice over the telephone while lounging in your pajamas at home and a six-figure income pours into your bank account—does not require anywhere near the effort and accountability of coaching through an organizational lens.

When vetting coaches who want to join the Partners International global network of coaches, a series of interviews quickly reveals whether or not coaches appreciate the more complicated approach contextual coaching requires (facilitating a coaching coalition, conducting structured interviews with critical stakeholders and co-creating reports with the leader being coached) and are willing to invest the extra effort to expand the benefits of coaching enterprise-wide. Among the most critical functions a coach must execute when facilitating a coaching coalition are (a) negotiating a consensus on the list of feedback providers for 360-degree-structured interview assessments conducted by the coach, (b) negotiating a consensus and drafting the list of questions the multiple raters will be asked by the coach, (c) conducting interviews, compiling the data and debriefing the coaching client, (d) reviewing the reports that the coach and coaching client jointly prepare at the beginning, middle and end of the engagement—action plan, mid-term update to the action plan and final report and (e) drafting an organizational analysis based on the data collected during coaching conversations and 360-degree-structured interviews—all without compromising the confidentiality of the leader being coached.

NEGOTIATING THE LIST OF 360-DEGREE-STRUCTURED FEEDBACK PROVIDERS

As mentioned earlier, once a coach is selected for an engagement, the contextual coach has two initial responsibilities vis-à-vis the coaching coalition: (a) negotiate and draft the list of feedback providers for 360-degree-structured interview assessments conducted by the coach and (b) negotiate and draft the list of questions the multiple raters will be asked by the coach. If this seems like an easy task, be assured it can be hair-raising. To the novice coach attempting to facilitate a coaching coalition for the first time might be stunned at how quickly contemporary or ancient grievances emerge between coalition members and how intense and inflammatory the grievances can be.

The leader being coached will have a list of feedback providers that includes best friends, parents, children (if they are speaking to them), co-workers with kindred spirits, fraternity brothers, sorority sisters, direct reports that worship the ground the leader walks on, etc. The leader's manager will suggest including some less amorous observers or, at the very least, some of the people with whom there seems to be friction or some level of contentiousness that leads to the kind of noise that alerted HR and the manager to the fact that there might be some corrective coaching in the leader's future. If the leader being coached and the leader's manager appear to be at odds with one another, add the third dimension to the chess game in the person of the organizational sponsor—most usually an HR business partner, internal talent consultant, learning and development manager or someone else who is big into the soft skills side of leadership development.

HR people are acutely aware of the political climate and landscape in the organization and want to restore order and silent running to the area that has experienced disruption. As a result, the HR business partner might have a name or two to suggest for the list of feedback providers that neither the leader being coached nor his or her manager has suggested. Obviously, the contextual coach needs to be a skilled negotiator in addition to being a skilled facilitator of a contentious team. The coach's objective is to facilitate the triangular negotiation until there is a reasonable consensus on the list of feedback providers. The more quality negotiating that goes on and the more consensus that is built, the greater the volume of the organization's voice, which is critical to setting the stage for a true contextually aligned and enterprise-wide beneficial coaching experience.

The best possible list of 8 or 10 feedback providers is the one that will produce the most objective perspective and intimate data. Because the other three corners of the coaching coalition have agendas to be served by the selection of their individual nominees for providing feedback, the contextual coach needs to guard against the HR business partner exerting too much political pressure, the manager exerting too much institutional authority or the leader being coached being too bifurcated, thereby contaminating or slanting the process to the point that the process impeaches itself.

ESTABLISHING THE LIST OF QUESTIONS FOR MULTIPLE RATERS

Structured interviews can be more valuable than 360-degree quantitative assessments in that the coach engages with the feedback provider live in person, over the telephone or through a video call. There are subtleties and nuances in the interaction between the contextual coach and the individual providing feedback through which the coach gets not only a rich sense of the affective condition of the relationship but also a host of information outside of the structured interview questions that the feedback providers cannot help but talk about (see Commandment 10). For these reasons, the relevance and precision of the questions in 360-degree structured interviews are critical and can reach far deeper into the truth of an organizational scenario than standardized questions. Generic questions from a drop-down menu or a one-size-fits-all instrument cannot compare to structured interviews in producing information and, more importantly, meaning.

Much of the same posturing among members of the coaching coalition that goes on in selecting feedback providers also takes place in the crafting of structured interview questions—and for similar reasons. The importance of asking the correct and/or most powerful questions possible is more acute if the coaching client is not only involuntary but also on life support in his or her organizational position. In lower-pressure, completely developmental (not corrective) scenarios, the precision and power of the questions is less critical. Not that every structured interview process in every level of coaching engagement is not important and that every coaching client, whether an established or emerging leader, is not worthy of the highest quality inquiry, but the more that is at stake, the more critical it is for the questions to be well targeted.

In terms of reliability, the structured interview questions (typically six to eight) need to be consistent from interview to interview. That does not mean that the coach cannot ask the all-encompassing question: 'What might I have asked you, but didn t' or 'Is there anything that you would like to share with me, but haven't?' That type of closing question can capture essential information about the leader being coached, the organization or both by granting licence to the feedback provider to go places he or she might not have considered when staying strictly between the lines of the structured interview questions that the coach helped facilitate consensus on in the coaching coalition.

In terms of validity, the fact that the coach works hard to facilitate a meaningful dialogue among the coaching client, the coaching client's manager and the organizational sponsor increases the probability that the structured interviews will measure what they are intended to measure. The potential downside of conducting structured interviews, which take precious time off the calendars of feedback providers, is that they are wasting everyone's time and accomplishing little if anything. This is why the validity of the structured interview process is so vitally important.

REVIEWING COACHING REPORTS

In addition to generating valid and reliable data that will inform the co-creation of the coaching action plan by the coach and the coaching client, the action plan is the blueprint that not only guides the coaching client's ongoing growth and development, but it also keeps the coalition intact. Two other major boxes are being checked at the same time. First, the confidentiality of the coaching engagement data is being protected because the coaching client approves the release of information that only he or she wants to be shared publicly. Second, the coalition members are committed upfront to monitor and support the ongoing work of the coaching client for fully actualizing the goals and desired outcomes of the plan.

With the organizational sponsor and the coaching client's manager engaged for the long term when the coaching coalition is originally formed, the value of the coaching engagement for the individual leader being coached and the organization that employs the leader becomes far more sustainable than an individual engage-ment that involves only the coach and the coaching client in any meaningful, ongoing manner. Besides negotiating who will be on the list of feedback providers and what questions the coach will ask the feedback providers, the coaching coalition's work continues when the coaching action plan is presented to the coalition by the coaching client.

Ideally, during the course of a coaching engagement, the coach-ing action plan will be reviewed by the entire coaching coalition and approved or revised and approved as close to the launch of the engagement as possible, at the mid-point and at the end of the engagement. In other words, the coaching coalition stays involved throughout the engagement and beyond. The term 'beyond' is particularly relevant here in the Buzz Lightyear sense of the term because the coaching engagement should not end when the internal or external coach is no longer involved.

Coaching action plans, mid-term updates and final updates to the action plans should always be examined by organizational sponsors and managers of the coaching clients as if the sponsors and managers are going to be the coaches beyond where the engage-ment coach completes his or her work. The plans they review and approve are plans they will be responsible for seeing through for as long as the coaching client is employed. Coaching is a protracted activity, not an acute solution. It is the responsibility of the coach-ing client, his or her manager and the organizational sponsor to make the emotional and behavioural changes sustainable, relevant and valuable to the organization for the long term.

THE LANGUAGE OF THE COACHING COALITION

Through a wide-angle lens, contextual coaching or coaching in the context of the organization is a holistic approach to executive coaching that balances and aligns the individual's need for leadership growth and development with the operational and strategic needs of the organization. As such, there is a lexicon around the practice. As coaching in organizational context simply means to coach through an organizational lens in which the individual coaching client and the organization sponsoring the coaching engagement are co-clients (see Commandment 8). In the contextual coaching process, none of the leadership competencies, principles or values that the organization subscribes to are left out of the engagement—especially those requiring the hardest work.

Because the coaching coalition is integral to the contextual coaching experience and keeping the voice of the organization alive and active in the coaching conversation, the language used by the members of the coaching coalition must be consistent with their roles. If for no other reason, consistent language will help the occupants of the four corners of the coaching coalition (see Figure 4.1) stay in character as they fulfil their functions and obligations to one another and to the organization as a whole.

As mentioned before, some call this working group a stakeholder or collaborative coalition. Regardless of exactly what it is called, the coaching coalition is critical to the success of any organizational contextual coaching engagement and, ultimately. the leader being coached.

To better ensure coaching engagement success, the constituents and key stakeholders need to be committed and willing to invest time and energy to the coaching process. Key constituents and stakeholders include any important participants in the coaching

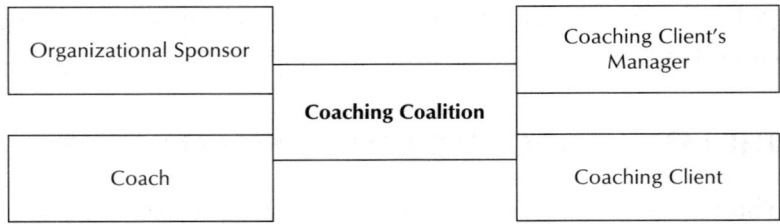

Figure 4.1 The coaching coalition has at least four corners and four distinct perspectives on the coaching engagement and the coaching client. There can be more than four members of the coaching coalition, but never less than four.

process and your coaching client's overall leadership development. They provide insight into the coaching client's goals as well as information throughout the coaching engagement that can deepen the experience for the coaching client, and help to monitor personal and professional development—while maintaining alignment to the organization's cultural context and strategic agenda. That is why the language of coalition is so important and an essential component of enterprise wisdom.

The voice of the organization is kept alive and active in the coaching conversation through the coalition members and the way each of them represents and articulates a different organizational perspective or point of view in the context of the organization's established leadership competencies, principles or values.

Each corner of the coaching coalition can, and often does, represent a unique point of view while still representing the voice of the organization (see Figure 4.1). It is easy to see the varied perspectives coming through the coaching coalition's conversations. Imagine that the coaching coalition is discussing communication skills, for example. The coach might share something like this:

During coaching engagements, I periodically paraphrase or restate what I hear my coaching clients say—using other words that make it clear that we're on the same wavelength and that I fully comprehend what I am being told. I also repeat her words back to her so we can be clear in our mutual understanding. Sometimes I point out when we have common experiences so

*my client feels more confident that I truly understand where she's coming
from. I've published books and articles before, and my coaching client writes a
lot of high-level documents. We both know what it is to stare at a blank screen
with a deadline looming. Knowing we both share that experience can help us
reframe our thinking.*

The coach's perspective on communication skills comes through
here. Remember that the engagement is not about the coach. It is
about the client. Many coaching purists will insist that coaches
should never disclose anything about themselves in coaching conversations. However, when the information about shared
experiences can strengthen trust, rapport and simpatico, knowing
that a coach has walked a mile in the coaching client's moccasins
can help a coaching client open up faster and potentially go deeper.
Shared experiences, even if not shared with the coaching client,
can help coaches ask more relevant, meaningful and powerful
questions.

The coaching client or leader being coached might say something
like:

*When I am presenting in meetings, I have a tough time keeping people focused
on the problem we're solving for. I'd like some help getting people to pay attention to what I'm saying, especially when they're my peers and I can't just order
them to do things. I really think that I'll get things done more collaboratively,
like my performance review calls for, if I can exert more influence when I'm
communicating.*

The coaching client's perspective on communication skills comes
through here. Whether or not the coaching client is frustrated that
his or her communication attempts are landing properly on the
intended ears or are creating the hoped-for impact, some sort of
improvement is called for. Perhaps the need to improve communication skills came from a performance review or a 360-degree
feedback (including but not limited to a structured interview
process). The better the coaching client can articulate not only the
need but also the benefits of (in this case) better communication,

the more skilfully the coach, coaching client's manager and organizational sponsor can provide the necessary support and thinking partnership to move the coaching client forward in a way that benefits the leader being coached and the organization.

The coaching client's manager might say something like this about communication skills:

> *I know it helps me as a manager for my people to tell me what's going on in a clear and concise way. That not only helps me manage better, but it also helps other departments work with us more effectively. I'll help you work on that. As for me, I know that I need to do a better job of being clear and concise with my messaging for all the reasons I just stated. Just last week, I changed my mind about something and didn't let everyone involved know that I had shifted gears or why. When I am confusing, ambiguous or inconsistent in my communication, it makes it tough on my team members, our partners across the enterprise and the organization as a whole.*

The manager's perspective and the organization's voice begin to come through a bit more powerfully here. Managers of coaching clients can quickly get caught, indicted and convicted of doing what they are trying to coach their reports to do more of or stop doing—if the coalition conversation stays alive and uses relevant and consistent language. Any experienced coach, organizational sponsor or manager of a leader being coached will testify that a great coach and a well-executed contextual coaching engagement helps every member of the coaching coalition grow, develop and become better in his or her job, especially in ways that benefit the organization as well as the leader being coached.

The organizational sponsor (perhaps a HR business partner) might say something like:

> *One reason the organization is investing in this coaching engagement and others like it is because we need cultural consistency in the way people communicate, especially leaders of teams. I have been asked to improve the ways I deliver feedback when managing coaching engagements, so this is something I'll pay close attention to. Even with individual contributors, it's important for all of us to continuously improve the way we give*

feedback and use respectful language when we do it. For the work that you do one-on-one in this department and with teams from other departments, we all need to model our leadership competencies around respectful and honest feedback.

The organization's voice comes through strongly here, albeit from a slightly different perspective when looking through the HR, talent or OD partner's lens. The keeper of all that is excellent around coaching resides in those who manage coaching functions in organizations. That is why contextual coaching begins not with the coach but with the organizational sponsor. A coach can come into an organization and practise contextual coaching all day long and not provide lasting, enterprise-wide impact if the coaching system inside the organization doesn't treat the coaching clients and the organization like co-clients (see Commandment 8) if a coaching coalition is not formed to keep the voice of the organization alive and active throughout the engagement, and organizational data is not captured and analysed from every coaching engagement (see Commandment 10). In short, if the organizational coaching function is not enterprise-wise.

A fabulous, overarching question that needs to be regularly asked by everyone in the coaching coalition, especially the coach, is: 'How is this coaching engagement helping this organization?' This must be a front of mind question for everyone in the coalition regardless of what the presenting issue for the coaching happens to be. The question itself is the first step towards keeping a systems-based focus and contextual alignment present throughout the coaching engagement. This is the organizational lens.

The more every coaching coalition member participates, the stronger and more comprehensive the organization's voice becomes. The more the organization and the individual being coached are aware and acknowledge their symbiotic relationship, the more effective both will be. The previously mentioned fabulous, overarching question regularly asked by everyone in the coaching coalition, especially the coach ('How is this coaching engagement helping this organization?'), becomes even more powerful as the members of the coaching coalition conduct a more authentic and animated coalition conversation using clear and contextually consistent language. The coaching coalition is not only the voice of the organization, it is also the lens through which the coaching engagement is observed and conducted.

CONTEXTUAL COACHING COMMANDMENT 4: CONCLUSION

Keeping the voice of the organization alive in every coaching conversation and aligned with the context of the global enterprise requires more than the mere establishment of a four-cornered coaching coalition (Figure 4.1) that includes at the very least the coach, the coaching client, the coaching client's manager and an organizational sponsor—usually an HR, talent or OD partner. Every member of the coalition must communicate and conduct him or herself in a manner consistent with a true systems approach to coaching in the organization. Each occupant of each corner of the coaching coalition needs to not only understand the unique perspective he or she brings to the coaching conversation, but also needs to understand that he or she is bringing a part of the organization's voice and language to the coaching engagement and representing the organization's best interest in this expensive investment. Each coaching coalition participant is contributing enterprise *wisdom* and needs to understand what that is and why it is so important.

Coaching through an organizational lens makes the coaching investment far more meaningful than coaching without organizational context. As mentioned before, what matters most is that a true support and encouragement team (coaching coalition) be established that will learn from the coaching engagement and carry those lessons forward once the coach is out of the picture to support the ongoing growth and development of the leader being coached and the organization as a whole.

Contextual Coaching Commandment

Co-create the Engagement

The Macro Perspective

Most individual coaching engagements that involve emerging or established executives are intensely focused on specific behaviour change. That is to say that the organization, through the eyes of the executive's boss, HR business partner or someone else of interest and/or influence, wants the emerging or established executive to stop doing something he or she is doing, start doing something he or she is not doing, or do more of the latter. Any coaching engagement, regardless of the presenting issue that initiates it, is a co-creation of the coaching coalition, most specifically, the coach and the coaching client.

In Commandments 3 and 4, the discussion focused on keeping the voice of the organization alive, present and participating in executive coaching engagements through the formation of a coaching (or stakeholder) coalition. As covered in Commandment 4, the coaching coalition has at least four members: the coach, the coaching client, the coaching client's manager and the organizational sponsor. As previously mentioned, organizational sponsors are most commonly HR people. Sometimes they can be OD or learning or talent partners. The important issue is to bring multiple perspectives to the coaching engagement that, considered together, will keep the interests of the organization represented, protected and promoted throughout the coaching engagement—from conception to completion.

Since executive coaching engagements are sponsored by organizations to help skill up, smooth out or, otherwise, enhance an emerging or established leader's ability to lead in a productive and profitable manner, the engagement is not a private affair between a coach and his or her coaching client. The leader being coached and the coach enjoy a special relationship—one that is marked by respect, trust, rapport, professional bonding and, of course, confidentiality.

Just because an organizationally sponsored coaching engagement is an experience shared among the members of the coaching coalition, it does not mean that it violates traditional coaching protocols, which include the privilege of confidentiality. Co-creation of a coaching engagement or an individual coaching session means that the experience and the work involved is shared among at least two people. However, coaching in the organizational context and for the benefit of the entire enterprise deliberately and openly pushes back some boundaries that might otherwise be assumed to be sacred.

The elevation in status of the individual receiving the coaching is consistent with the belief that a coaching client is a privileged individual in whom the organization has chosen to make a significant and often sizeable investment. Common logic would suggest that someone in whom an organization is willing to invest a large sum of money must add significant value to the organization. Executive coaching is arguably the single most expensive investment an organization makes along the leadership talent development continuum.

All this to say that an organization has a right to expect results—a return on investment (ROI), if you prefer. What exactly is the financial ROI from executive coaching? Once corporate or organizational accountants or financial policymakers can put a number on what an emerging or established executive adds to the bottom line in actual dollars on a daily, weekly, monthly, quarterly or annual basis, the conversation can begin on what the actual financial increase is from coaching. What is the actual ROI from having an employee cafeteria on sight? It is assumed that people are more efficient when employees can get back to their desks sooner. But is it? Where are the studies and the sacred numbers to prove the theory?

Companies invest in gymnasiums, extra-curricular sports and other recreational activities. Is there ROI data to justify those expenditures? How about investments in office decor and community projects? None of this is written to suggest that firms do not serve good purposes by doing these sorts of things. In fact, these expenditures might indeed add to the bottom line in some circuitous manner. The author simply hasn't seen or heard of Kaunas demanding to see evidence of a palpable ROI on the company softball team.

Without a baseline dollar figure that everyone can agree to, there is no possible way to have a legitimate conversation or calculation of how much that dollar figure has increased or decreased as a result of executive coaching. Even if such a calculation could be made, how would all of the independent variables and other mitigating influences be sufficiently scrubbed to ensure that no other influencing factors have contaminated the calculation? The value of coaching emerging or established leaders/executives is predicated on the assumption that the emerging or established leaders/executives are worth what they are being paid and adding corresponding and commensurate value to the organization. As such, making them more effective at what they do adds a multiplier effect to what they are being paid to do.

Having put the issue of ROI of coaching to rest, the act of co-creating the coaching engagement, that is the entire coaching process for the leader receiving the coaching, is an important step towards ensuring a maximum ROI for both the individual leader receiving coaching and the organization. Another way of saying that yet again is: contextual coaching, when excellently executed, aligns what emerging and established leaders do best with what their organizations need most. That is why co-creating the engagement is, at least a 50 per cent macro- or big-picture endeavour. Together, every member of the coaching coalition discusses what is going to take place throughout the engagement and comes to agreement on how the engagement design will most benefit everyone involved.

The macro perspective on coaching emerging and established leaders requires that expectations be set and agreed to at the inception of the engagement among the coach, coaching client, the coaching client's boss and the organizational sponsor that might cause coaching purists to blanch. 'What do you mean information from 360-degree-structured interviews and confidential coaching conversations will be shared with the coaching coalition', they demand incredulously, 'and even those who provided the 360-degree feedback to begin with?'

Yes, whatever data the coaching client agrees to release will be valuable data for all to learn from. Transparency, honest disclosure and authenticity are desirable qualities in human development in general, not simply in coaching emerging and established leaders. Therefore, leaders being coached will demonstrate more their emotional maturity as human beings and leaders of human beings the more they are willing to be self-disclosing, transparent and authentic. This expectation should be articulated by the contextual coach and the organizational sponsor at the onset of every engagement.

The emerging or established leader being coached can invoke confidentiality and limit how much he or she is willing to share. That is the coaching client's prerogative and privilege. Trained, credentialed and qualified coaches will forever defend that prerogative and privilege, even when corporate Kaunas pound their fists on their desks and demand the coach spill the beans on the leader being coached. 'We paid for the data', the Kauna bellows, 'and you're going to darn well disclose it'.

Not.

True, the organization paid for data collection and one might surmise the organization owns the data as a result. But in a sometimes-awkward perversion of consumer logic, the data and the engagement itself belongs to the emerging or established leader being coached. The need to uphold the prerogative and privilege of confidentiality in favour of the leader being coached is so that coaching emerging and established leaders will not be used as a means of managing people out of organizations or discovering cause to terminate.

If data collected in 360-degree-structured interviews (or any other type of self- or multi-rater assessment) is used in such nefarious ways, coaching will forever lose all credibility and power to transform leaders in positive ways. The same is true of those who provide feedback for emerging or established leaders in qualitative or quantitative assessment processes. If they cannot be assured that what they share will be held in strictest confidence, including not revealing source identity to the leader being coached, then the source of truly valid, reliable and objective feedback will be completely compromised and dry up. Even more data will be lost that bears tremendous organizational reconnaissance value if confidentiality is compromised (see Commandment 10).

As mentioned in Commandment 3, the coach must be organizationally savvy (enterprise-wise) and function as a skilled facilitator to make sure that all voices are heard and acknowledged as the coaching engagement is designed. That's the only way the voice of the organization can be heard, whereas the basic outline of executive coaching engagements remains similar from one engagement to the next, specifics of what happens inside the engagement are almost never the same from one engagement to the next. That's the micro focus that will be described in Commandment 6.

This macro perspective—setting the expectations among the coach, the coaching client, the coaching client's manager and the organization—is essentially how the engagement framework is built. And the contextual framework will be consistent from one engagement to the next across the organization, thus ensuring enterprise-wide continuity and quality assurance as leaders are developed. If executive coaching is used to build the leaders who will build your business, you need to take steps to ensure that the framework for coaching engagements is aligned with your organization's leadership development strategy, which should, in turn, be fully aligned with your organization's global business strategy.

If you are the individual responsible for managing the coaching function in your organization, you must hire organizationally aware coaches and be a good teacher for your coaching clients and their managers to make sure everyone understands that every coaching engagement across your organization marches to the beat of your organizational leadership competencies, values, priorities and/or disciplines.

Every coaching report that's filed (and there should be no less than an action plan with a mid-term and final update) paints a backdrop of how the leader being coached is growing and developing in the organizational context. It cannot be said often enough, the essential question that cuts to the chase with any coaching engagement is, 'How is this helping our organization?'

Specific details, such as how many face-to-face sessions will be conducted between the coach and the coaching client, how often, how many reports will be developed collaboratively between the coach and coaching client, how often will the coalition meet together to discuss and approve the reports are all macro issues when it comes to engagement design. Most contextual coaching engagements will involve a 360-degree assessment comprised of the coach conducting a series of structured interviews. As also mentioned in Commandment 4 about the coaching coalition, the coalition negotiates which feedback providers will be approached to provide multi-rater data and which questions will be asked to ensure the most salient challenges are surfaced for the coaching.

As discussed at the beginning of this chapter, these are all macro issues of co-creating the executive coaching engagement. Commandment 6 will deal with the micro issues of co-creating the individual coaching sessions. The reason alignment is emphasized so often because the macro design of engagements that ensures the organization is continuously engaged in coaching emerging and established executives must resonate with the micro challenge of making sure the individual leader's unique growth and development needs are successfully addressed, which they cannot be unless the macro context of the engagement is established. That is, in absence of the cultural and strategic context in which the emerging or established leader is functioning, the growth and development of the leader being coached will be severely limited. And so goes the dance of executive coaching, where the best interests of individual leaders must align with the best interests of their organizations.

MACRO PERSPECTIVE REQUIRES A SYSTEMS PERSPECTIVE

One core thesis behind the concept of organizational behaviour (OB) is that human behaviour in isolation changes when an individual functions as part of an organizational system and vice versa. The implications of this for coaching emerging and established leaders and executives in organizations are enormous. For example, leading OB theorists such as Chester Bernard and Herbert Simon contend that decision-making happens differently in group settings versus individual settings. At its core, coaching emerging and established leaders—which is to say causing change in the form of behaviour modification—is about making different and better decisions. In a system, a single decision unleashes energy that usually impacts every other dimension of the system.

In organizational settings, the interface between individual human behaviour and the organization as an aggregation of individuals, groups and sub-groups, is a study in complex systems. Currently, most coaching in organizational settings is still approached in a one-off, detached, fragmented and isolated manner that lacks true strategic organizational alignment or enterprise wisdom. To use the language established earlier in this treatise, most coaching of emerging and established leaders in complex organizational systems lacks the necessary strategic vision and alignment to deliver maximum enterprise-wide improvement in decision-making and other leadership behaviours capable of propelling organizations forward towards their espoused goals, objectives and fulfilment of their global strategic agenda.

One Partners International client with more than 100 years of major organizational and marquee-name recognition in the marketplace and Fortune 100 credentials on the street spends millions of dollars on executive coaching each year and yet has no consolidated nor aligned enterprise-wide framework or process for coaching their emerging and established leaders. What takes place in one coaching engagement might or might not have anything whatsoever to do with a coaching engagement taking place across the hallway or on the other side of the world in terms of how the corporation has defined leadership excellence. That is to say that each executive coaching engagement focuses only on the specific behavioural goals and objectives unique to the emerging or established leader being coached (see the micro perspective described in Commandment 6).

In this major international corporation with more than 50,000 employees worldwide, coaching coalitions are only formed if a specific HR business partner feels it is necessary. Contextual coaches regularly request the formation of actively engaged stakeholder coalitions, but the requests are seldom honoured. 'Everyone is too busy', the coach is told. Coaching action plans are consistent across the enterprise but only cover coaching goals and objectives unique to the individual leader being coached. There is nothing in the coaching action plans at this firm that pins the desired individual goals and outcomes to the overarching leadership competencies, priorities, success factors, disciplines, values or other monikers for the way the organization has defined leadership excellence.

Nothing in the organization in question aligns what their leaders do best with what the organization needs most. Any correlation between the two is merely coincidental or through the deliberate efforts of a contextual coach working on his or her own initiative to enhance the organizational value of the coaching services being delivered. There simply is no macro focus. This is due to the old-school notions about coaching being about the coach and 'coachee' disappearing together behind a veil of secrecy or beneath a cone of confidentiality to do secret work that will return the emerging or established leader to the organization one to three years later in a radically transformed state that might or might not have anything to do with what the organization truly needs from the leader being coached. Again, the macro focus was forgotten and/or neglected altogether. The voice of the organization was silenced.

As mentioned in Commandment 1, gaggles of mostly unschooled (in the craft of coaching), overstarched and overimpressed (with themselves) master coaches (not ICF MCCs) convince mid-level HR managers, directors and VPs that the masters are the Solomons of coaching, keepers of all coaching wisdom and knowledge, and proceed to dictate policy. The tail still wags the coaching dog in all too many major organizations who are convinced (by the Svengali-like independent coaches) that there is some magic formula to coaching executives that only they, the self-proclaimed wizards of coaching, possess.

Whatever! No matter how magical and transformative the Svengali coaching might be, if it is not conducted in complete alignment with the global strategic agenda of the organization paying to coach the emerging or established leaders, a great deal of money is being wasted on executive coaching in the form of a diminished return on the coaching spend. The renewed rant about Svengali coaches is born from frustration with those managing the coaching function in organizations who still allow the tail to wag the coaching dog.

The ideal leader of a coaching function in an organization is someone who is:

1. Formally trained as a coach
2. Independently accredited and credentialed as a coach (ICF for example)
3. In possession of a graduate degree in OD and/or OB

4. Someone with business-side P&L experience
5. A student of theories and evidence-based psychological foundations of coaching

Credit HR consulting, talent development, career transition and executive coaching entrepreneur, Amy Friedman, with asking the simple question, 'How is this helping the firm?' Six words that explain with tremendous concision the importance of maintaining the micro focus parallel dimension of macro focus. Even if the coach of an emerging or established leader can make a strong case for how the organization's coaching investment is building a leader who will, in turn, build the business (which is a great thing), how well can the coach articulate and run across the taxonomy to apply how the coaching of one individual emerging or established leader is deliberately and intentionally aligned with the enterprise-wide leadership development strategy?

Revisiting Simon and Bernard's theories about individual versus corporate decision-making, creating a culture of coaching means that the wisdom that comes from a rich combination of experience, exposure, research and inquiry informs sustainable solutions as opposed to individuals seeking the course of least resistance—aka groupthink. In cultures where powerful questions are not asked in the cultural context of the organization, individual leaders, emerging or experienced and established, can and often do engage in groupthink solitaire. When quality coaching helps tap internal reserves and reservoirs of experience, exposure, instinct and/or intuition in emerging and experienced leaders, decisions are more sound and sustainable. When coaching of emerging and experienced leaders is consistently enterprise-wide, the continuity of quality coaching makes sound and sustainable decision-making more consistent and frequent.

Coaching of emerging or established leaders is not complete until the macro interests of an organization are served alongside (read: aligned with) the micro interests of the individual. As a discipline that is at least 50 per cent organizationally focused, contextual coaching embraces much of the thinking discipline found in organizational psychology, the execution discipline found in OB and the strategic planning discipline found in organization design and development. Most importantly, complete contextual coaching incorporates the organizational dimensions of all three and aligns them with the thinking discipline found in individual psychology, the execution discipline found in individual behaviour and the strategic planning discipline found in the organization design and development dimensions of individual performance. Complete contextual coaching also embraces important aspects of social sciences and economics to provide a well-rounded coaching experience through an organizational lens.

CONTEXTUAL COACHING
COMMANDMENT 5: CONCLUSION

The macro perspective establishes the expectations between the coach, coaching client and the organization. As mentioned at the beginning of this chapter, most individual coaching engagements that involve emerging or established executives are intensely focused on specific behaviour change. Maintaining the macro perspective throughout a contextual coaching engagement ensures that an organizational framework will be built and maintained to keep the organizational context intact, regardless of what type of individual coaching is taking place inside the frame.

An organization can have a gaggle of Svengali-style coaches running the hallways and practising their secret magic and still keep the overall transformative power of coaching emerging and established leaders flowing—as long as the macro perspective is maintained vis-à-vis the contextual and cultural process and framework. At Partners International, it is called 'The Art of Alignment'. Contextual coaching consistently aligns individual and organizational interests of emerging and established leaders with their organization's interests through the coaching application of enterprise wisdom.

Contextual Coaching Commandment

Co-create the Engagement

The Micro Perspective

In Commandment 5, the discussion continued from Commandment 3 about keeping the voice of the organization alive, present and participating in executive coaching engagements through the formation of a coaching (or stakeholder) coalition, as described further in Commandment 4. The coaching coalition's primary function is to ensure that the interests of the organization are at least equally represented, protected and even promoted throughout coaching engagements alongside the interests of the emerging or established leader being coached. In Commandment 6, the emphasis shifts from the overall, organizationally focused macro coaching engagement to the individual focus in micro coaching sessions.

A holistic coaching engagement paid for by a business or other organization represents the overall coaching programme or event for an emerging or established leader being coached and needs to be aligned contextually with the sponsoring organization's leadership development strategy, as well as its overarching organizational strategic agenda. One mantra to put on your conference room wall is, 'A successful business strategy begins with a solid talent strategy'. Some might argue that the mantra should be reversed. Perhaps. The point is well taken either way. The leadership development strategy in an organization (as a component of an overarching talent development strategy) and the global business strategy must be inexorably linked. The coaching coalition works together to monitor and guide coaching engagements to ensure that the engagements are consistently aligned with organizational leadership *and* business strategies.

As opposed to the work of the coaching coalition, which focuses on alignment between the voice of the organization and the growth and development of the emerging or established leaders, the individual coaching sessions, although professionally oriented, are much more personal and involve only the coach and the coaching client. As discussed in Commandment 5, regarding the macro perspective, the language around coaching is shifting and some might say, maturing.

Some now refer to the coach and coaching client dyad as 'the practitioner and the participant' or 'the coach and the leader'. The earlier rant on the term 'coachee' notwithstanding, others would still insist on referring to the dyad as 'coach and the coachee'. Regardless of how those involved in coaching engagements and coaching sessions are labelled, what transpires between them must still be aligned with the sponsoring organization's strategic agenda. However, it is the more intimate work between the coach and the emerging or established leader receiving coaching that ultimately accomplishes said alignment while still enabling growth and development of the coaching client against his or her individual coaching goals and objectives.

In the macro work of the coaching coalition, as it collectively creates the coaching engagement, the primary focus—or at least equally shared focus—is on the alignment of the engagement to the organization's leadership and business strategies When the coach and coaching client co-create each coaching *session*, the more intimate micro focus is on the individual leader's growth and development agenda. Even during their more intimate work, however, the coach and coaching client remain mindful of contextual alignment. Although the privilege of confidentiality is honoured, the organization's needs are never out of mind.

GUIDING THE SESSIONS

The ICF has done a comprehensive job of bringing together guidelines and best practices for non-directive coaching techniques. The ICF list of 11 core competencies, if practised properly, will help, guide and enhance any coaching session as well as serve as foundational and operational architecture for entire coaching engagements. When seeking consistent quality of executive coaching across an organization, the ICF core competencies are an excellent standard to apply.

The context of what leaders should look like—and ideally how they should show up, present and conduct themselves—is a matter of establishing leadership competencies, values, priorities and/or values that align with the organization's cultural and strategic agenda. The individual coaching sessions as well as the coaching engagements should be conducted in that context. All of the ICF core competencies can and should be deployed when coaching in complex organizations. A brief overview of how that can look follows:

THE ICF'S 11 CORE COMPETENCIES AS PRACTISED IN COMPLEX ORGANIZATIONS

A. Setting the Foundation

1. Meeting Ethical Guidelines and Professional Standards

These are well defined by the ICF and can be studied on their website.[1] The ICF, like other accrediting bodies in the field of coaching, takes the issues of ethics and professionalism very seriously and has set in place guidelines and standards that

---

[1] See http://coachfederation.org

any business or organization that employs internal or external coaches can rely on to represent the best practitioner conduct that can be expected in the practice of coaching emerging or established leaders. The ICF's exhaustive work in the area of ethics and professionalism in coaching should be a role model for other credentialing bodies as well as any coach training programme. The ICF preamble to their ethical guidelines and professional standards narrative makes this dedication to superior standards evident:

> ICF is committed to maintaining and promoting excellence in coaching. Therefore, ICF expects all members and credentialed coaches (coaches, coach mentors, coaching supervisors, coach trainers, or students), to adhere to the elements and principles of ethical conduct: to be competent and integrate ICF Core Competencies effectively in their work.
>
> In line with the ICF core values and ICF definition of coaching, the Code of Ethics is designed to provide appropriate guidelines, accountability and enforceable standards of conduct for all ICF Members and ICF Credential-holders, who commit to abiding by the following ICF Code of Ethics.

As an overview of the complete ICF treatise on ethical behaviour for coaches adopted by the ICF Global Board of Directors in June 2015, the correlations to and applications of coaching in businesses and organizations are often self-apparent.

In Part I of the ethical commentary, the ICF provides its definition of coaching:

> Coaching is partnering with clients in a thought-provoking and creative process that inspires them to maximize their personal and professional potential.

While other definitions of coaching in simple and complex organizations abound and can easily be found on the Internet, they all point into the wind of helping professional men and women conduct themselves in more influential and inspirational ways that promote the best interests of their organizations and constituencies. ICF-credentialed coaches, as all coaches should do, pledge to practise in accordance with a set of rigorous standards that create accountability and establish credible guidelines for professional coaching relationships. The ICF sets forth that a professional coaching relationship exists, 'when coaching includes an agreement (including contracts) that defines and clarifies the responsibilities of each party'.

The ICF's ethical guidelines and professional standards help clarify roles in coaching relationships. In terms of coaching in organizations, the ICF recognizes the importance of distinguishing between coaching clients and organizational sponsors, as described in Commandment 4 about the roles of coaching coalition members. When coaching in organizations, for example, whether a coach is working as an independent external coach, a representative of an external coaching provider organization or an internal coach, the true fiduciary relationship exists between the organization funding the coaching engagement and the coach or coaching provider. The coaching client, executive, participant or however the organization refers to the emerging or established leader being coached is not the customer but rather the end user.

All of the privileges that are customary for a coaching client to expect remain intact, including but not limited to coach–client confidentiality, ownership of coaching conversation and 360-degree-structured interview data. Even so, the organization is party to (if not the author of) the professional covenant and contract for the coaching engagement. This is all the more reason to promote consistency and continuity throughout all coaching engagements across the enterprise through adherence to a rigorous set of ethical guidelines and professional standards like those the ICF has established in the ICF core competencies. In life coaching, where the individual being coached and the coach contract directly with one another and the coaching fee is paid out of the client's personal resources, an organization that the coaching client is working for does not have a place in the coaching coalition unless invited by the coaching client and the fiduciary relationship is directly between the coach and the coaching client, who is also the end user.

The ICF holds that 'In [cases where], the client and sponsor are the same person, [they] are jointly referred to as the client. For purposes of identification, [the] ICF defines these roles as follows: The Client [is] the person(s) being coached. [The] sponsor is the entity (including its representatives) paying for and/or arranging for coaching services to be provided. In all cases, coaching engagement agreements should clearly establish the rights, roles and responsibilities for both the client and sponsor if the client and sponsor are different people'.

In its online ethics narrative (http://www.coachfederation.org/ethics), the ICF goes on to define the roles of students, coaching supervisors and coach mentors in learning the coaching process or enhancing and developing coaching skills. The issues ICF lists have been slightly broadened later to encompass all of the principal parties in an organizational coaching engagement. However, the micro focus of an organizational coaching engagement is the primary consciousness at this moment even though the macro implications are also present and evident.

The following list is inspired by what is perhaps the world's most comprehensive single resource for coaching knowledge and application. The ICF provides definitions, descriptions and methods for addressing issues that include, but are not limited to:

Section One: Professional Conduct at Large

- Commitments and accountability around all interactions, including coach training, coach mentoring and coach supervisory activities
- Commitments to take the appropriate action with coaches, coach trainers and coach mentors or supervisors, and to contact ICF to address any ethics violations or possible

breaches as soon as the possibility of such violations becomes apparent

- Communicating and creating awareness in others, including organizations, employees, sponsors, coaches and others who might need to be informed of the responsibilities established by codes of ethical conduct and professional behaviour
- Avoidance of unlawful discrimination in occupational activities, including age, race, gender orientation, ethnicity, sexual orientation, religion, national origin or disability.
- Commitments to make verbal and written statements that are true and accurate about what coaches offer appropriately as coaching practitioners and the coaching industry as a whole
- Accurate identification of coaching qualifications, expertise, experience, training, certifications and coaching credentials
- Recognizing and honouring the efforts and contributions of others and claiming only the ownership of original material
- Understanding that violating the previous standard may lead to legal remedies by a third party
- Striving at all times to recognize personal issues that may impair, conflict with or interfere with performance of coaching responsibilities or professional coaching relationships
- Commitment to promptly seek relevant professional assistance and determine the action to be taken, including whether it is appropriate to suspend or terminate coaching relationship(s) whenever the facts and circumstances necessitate
- Recognizing that the Code of Ethics applies to all relationships with coaching clients, emerging and established leaders, students, mentees and supervisees
- Conducting and reporting research with competence, honesty and within recognized scientific standards and applicable subject guidelines

- How to maintain, store and/or dispose of any records, including electronic files and communications created during coaching engagements in a manner that preserves confidentiality, security, privacy and complies with any applicable laws and agreements
- Using ICF Member contact information (email addresses, telephone numbers, etc.) only in the manner and to the extent authorized by the ICF

Section Two: Conflicts of Interest

- Clarifying roles for internal coaches including setting boundaries and reviewing with stakeholders the conflicts of interest or dual roles that may emerge between coaching and other organizational role functions
- Disclosing to clients and organizational sponsors all anticipated compensation from third parties that might result from referrals of clients or compensation for receiving clients
- Honouring equitable coach/client relationships, regardless of the form of compensation

Section Three: Ensuring Professional Conduct with Clients

- Ethically speaking what is known to be true to clients, clients' managers, prospective clients and sponsors about the potential value of the coaching process
- Carefully explaining and striving to ensure that, prior to or at the initial (coaching coalition) meeting, coaching client, coaching client's manager, organizational sponsor(s) and coaches understand the full nature of coaching
- Crafting a clear coaching service agreement with all parties to the coaching engagement before launching the coaching engagement

- Holding responsibility for awareness of and setting clear, appropriate and culturally sensitive boundaries that govern interactions, physical or otherwise, that might be part of a coaching engagement
- Avoiding any inappropriate relationship or dual role with current clients, organizational sponsor(s), coaching students, mentees, supervisees or any other parties to a coaching engagement
- Taking appropriate action to provide a safe environment overall for the coaching engagement and all parties involved or affected
- Respecting the coaching client's right or the right of the sponsoring organization to terminate the coaching relationship at any point during the process, subject to the provisions of the coaching agreement
- Remaining alert to indications that there is a shift in the value received from the coaching relationship
- Encouraging changes to be made if the client, client's manager, organizational sponsor or the organization at large would be better served by another coach or other resource

Section Four: Maintaining Confidentiality/Privacy

- Maintaining the strictest levels of confidentiality with the information of the coaching client, coaching client's manager and organizational sponsor unless release is required by law
- Crafting a clear agreement about how coaching information will be exchanged among all parties to the coaching engagement
- Cleary specifying and reaching agreement up front from all parties to the coaching engagement about the conditions under which confidentiality may not be maintained (e.g., illegal activity, pursuant to valid court order or subpoena; imminent or likely risk of danger to self or to others; etc.) and ensuring all parties to the coaching engagement agree in writing to that limit of confidentiality

Section Five: Continuing Development

- Continuing development of professional skills as a coach, organizational sponsor of coaching engagements or any other role responsible for influencing the quality of the coaching experience

Before moving on, let us revisit the ICF Pledge of Ethics for coaches:

> As an ICF coach, I acknowledge and agree to honor my ethical and legal obligations to my coaching clients and sponsors, colleagues, and to the public at large. I pledge to comply with the ICF Code of Ethics and to practice these standards with those whom I coach, teach, mentor, or supervise.
>
> If I breach this Pledge of Ethics or any part of the ICF Code of Ethics, I agree that the ICF in its sole discretion may hold me accountable for so doing. I further agree that my accountability to the ICF for any breach may include sanctions, such as loss of my ICF Membership and/or my ICF Credentials.

Once again, broadening the groundwork the ICF has established, the following two bullets could be added to the ethics conversation:

- Pledging to honour all ethical and legal obligations (ICF or otherwise) to the coaching engagement and all participating parties
- Keeping everyone involved in the coaching engagement accountable to the organization and the ICF or other standards-establishing body for any breach that may include sanctions, such as loss of memberships and/or credentials.

The remaining ICF core competencies are as follows. They are expanded and embellished with relevant expansion given to provide the following organizational context—co-creation of coaching engagements for emerging or established leaders being coached to ensure continuous alignment to achieve maximum value for both the emerging or established leader and the organization sponsoring the coaching engagement.

2. Establishing the Coaching Agreement

Every session needs to be co-created between the executive coach and the emerging or established leader receiving the coaching. Every executive coaching session has an agreement between coach and leader on what the session outcomes should be, even if the agreement is oral. The written action plan and the mid-term and final updates to the action plan reflect the expectations and the work being done inside the overall coaching engagement and are signed off on by the coaching coalition members. Contextual alignment to the organizational strategic agenda is always the framework or backdrop when the coaching is conducted in organizational context.

B. Co-creating the Relationship

3. Establishing Trust and Intimacy with the Client

This is essential for the intimate micro coaching session work that the executive coach and the emerging or established leader being coached do together. In addition to trust and intimacy between the executive coach and leader, trust and respect need to be established for all members of the coaching coalition and, hopefully, become a mainstay of the entire enterprise.

4. Coaching Presence

In session work between the executive coach and the emerging or established leader receiving coaching, it is imperative that the coach be totally present and available emotionally and intellectually for the coaching client, regardless of the issue and overriding contextual framework. It is the coach's responsibility to every party invested in the success of the coaching engagement to remain focused.

C. Communicating Effectively

5. Active Listening

This is a skill that helps everyone in the workplace and beyond. It is not reserved only for the micro one-on-one coaching sessions or the work of the coaching coalition. Active listening is essential at both the micro- and macro-levels if the coaching engagement is going to succeed.

6. Powerful Questioning

Challenging conventional or unconventional thinking that might be binding up a leader is one responsibility of an executive coach. But it is also a skill that can unleash new, more reflective, better and broader thinking virtually anywhere—including when co-creating coaching engagements. Executive coaching is largely a cognitive endeavour.

7. Direct Communication

This is another skill that has broad value and application, especially in formal and complex organizations as well as interpersonal relations. Coaching sessions are good opportunities to learn and begin practicing direct communication skills and techniques. The concept of direct communication, especially in business and organizational settings, can also be studied in *The Art of Constructive Confrontation: Increasing Accountability and Reducing Conflict* by John Hoover and Roger DiSilvestro.[2]

D. Facilitating Learning and Results

8. Creating Awareness

The heightened individual and organizational awareness that will, hopefully, sweep the organization and broaden peoples' thinking

---

[2] John Hoover and Roger DiSilvestro, *The Art of Constructive Confrontation: Increasing Accountability and Reducing Conflict* (Hoboken, NJ: Wiley, 2005).

often begins in intimate coaching session conversations. The way that powerful questions break through mental and emotional blockages and bifurcations to promote reflection is one way that coaches help their coaching clients create awareness.

9. Designing Actions

Operationalizing the ideas and new thinking that emerge from coaching sessions and making them real, palpable and authentic is a primary goal of coaching. Turning reflective thinking and new awareness into new behaviour conclusively demonstrates how the micro focus work that takes place in coaching sessions for emerging or established leaders and across the entire coaching engagement aligns with the broader organizational outcomes as established in the engagement's contextual framework.

10. Planning and Goal Setting

Once again, the executive coach and the emerging or established leader being coached begin the work of mapping out specific objectives to be achieved to turn new awareness into real outcomes. From the micro-level to the macro-level, the alignment between individual plans and goals and organizational plans and goals should ideally be in the context of the organization's desired culture and strategic agenda.

11. Managing Progress and Accountability

Osmosis is not a commonly accepted coaching technique. If it were, powerful questioning would not be necessary. Coaching, as defined by the ICF, is more inherently heuristic in that the answers emerge largely from the coaching client's experience, education and common sense. This is to say that the new learnings must represent incremental or large-scale progress and be memorialized in order to keep the coaching client accountable for his or her growth and development. This 11th core competency from the ICF is particularly valuable when considering that there is a contextual frame-work within which organizational coaching will be conducted at both the micro- and macro-levels.

CONTEXTUAL COACHING COMMANDMENT 6: CONCLUSION

When co-creating the individual executive coaching sessions at the micro-level and with a micro focus and perspective, expecta-tions need to be established and agreed upon between the coach and the emerging or established leader receiving the coaching. When co-creating the entire coaching engagement, the coach, the leader, the leader's manager, the organizational sponsor and any other members of the coaching coalition must negotiate and come to agreement on what the outcomes should be and how they will align with leadership competencies, values and/or disciplines established for the organization, all based on the organization's overarching strategic agenda.

Most individual coaching engagements that involve emerging or established leaders are intensely focused on specific behaviour change. They are, therefore, much more narrowly focused by design. Having said that, all organizational coaching is conducted with one eye on the larger entity. Complete contextual coaching also embraces important aspects of social sciences and economics to provide a well-rounded coaching experience through an organiza-tional lens. The individual work, no matter how powerfully transformative, is most valuable when conducted in the context of the organization's global business agenda.

Contextual Coaching Commandment

Establish and Maintain a Coaching Culture for a Well-coached Company

A coaching culture in an organization means a well-coached company. A well-coached company means that coaching is for everyone and everyone is for coaching. Enterprise-wide support for coaching means coaching in the organization is enterprise-*wise*.

A coaching culture is formed when an organization offers multiple types of coaching (internal, external, team and group) and fosters the expectation that all emerging and established leaders will coach their employees. A coaching culture means adopting and articulating curiosity, inquiry and thinking partnerships as the shared values, beliefs and expectations enterprise-wide and then consistently practising them globally. A coaching culture asks for ideas and input instead of telling and giving orders. A coaching culture works inside out and bottom-up instead of the old-school notions of outside-in and top-down. Coaching cultures build the leaders who build businesses based on the best thinking from the highest potential people. Coaching cultures access the whole person and create sustainable solutions by accessing the truth that dedicated men and women carry inside themselves until someone grants them permission and encourages them to speak it.

Commandment 5 was about the macro perspective that puts all of the aforementioned in organizational context. As a provider of contextual coaching services, I am always looking for coaches who are constantly on the new frontier looking to help coaching clients add value to the organizations they serve. Working to develop enterprise-wide and enterprise-*wise* cultures of coaching makes enterprise-wide enhancement of habits, skills and attitudes pre-emptive rather than reactive. Too often our Partners International telephone rings *after* an executive has been promoted into a position he or she is not qualified and/or experienced enough to successfully occupy. In such cases, our coaching services are often requested to instil five or more years of leadership maturity in six months or less. A true coaching culture would never allow that to happen.

Instilling five or more years of leadership maturity in six months or less is a tall order under any circumstances. Instead of waiting until emotional and material damage has been done, relationships broken and dissention sewn far and wide, a deliberate and healthy culture of coaching helps to keep people at all levels of the organization continuously engaged and working on habits, skills and attitudes—individually and corporately—as a way of doing business, not merely dealing with difficult and challenging behaviour after the fact.

Unless your organization is consciously, systematically and strategically building and sustaining a culture of coaching, summoning an internal or external coach to contend with a dysfunctional behaviour is more likely to resemble a 911 call rather than pre-emptively and strategically developing leadership strengths. Note that in Appendix A later in the book, there is an exhaustive list of organizationally aligned overutilized, underutilized and optimally utilized strengths. A proactive culture of coaching focuses energy and resources on creating thinking partnerships, accelerating performance and making good talent better rather than waiting for things and people to crash and require correction or rescue.

In our experience as a provider of organizationally aligned executive coaching services framed in the context of the enterprise leadership development strategy, some of the most frequently cited reasons for coaching are:

1. To enhance executive presence
2. To develop leadership potential
3. To help executives deal with stress
4. To address habits, skills and attitudes
5. To prepare high-potentials for promotion
6. To prepare high-potentials for succession
7. To improve intrapersonal communication
8. To help find assistance with personal problems[1]
9. To soften critical or abusive leadership behaviours
10. To help people understand and better fulfil their roles
11. To interpret 360-degree feedback and put it to good use
12. To help the individual transition to a larger or stretch role
13. To interpret and put to good use self-reporting assessment data
14. To help the individual navigate a major organizational transformation or crisis
15. To help shape perceptions and expectations to improve attitudes and relationships

Why should an organization adopt one-on-one coaching? Aren't training and development or organizational learning solutions enough? You will never get anyone in the talent development business to criticize the practice of organizational learning. Partners International occupies as much space in the organizational education and strategic team alignment universe as we do in executive coaching. There has never been an executive, artist or athlete who did not improve on his or her natural talents and

---

[1] Perhaps simply by referring the emerging or established leader being coached back to the organizational sponsor and/or employee assistance programme.

abilities with expanded knowledge and practice. There has never been an organization that performed better over time in a state of ignorance than in a state of enlightenment.

Training and development activities are good. But coaching is better. It is the difference between classroom learning for children and having a private tutor who is a subject-matter expert. It is the difference between attending golf, tennis or skiing clinics versus private lessons.

In terms of developing talent and leadership in organizations, the best possible outcome results from a combination of group training and development opportunities plus one-or-one coaching. In action coaching, action learning or what we refer to as strategic team alignment, it is the combining of real-time learning activities with individual coaching that gives the entire learning experience maximum traction and transformation. If organizational learning is an effective topical ointment, coaching is a fast-acting, quick-dissolving gel tablet with a concentrated dosage. Perhaps even an IV drip.

No single form of training and development gets a business person's attention as completely as coaching. No single form of organizational learning addresses an individual business person's complete range of developmental needs as completely or comprehensively as coaching. No other form of workplace intervention offers more hope of radical performance improvement than coaching.

Nothing can transform an entire organization's way of doing business faster than coaching. Nothing cascades best practices and best thinking more powerfully and sustainably as a cultural coaching construct. Massive doses of training, learning and development or team development can spread the word enterprise-wide fast. But the hyperbole will dissipate into the ether even faster if the message isn't turned into a way of living and doing business.

Training human beings, as when training other carbon-based life forms, is about learning to do new things and familiar things in new ways. But transforming learnings into ways of living and doing business requires the new behaviour and thinking to become personal. Truly transformed thinking and behaviour is more than just doing new things, it requires a new way of being. Training, learning and development, as good and helpful as they can be, are much more about doing and less about being. At its core, coaching is less about the human doing and more about the human being.

Coaching is action learning and action learning's antecedent discipline, action research, at its very best. Completely real-time and real-world, individual coaching is a continuous living tutorial on habits, skills and attitudes—all in the context of the organization—especially in the social and professional interactions of organizational life.

Consider what executive coaching is most commonly needed for: to fully groom and prepare people for the new roles and responsibilities the organization needs them to assume or when disruptive executive behaviour has reached critical proportions and organizational policymakers are faced with the daunting prospect of severing ties with an expensive sample of senior talent—often a top revenue producer.

THE DOUBLE-EDGED SWORD

This book does not fully address why so many organizational policymakers promote so many men and women who have no background, training, coaching, natural instincts or talent to manage people into roles where they are responsible for leading and inspiring dozens, hundreds and even thousands of unfortunate employees who never imagined reporting to such extreme incompetence. That might sound harsh, but the number of times executive coaches have repressed the impulse to ask such organizational policymakers, 'What in the lower realms were you thinking?' outnumber the stars. As many heads of organizational coaching practices tell us, the bitter-yet-honest truth is that coaching done as a result of improper promotions is often no more than a Band-Aid on a massive wound—it might slow or even stop the bleeding—but it rarely heals the wound.

The other side of that double-edged sword is sharper than the insanity of promoting incompetents into positions of tremendous institutional authority where what they either don't know or think they know but don't destroys careers, lives and millions in profits. The reasons so many organizational policymakers make such organizationally devastating and obscenely expensive decisions when filling top-of-the-house positions are varied. Some are promoted due to nepotism. Others are promoted because their personalities and attitudes are so explosive and volatile that organizational policymakers fear them and would prefer to cower and grant a promotion than to grow a spine and say, 'no' to an obviously insane promotion.

Most often, organizational policymakers see a top-producing salesperson, a genius software writer, a top-notch scientist, engineer or physician and somehow conclude that they have a great leader at their hands. However, nothing has been proven more often than someone who is exceptionally talented at something is by nature antithetical to leading others to do that something. An amazingly talented technician will not by osmosis be an equally talented, nurturing, encouraging and inspirational leader once he or she is promoted. The fact that this technique of selecting people for promotion fails nine times for every one time it succeeds seems to be lost on people who claim to make data-driven decisions.

The data is painful no matter how you slice it. Swinging the sword in one direction chops off the most talented, experienced and productive people on the payroll, severing them from the work they love and that delivers the highest possible value to the organization from their efforts. Depending on the industry, the first swing of the promotion sword can often lop off the aforementioned top-producing salesperson, genius software author, top-notch scientist, engineer or physician. In short, the greatest talent and potential are no longer available to the organization because they were promoted *away* from their area of expertise and competence. You might as well have pushed them in front of a bus as far as their post-promotion usefulness to the organization is concerned. They might show up for work as the new boss, but they are bandaged and hobbled with splints.

Just as you might begin to realize the tremendous blow to production, performance and profitability that has been dealt by an ill-advised promotion, the double-edged sword swings the other direction and beheads any hope of skilled and effective leadership emanating from the offices the former top-producing salesperson, genius software writer, top-notch scientist, engineer or physician now occupies—offices that should be filled with, hopefully, strategic leaders who inspire, motivate and bring out the best in everyone within their spans of control. In short, the ill-advised promotion caused the loss from the organization of the best producers in their fields and placed enormous institutional authority in the hands of rank amateurs when it comes to leading others.

The unfortunate truth is, when it comes to top-of-the-house promotion decisions, allowing only the 'right people' into 'the club' takes precedent over qualifications, talent and ability. How Kahunas keep their inner circle pure is worthy of its own book. In fact, the entire issue of institutionalizing incompetence versus the more logical practice of institutionalizing incompetents is described in the book *How to Work for an Idiot: Survive and Thrive... Without Killing Your Boss.*[2] For the purpose of illustrating the immense value in creating and sustaining a coaching culture, there is nothing like setting the bar in the right place for leadership behaviour that aligns what people do best with what the organization needs most.

---

[2] John Hoover, *How to Work for an Idiot: Survive and Thrive...Without Killing Your Boss,* 2nd Ed. (Franklin Lakes, NJ: Career Press, 2011).

HOW DOES A COACHING CULTURE HELP TO AVOID THE DOUBLE-EDGED SWORD?

'Why such a bleak tale of despair?', you ask. 'Surely, not all senior-level promotions are that catastrophic or damaging to the organization'.

True. Most promotions barely blip the radar. They do not wrinkle the bedcovers. They do not cause noise in the system. They protect and promote the status quo. They don't change a thing because they ain't got that swing. Everything remains cool, calm and copasetic. But without such bleak scenarios, the executive coaching industry would be slashed to a fraction of its current size.

With rare exceptions, organizations are far more willing to pay large fees for coaching executives who are blipping the radar, wrinkling the sheets, causing noise in the system and upsetting somebody's apple cart. The big money paid out on a per engagement basis for coaching in for-profit, not-for-profit and public-sector organizations is to reduce friction and restore balance to a system that has for some reason been unbalanced by whomever has been identified as the leader in need of coaching.

Truth be told, coaching is often provided for scapegoats rather than the true disruptive influences. Reading all of this might cause you to think the author is delusional or that the organizational policymakers who make ill-advised promotions are delusional. In truth, both feel perfectly justified in thinking what they think and doing what they do. So, what is the best organizational hedge against discovering people are in positions they are not qualified to occupy? Coaching. Not merely coaching scapegoats, but, building a *coaching culture* that eliminates the need to identify scapegoats. A well-thought-out and executed coaching culture could render blame-throwers extinct and cause the closure of scapegoat identification departments in many organizations.

In the same way that *The Art of Constructive Confrontation*[3] promotes reducing conflict by confronting problems early and often, the noise and disruption in the enterprise-wide corporate system can be avoided by pre-emptive coaching of emerging and established leaders by well-trained, independently credentialed, organizationally aligned and enterprise-*wise* internal and external coaches. As mentioned earlier, some of the basic tenets of coaching include curiosity and inquiry. 'Why is this person right for this position?' 'Does this person have the attitudes, skills and habits to succeed in this new position?'

COACHING PUMPS UP LEADERSHIP DEVELOPMENT PROGRAMMES

When there are only seconds left on the clock to preserve a monumental investment in human capital—that is keeping a senior executive from derailing or setting the senior executive back on the rails after he or she has derailed—one does not send the senior executive to an instructor-led classroom or an online course to bring about change. It means calling in an executive coach. When the *whole team* needs a powerful intervention or performance acceleration, the answer to the problem is dialling up strategic team alignment with individual coaching for each team member.

Coaching can make emerging leaders succession ready and fully prepared for the challenges they will face in future positions. If exposed to coaching early enough and given opportunities to observe and practise coaching skills, emerging leaders will develop an adaptive capacity for problem solving and leading people with sufficient skills to avoid the need for corrective coaching when they become experienced and established leaders. But coaching is expensive.

---

[3] Hoover and DiSilvestro, *The Art of Constructive Confrontation*.

Some of the best programmes we have deployed and seen deployed include leadership development in the form of strategic team alignment with a coaching component. In short, truly transformative leadership development programmes provide participants with accelerated or abbreviated coaching exposure to ensure the leadership messaging becomes personal and cascades throughout the organization. The addition of coaching to leadership development programmes takes the topical ointment medication that training and development is and intensifies its effectiveness and potency to that of a hypodermic injection.

Group Coaching Is a Strategic Solution to Create a Coaching Culture

While many organizations identify high-potential emerging leaders and make the investment in individual coaching to prepare them for expanded responsibilities, the amount of qualified coaching that is offered to emerging leaders is still insufficient to instil a coaching environment in most organizations. More and more organizations are opting for group coaching as a low-cost alternative to individual coaching engagements. Group coaching, which should never be confused with team coaching or team development with intact teams, is truly an individual coaching experience in a group setting.

A quick look back on the ICF Core Competencies is appropriate as the overview conversation about group coaching begins. As mentioned in Commandment 6, to articulate the shared values, beliefs and expectations across the enterprise and then to consistently coach to them wherever in the world the coaching is taking place, there is no better or comprehensive list of coaching competencies than the list compiled by the ICF:

1. Meeting Ethical Guidelines and Professional Standards
2. Establishing the Coaching Agreement
3. Establishing Trust and Intimacy with the Client

   4. Coaching Presence
   5. Active Listening
   6. Powerful Questioning
   7. Direct Communication
   8. Creating Awareness
   9. Designing Actions
   10. Planning and Goal Setting
   11. Managing Progress and Accountability

CONTEXTUAL COACHING COMMANDMENTS OF GROUP COACHING CIRCLES

Like contextual coaching, group coaching has a framework and process to follow that ensures that, with the involvement of a coaching coalition, the integrity of the process is preserved and the value to the individual coaching client equals that of the organization sponsoring the coaching. Here are 12 highlights of group coaching circles:

   1. Group coaching is most powerfully administered to groups of participants from different departments who do not report to the same manager—and certainly not to one another.
   2. Group coaching circles can be organized by corporate level, discipline, role or another designation, as long as the group coaching circle participants are not members of an intact group. Technically, an intact team can be coached, but such an intervention is much more likely to resemble action learning or strategic team alignment.
   3. Group coaching circles can be open enrolment, populated by nomination from managers or a combination of both, depending on how the organizational coaching practice is managed.
   4. Group coaching typically takes place in circles of three to six participants. Four is usually ideal.

5. Group coaching sessions are typically from 90 minutes to 2 hours in length. Session length is divided among the group coaching circle participants and each one has a proportionate amount of time to do their own individual work with the group coaching circle coach, in the presence of their fellow group members.

6. Participants in group coaching circles work directly with the group coach while being observed by the other participants in the group coaching circle. This observation is designed to help all group coaching circle participants learn coaching skills and techniques and spread familiarity with and popularity of coaching throughout the organization.

7. Observing participants do not interrupt during the identified participant's allocated time.

8. Observing participants offer feedback only if the identified participant requests it.

9. When giving feedback, observing participants only ask questions and follow coaching protocols to promote self-awareness in the identified participant.

10. Participants in the group coaching circles must participate as participants and observers within the protocols of complete coaching, acknowledging and asking permission from their group coach and their fellow participants when they want to suspend proper coaching protocols to ask for clarification or comment on the process.

11. Each participant in a group coaching circle drafts a coaching action plan with the group coach's assistance and presents the plan to his or her manager and organizational sponsors (such as HR business partners or talent development specialists as described in Chapter 4) for input and approval.

12. The coaching action plans for each participant are updated at the mid-point and at the end of the engagement and are re-presented to the coaching coalition at those intervals for input and approval as in a regular coaching engagement.

It is clear that group coaching is different from what many practitioners do when facilitating team building or what are most commonly referred to as team-coaching activities. Like much of the executive coaching industry, language is loose and often ambiguous around group and team development. Those same practitioners engaged in building and/or developing teams will sometimes refer to what they do as group coaching. The explanations given ahead distinguish between when the craft of coaching is used in a group setting versus when group facilitation techniques are deployed in group or team development activities. Both strategic team alignment and group coaching build community, but in different ways. Group coaching follows the most commonly accepted rules of coaching as opposed to mentoring, consulting, learning and development, training and team development motifs. The presence of, and option to participate in, group coaching is a sure indicator that coaching in the organization is enterprise-*wide*.

Strategic team alignment (and some forms of team coaching) focuses on the team. Team coaching is truly the process of solidifying, synchronizing and stabilizing group behaviours that align with the organization's leadership development initiatives and leadership competencies. Leaders and their team members focus on the strategic alignment between the team leader, team members and the way their company has defined excellence in individual leadership accountability and team performance. A qualified team alignment coach facilitates the sessions and draws real-time, real-business correlations between the interactions among team members, with the team leader and with the rest of the organization that illustrate the practical application of the leadership competencies. Strategic team alignment sessions respect organizational hierarchy and are virtually without exception intended for intact teams.

Group coaching focuses on the individual in a group setting. Unlike team coaching, which focuses on the team as a unit with its roles and responsibilities intact, group coaching provides a safe and structured environment for individual growth and development with a qualified group coach conducting sessions through group process. Although the agenda of group coaching is based on and rotates through everyone's individual needs, an underpinning contextual framework keeps all individual work strategically aligned with the organization's leadership competencies. As described earlier in the 12 highlights of group coaching, each participant has his or her own action plan. In group coaching, leaders from a variety of departments can join in monthly or semi-monthly group coaching sessions selected by corporate level, discipline, geography or other criteria.

While group coaching does not deal with intact groups, the group being coached (or coaching circle) is an intact group in that it respects confidentiality, mutual respect and formal group process. If participants from various corporate levels are part of the same group coaching circle, they check their rank at the door as they model building trust, openness to feedback and other leadership priorities. In an open-enrolment setting, each group coaching circle session is self-forming and not time-bound as opposed to a group coaching circle being formed for a specific period, typically six months or a year.

Attending a specific number of sessions is not required unless the group is closed as described earlier. Each monthly open group coaching circle is likely to be larger or smaller than the previous or following month and be comprised of a variable set of participants. As mentioned, group coaching circles with permanent enrolments can be formed for specific periods of time. After a group coaching circle ends a six-month term, for example, a new term can begin what is likely to be a slightly reconfigured membership. There is no hierarchy in group coaching circles. Not even the group coach is considered to occupy a higher plain with a disparity of power over the group coaching circle participants. Ergo, the term 'coachee' is not any more appropriate for group coaching circles than it is for any other type of coaching.

CONTEXTUAL COACHING
COMMANDMENT 7: CONCLUSION

As defined at the top of this chapter, a coaching culture means adopting and articulating curiosity, inquiry and thinking partnerships as enterprise-wide shared values, beliefs and expectations— and then consistently practising them across the organization— globally if necessary. A coaching culture asks for ideas and input instead of telling and giving orders. A coaching culture works inside out and bottom-up instead of the old-school notions of outside-in and top-down. Coaching cultures are about partnerships and equals supporting equals, not disparities of power. Coaching cultures build the leaders who build businesses based on the best thinking from the highest potential people.

If your mid-level to senior-level executives practised the ICF competencies as a matter of daily corporate leadership culture, you could, figuratively speaking, put the executive coaching industry out of business with your own coaching culture. I say, 'figuratively speaking' because executives, like entire organizations, always want to be better. That means there will always be a place for external, objective, executive coaches, free from the bonds of internal political agendas—especially coaches and managers who coach to align what leaders do best with what organizations need most.

The top-down support for a bottom-up exercise in brilliant listening, powerful questioning and curious inquiry will be the blood in the veins of a coaching culture. Training in coaching skills is good. But the ability to observe and practise masterful coaching as a group coaching circle participant is even better. In all likelihood, the best possible way to expose an organizational population to real executive coaching and provide the opportunity to practise coaching skills is group coaching. Nothing builds a coaching culture faster than ample group coaching opportunities. That is enterprise-wisdom at its best.

Like the *Art of Constructive Confrontation*[4], the way to reduce conflict and increase accountability enterprise-wide is to coach early and coach often, regardless of who is doing it. The way to avoid calling coaches into caustic and even catastrophic scenarios is to challenge ill-advised promotions through pre-emptive coaching and ensuring emerging leaders are succession ready long before picking up the telephone and calling a coach who is, by then, likely to be too little, too late. If you truly want to achieve competitive supremacy, make the commitment and the investment to be the best-coached company in your industry.

---

[4] Ibid.

Contextual Coaching Commandment

8

Keep the Leader and the Organization as Co-clients at All Times

As discussed in Commandment 4, the organization needs to have a voice in what it is paying for in terms of leadership development. Coaching at the executive level is usually the singular most expensive investment organizations make in developing leaders on an individual-to-individual basis. The voice of the organization is kept alive and audible in executive coaching engagements through the work of the coaching coalition described in Commandments 3 and 4. That means, at a minimum, the participation of the coach, the leader being coached, the leader's manager and the organizational sponsor is established as a formal expectation throughout the engagement.

The coaching coalition members come together initially in a dialogue facilitated by the contextual coach to contract for the engagement, set expectations and determine who will be on the list of feedback providers during the structured interviews conducted by the coach. The coaching coalition also discusses and ultimately decides upon what questions the contextual coach will ask each of the feedback providers in the structured interview process. Then the coach debriefs the 360-degree-structured interview feedback with the leader being coached and works with him or her to co-create an action plan for the coaching engagement that will be presented to the coaching coalition for approval.

The coaching coalition meets again to review, discuss, modify and approve a mid-term update to the action plan and a final report.

As discussed, the participation of every member of the coaching coalition ensures that the voice of the organization is present and participating throughout the coaching engagement, especially if the aspirational leadership competencies, values, disciplines, priorities, success factors or however the definition of leadership excellence in an organization is described are used as an enterprise-wide framework for coaching emerging or established leaders. Coaching emerging or established leaders must be done with equal respect for the organization sponsoring the coaching and the individual leader receiving the coaching. That is enterprise-wide wisdom.

Why is there so much emphasis on co-client status for the emerging or established leader being coached and the organization? The idea came out of training in marriage and family therapy (MFT). MFT, as anyone close to psychological counselling or clinical social work knows, is rooted in systems theory, specifically, family-systems theory. When partner number one comes into the counselling room for couple's therapy, he or she is not the therapist's client. When partner number one's significant other comes into the counselling room for couple's therapy, he or she is not the therapist's client either.

The marriage and family therapist's client is the marriage or covenant relationship between the two individuals. Oftentimes, therapists refer to couples as co-clients because of the shared status of their relationship. When two or more people join in a relationship, voluntarily or involuntarily, an organizational system is formed. An entity is created that is more than the sum of the individual parts. Anyone who is coaching an emerging or established leader (or anyone for that matter in an organizationally sponsored coaching engagement) is coaching the relationship between the leader being coached and the organization. The organization is not only a co-client, as the individuals in a relationship or marriage counselling scenario are, but the organization is arguably the primary client.

This understandably flies in the face of those who have defined coaching engagements as individual and intimate relationships between the leaders being coached and their coaches with the organization and those representing the organization's interests held at a safe distance. Many practitioners prefer to allow access only to the coaching process and what is transpiring, if and when the leader being coached and his or her coach elect to allow the cone of confidentiality to be lifted and/or and the curtain of confidentiality to be pulled back.

In contextual coaching, confidentiality is honoured. The coaching client or leader being coached always owns the engagement and his or her 360-degree feedback data. Moreover, the feedback providers who make the 360-degree feedback process so valuable through their objective observations about the emerging or established leader being coached must also be extended the privilege of their own confidentiality. This is the huge difference between a Big Five consulting firm conducting focus groups and a coach conducting a personal interview. Nothing said in a focus group is confidential. If feedback providers, like coaching clients, are not assured of confidentiality in what they say, there will never be sufficient trust to produce truly reliable feedback. Without reliable 360-degree feedback, coaching action plans will be compromised and the overall ability for the coach and coaching coalition to address the most pressing developmental or corrective needs of the emerging or established leader can not be effectively addressed.

As Commandment 10 will make abundantly clear, 360-degree-structured interviews gather data not only on the emerging or established leader being coached but also on the organization. It is not the primary purpose of 360-degree-structured interviews to gather data on the organization, but to ensure objectivity and diverse organizational perspective on the emerging or established leader being coached. However, those invited to provide 360-degree-structured feedback can not help themselves but to expand the conversation to include insights and perspectives on the organization itself.

These insights and perspectives feed enormously valuable organizational analysis, especially around leadership and talent development. More than that, the feedback from 360-degree-structured interviews is far more reliable than data gathered in focus groups and surveys administered by MBAs from consulting firms. The fact that—hopefully—trained, credentialed, experienced and naturally inquisitive coaches are gathering the data suggests far more probing and transparent information will be the basis of the contextual coaching action plan and organizational analysis report.

Back to the co-client status between the emerging or experienced leader being coached that launched this sidebar on confidentiality and reliability of data gathered in 360-degree-structured interviews, the expectation-setting stage of creating the engagement with the coaching coalition makes it clear that the organization is indeed a co-client unless the leader being coached refuses to include it or the organizational sponsor or leader's manager do not allow it, in which case the executive coaching engagement is compromised from the start. Unless the coaching is part of an employee assistance programme, the exclusion of the organization and its overarching corporate interests is suspect to say the least.

It is difficult to conjure a scenario in which an organizational leader can be coached for success outside of the cultural, structural and/or political context of the organization that pays the leader's salary and funds the coaching. Many coaches feel as if they can coach organizational leaders successfully without aligning what the leaders and their organizations need most, both individually and collectively. But if the voices of the organizational sponsor and the coaching client's manager are removed from the conversation, who speaks for the needs of the organization in the 'marriage' between the emerging or established leader and the organization he or she works for?

Coaching clients need to find their authentic voices in the workplace and coaches are great thinking partners in that process. But for a coaching conversation to be genuine and authentic, the organization's voice must be heard and acknowledged as well as the individual's. Imagine a marriage and family therapist counselling a couple and only allowing one of them to speak or even be present for the therapeutic conversation. How authentic would that be? Could that process truly be called credible? What if only one party to the relationship were even involved, other than to write a cheque to pay for it? It is the sound of one-hand clapping.

Despite what appears to be common sense in organizational coaching engagements for emerging or established leaders, the coach and the leader being coached all too often continue to disappear completely behind the curtain of confidentiality and cannot be heard at all underneath the cone. When they re-emerge 6–12 months later (or more), oftentimes no one truly knows what was supposed to be accomplished much less what, if anything, *was* accomplished.

Life coaching and employee assistance counselling are horses of a different colour. If an executive leadership coach shows up riding a life coaching or EAP horse—and tries to convince you that all horses are the same—and the organization and the coaching client will derive equal value from the coaching spend—beware. One of the co-clients might be in danger of being excluded and tremendous organizational value lost.

Regular reporting in the form of an action plan, mid-term update of the action plan and a final report is designed to keep every member of the coaching coalition abreast of the progress of the engagement and the voice of the organization present and participating. More than merely informing coalition members, each presentation of an updated report gives coalition members—that is to say the voice of the organization—the opportunity to be heard and weigh in on important issues. This produces excellent feedback and ongoing guidance to the coach and the emerging or established leader being coached.

As mentioned earlier, confidentiality is a privilege. Add that to the fact that coaching is a luxury. Both serve important purposes and can produce powerful results. A coaching engagement with one client absent and/or one client's voice muted is likely to be as effective as the aforementioned proverbial one-hand clapping. Contextual coaching is about context. The emphasis with systems theory shifts focus from individual parts to the organization of parts, recognizing that interactions between the parts are not static and constant but dynamic processes.

CO-CLIENT SIMPLICITY AND ORGANIZATIONAL COMPLEXITY

If there is more than one party in a relationship (which, by definition, there must be in order for it to be called a relationship), there is a *system*. The greater the number of components, the more complex the system. A general systems perspective examines the way components of a system interact with one another to form a whole. Rather than merely focusing on each of the separate parts, a systems perspective focuses on the connectedness and the interrelation, interdependence and alignment of all the parts. The co-client relationship between the emerging or established leader being coached and the organization is a complex organizational dynamic, even if the minimum number of people active in the relationship include only the emerging or established leader being coached, the coach, the leader's manager and an organizational sponsor.

These four individuals in and of themselves represent a system more than just twice as complex as the coach–leader dyad. Once a third person is added to the system, there are three relationships: coach–leader, coach–third-party and leader–third-party. By the time a coaching coalition reaches its optimal size of four, the four corners being the coach, the coaching client, the coaching client's manager and an organizational sponsor, there are six relationships.

All of the relationships have dynamics of their own. Once a 5th person is added to the system, the number of relationships increases to 10. It is easy to see how quickly a relatively simple system can become complex. These interrelational dynamics are impacting the work of and the experience of everyone in the system.

So, how broad is the coach's responsibility when a system quickly becomes complex? When coaching through an organizational lens, an external coach has what is possibly the least responsibility for managing relationships (in terms of sheer numbers). An internal coach's world is different, sometimes extremely more complex because of the overwhelming number of relationships he or she is involved in organizationally. In short, internal coaches in organizations interact officially, unofficially, directly and indirectly with far more people inside the enterprise than external coaches do.

Although all coaches in organizational settings are responsible for being aware of and managing multiple relationships, to what degree all of those additional relationships compromise or enhance the objectivity of the internal coach's coaching effectiveness is difficult to assess. It could be argued that the *usually* more experienced, better-credentialed and trained external coach has fewer relationships and, therefore, can remain more objective and effective. Often, when an organization uses a combination of internal and external coaches, the externals are used for the more senior leaders and the internal coaches for more junior people. This would suggest that externals are considered more effective, if for no other reason, because the external coach is less likely to be influenced by organizational politics that thrive among the myriad of complex and often tangled relationships.

It is also important to mention that with multiple, complex relationships comes an exponential increase in expectations. Knowing that expectations, especially unspoken expectations, are the tripwires of relationships and resentments waiting to happen, it is extremely important to pay attention and map them. Many emerging, but mostly established, leaders being coached push back on the notion of 360-degree-structured interview assessments, calling them witch-hunts and interrogations.

The best way to reframe these notions, which unfortunately have some historical basis in truth, is to point out to the coaching client that 360-degree-structured interview assessments are excellent ways to expose unspoken expectations. That means forewarned is forearmed. What could be more valuable than navigating the treacherous waters of corporate politics than knowing the expectations of critical stakeholders with career-changing institutional authority? It is like Tom Cruise putting on those special glasses in a *Mission Impossible* movie that reveal all of the otherwise invisible laser beams in a high-security area he is trying to enter. Once you can see the laser beams, you can avoid tripping them. What better way to build and sustain relationships and advance one's career? What a great benefit of achieving co-client status with the organization.

COMPOSITE PERSONALITY IN SIMPLE AND COMPLEX SYSTEMS

What was just described as relationship complexity in organizations has a companion dimension in personality. Coaching emerging and established leaders in organizations has a great deal to do with personality. There are hundreds of personality assessments on the market and dozens of them find their way into executive coaching engagements. They are largely self-reporting instruments that inform coaches, coaching clients and the rest of the coaching coalition about which dimensions of personality most impact the way emerging or established leaders conduct themselves in organizations and why.

Without delving deeply into what a typology or personality assessment accomplishes and/or the value it brings, it is important to understand that the most important personality—the composite personality that emerges when two or more people are combined in relationship—is never measured to our knowledge except in the ComposiTEAM® process.[1] Suffice to point out here that the

---

[1] John Hoover and A. DiSilvestro, *Unleashing Leadership* (Franklin Lakes, NJ: Career Press, 2005).

combinations of related parties remain separate, regardless of how many there are. A typical way that a personality assessment illustrates the relationships between personalities it measures is to produce a scattergram that informs a conversation about how every dot relates to every other dot—one at a time.

The notion of composite personality is that there is an over-arching, phantom personality that appears when two or more personalities are combined in relationship such as a work group or team. The composite personality is not an aggregate of how every individual personality relates to every other personality as in the four-cornered coaching coalition relationship example where there are six immediate relationships:

1. Coach to coaching client
2. Coach to coaching client's manager
3. Coach to organizational sponsor
4. Coaching client to coaching client's manager
5. Coaching client to organizational sponsor
6. Coaching client's manager to organizational sponsor

The composite or phantom personality is the composite combination of all relationships. To use the coaching coalition example again:

1. Coach to coaching client produces a third composite personality that is the combination of both
2. Coach to coaching client's manager produces a third composite personality that is the combination of both
3. Coach to organizational sponsor produces a third composite personality that is the combination of both
4. Coaching client to coaching client's manager produces a third composite personality that is the combination of both
5. Coaching client to organizational sponsor produces a third composite personality that is the combination of both

6. Coaching client's manager to organizational sponsor produces a third composite personality that is the combination of both

7. Coach, coaching client and coaching client's manager produces a fourth, composite personality that is the combination of all three

8. Coach, coaching client and organizational sponsor produces a fourth, composite personality that is the combination of all three

9. Coaching client, coaching client's manager and organizational sponsor produces a fourth, composite personality that is the combination of all three

10. Coach, coaching client's manager and organizational sponsor produces a fourth, composite personality that is the combination of all three

11. Coach, coaching client, coaching client's manager and organizational sponsor produces a fifth, composite personality that is the combination of all four

'Appears' is perhaps a poor choice of words because the phantom or composite personality is rarely apparent any more than staring at the side of an unmined mountain reveals whether there are gold deposits hidden inside or any more than staring at parched earth reveals whether or not there is water below. When leading a team, the personality that is most essential to lead is the phantom or composite personality because it is the personality that all of the individual personalities created. If a manager attempts to manage four separate personalities on a team of four (forgetting that the manager is yet another personality that forms a composite personality from the five related personalities), he or she is going to be frustrated by why the team is not responding the way the manager's attempts at managing individual personalities 'should' work out.

Phantom or composite personality is a subject for another book, like *Unleashing Leadership*, where the concept was first introduced. However, when considering co-client status between emerging or established leaders being coached and their complete organizations (the topic of this chapter), the phantom or composite personality must be considered. An organization's phantom or composite personality (with a mind of its own) is otherwise known as the organization's dominant culture. Coaching emerging or established leaders cannot be complete until the coaching takes place in true organizational, cultural and strategic context.

CONTEXTUAL COACHING COMMANDMENT 8: CONCLUSION

Coaching outside of cultural context is irresponsible and drastically diminishes the value and impact of the engagement. Coaching that is not culturally aligned and/or aligned with the organization's strategic agenda is incomplete coaching. Co-client status between the emerging or established leader being coached in all of his or her individual goals and objectives and the organization's cultural and/or strategic context results in complete, enterprise-*wide* and enterprise-*wise* coaching.

To ensure the coach, the leader being coached, the leader's manager and the organizational sponsor do not become myopic and insular in their thinking and engagement, all parts of the system, all four corners of the coaching coalition (see Commandment 4) must deliberately strive to maintain co-client status for the leader being coached and the sponsoring organization at all times. This requires the skill and ability to build and sustain meaningful and strategic relationships.

Sometimes the co-client status can be affirmed by members of the coaching coalition by simply scribbling Amy Friedman's proverbial contextual coaching question on their palms, occasionally opening their hands, looking at one another, and asking, 'How is this helping the organization?' Never forget that contextual coaching is the art of aligning what leaders do best with what their organizations need most. In relationships, partnerships and strategic alliances, it takes two hands to applaud.

Contextual Coaching Commandment

Keep the Leader and the Organization as Co-beneficiaries

Contextual Coaching Commandment 9 twists the lens on the notion of the leader being coached and the organization sharing co-client status. Taking the conversation a bit further, the coaching coalition must discuss how much of a benefit the organization and the leader being coached will derive from the expensive engagement. Before a coalition is ever fully formed (i.e., before a coach is selected), the emerging or established leader, the leader's manager and the organizational sponsor must consult with one another to decide if coaching is even the right solution for what is ailing or facing the organization and the relevance of that to the established or emerging leader.

There are many other leadership development things that can be done with that money. None of the alternatives will provide as intense and intimate of a learning journey as executive coaching. But coaching might be overkill. If executive coaching is considered a pejorative that is stigmatized in an organization, as it is in many if not most organizations, it might be difficult to convince the leader to be coached to voluntarily 'submit' to the humiliation of being coached. Despite the happy face that so many organizations, associations and coaches try so hard to hang on all executive coaching, we rarely see the happy dance when established leaders are informed that the organization thinks it 'would be a good idea to consider a coach'. There aren't enough grains of sand on the beach to count how many times we have heard established leaders say, 'I couldn't be more pleased to have a coach', through teeth clenched so tightly that the enamel is turning to chalk.

Those sound like strong words, but men and women in positions of leadership can do the math. If they look around and see that only the 'problem' people are getting coached, why should they raise their hands to volunteer for or agree to coaching? It can be a tough proposition to get a leader in a non-coaching culture to cooperate. If he or she feels compelled or coerced to be coached, his or her degree of vulnerable self-disclosure and transparency is likely to be limited.

In sort of a glass-half-full or glass-half-empty reasoning scheme, a conservative college football coach once said, 'When you pass the ball, three things can happen and two of them are bad'. Needless to say, his team rushed the ball a lot—most of the time with little success. His offensive scheme was, in a word, predictable. The student section used to chant, 'Rush to the right. Rush to the left. Rush up the middle. Punt'. It was not very entertaining football. Using similar reasoning, the following expands on the four levels of motivation for coaching from Commandment 2:

1. Level one: Voluntary and enthusiastic—coaching as opportunity

   - Emerging or established leaders and other potential coaching clients raise their hands and ask for a coach because they are eager to grow and develop as leaders, and they see coaching as a positive and powerful tool to help them get better.
   - Emerging or established leaders recognize the desire of corporate policymakers to establish and maintain a coaching culture and freely choose to join the effort to make that so. We love it when that happens.

2. Level two: Glass half-full—Coaching as an acquired taste (compliant-but-likeable)

- Coaching engagements are recommended by others (like the boss maybe) and the coaching client comes to appreciate coaching as a rare and unique opportunity as he or she gains more experience and value from it.
- Coaching engagements are included as part of team leadership training, action learning or strategic team alignment events, and the leaders being coached consider the coaching to be a positive extension of and way to become more comfortable with and receptive to the training. These emerging or established leaders often sign up for additional coaching sessions when additional elective sessions are offered. We love it when that happens, too.

3. Level Three: Glass half-empty—coaching as a necessary evil (compliant-but-disagreeable)

- Coaching engagements are recommended by others (like the boss or HR). Coaching clients do not like the idea of coaching after seeing only 'problem' people getting coached, and might find it intimidating and/or pejorative. They fear that they might be stigmatized by the process. But they will go with the programme and possibly pick up a positive leadership technique or two, realizing that it is wiser for them politically to cooperate than to push back.
- Coaching engagements are included as part of team leadership training, action learning or strategic team alignment events and the leaders being coached consider the coaching to be annoying but required for graduation. They go through the motions and tolerate coaching, but will get off at the first exit. No elective sessions for these folks.

4. Level Four: involuntary—coaching as punishment (or worse; coerced)

- The coaching client is compelled to participate in a coaching engagement that he or she doesn't feel is necessary, justified or makes any sense given his or her long-term successful performance with the organization (usually in an operational or transactional capacity), or what he or she perceives to be long-term successful performance with the organization without needing to deal with anything as silly as strategy. Coaching clients can feel as if they are being singled out in a witch hunt and are being used as scapegoats for the poor leadership or performance of others (like maybe the boss who recommended the coaching). These coaching engagements can, and often do, turn out successfully. However, highly talented and skilled coaches are required; coaches who can coach in the context of the organization and convince both the emerging or established leader being coached and the organization that they are better off aligned than misaligned. There can be thick ice to break through or melt.

- Coaching is truly a CYA attempt by an organization that has predetermined the leader is going to, as we used to say at Disney, 'find [his or her] happiness elsewhere'. No legitimate coach would knowingly participate in such a ploy. But it continues to happen. And leaders being forced out usually know it. This does not help build a positive image for executive coaching. But it does get a lot of attorneys' telephone numbers programmed into employees' speed dials.

Coaches, managers of emerging and established leaders being coached, and, especially, organizational sponsors of coaching *must* establish an authentic value proposition around coaching. It is the old 'what's in it for me?' question, answered with a compelling case of how growing and developing as a leader is good for both the individual and good for the organization. In fact, tying the individual leader's leadership growth and development to revenue growth and profitability of the organization makes coaching a no-brainer. What reasonable person would opt out?

If the organizational sponsor is well versed with the diagnostics of coaching or has attended Fielding Graduate University's *How to Manage the Coaching Function in Organizations* or NYU's *Foundations and Theories of Coaching*, he or she will be able to advise the leader, leader's manager and any other invested stakeholder with well-articulated apologetics for why organizations get better right after their leaders do. The principle is universal. To review: Children get better right after their parents get better. Students get better right after their teachers get better. If a person wants to be a respected, effective, legacy-leaving leader, that alone is worth the coaching investment on the part of the organization.

On the competitive rungs of the leadership ladder, any advantage should be welcomed. If a horrific-but-maniacal weekend golfer is swatting at balls on the driving range and Tiger Woods' golf coach wanders by and asks, 'Would you like a free piece of advice or two?' Would a bad golfer, but otherwise reasonably intelligent human being, say, 'No'? If you are the club champion and Tiger Woods' golf coach wanders by and asks, 'Would you like a free piece of advice or two?' Would even an already good golfer really say, 'No'? Tiger Woods doesn't say 'No'. He hired the coach and continues to pay big money for the privileged experience of being coached.

If you are an organizational leader, leader's manager and/or guide and manage the coaching engagements for your organization, it's important to point out to the leader about to be coached that this isn't 'free advice' by any means. Coaching purists would correctly point out that coaching is never about advice giving, free or otherwise. Financially speaking, coaching emerging and established leaders in organizations usually means a nice chunk of EBITA is being invested in a unique and potential-packed opportunity for the leader. Free to the leader? It is free except for the blood, sweat, tears, vulnerability, risk taking and deep reflection that produce a more impressive, stronger, more agile and more resilient influencer on behalf of the organization. That is usually the skin-in-the-game that belongs to the leader being coached.

Note to the emerging or established leader being coached: coaching, at the core of its craft, is not about you becoming someone else. It is about becoming the best *you* possible. You, after all, are all you and your coach have to work with. So, you and your coach go to work reflecting, exploring, questioning and practising how to be everything you have the gifts, talents, intelligence and wherewithal to be.

To derive maximum value from the organization's coaching spend, the organization and the leader being coached must mutually benefit from every coaching conversation, as well as the entire engagement. The more invested in time and attentiveness the balance of the coaching coalition is (the organizational sponsor and the leader's manager), the more powerful the outcome is for all stakeholders. That's a power proposition that's hard to say 'No' to.

CO-BENEFITS

To leave as little as possible to the imagination—better said—to establish a solid foundation for understanding the shared benefits for the individual and the organization when coaching through an organizational lens, it helps to understand what the term 'benefit' means, both as a noun and a verb. For starters, a benefit is a good thing as opposed to a detriment or liability. In terms of organizational leadership development, the whole purpose is to make emerging and established leaders *better* leaders. That might seem axiomatic, but the things we do in the name of leadership development can leave one scratching one's head. Most specifically, coaching.

If coaching leaders is a good thing, then how does the entire idea become so quickly soiled in organizations? As discussed, when only (or mostly) problem children receive coaching in organizations, it is not hard to connect the dots. Getting a root canal is a good thing if the nerve in your tooth needs to be removed. After the root canal is over and the tooth no longer hurts, it is definitely a good thing. If the coaching engagement was initiated because the organization itself was experiencing pain, then the organization can claim the benefit of the good thing when the pain goes away.

The trend we see is that not only long-tenured, established leaders can be abrasive, but younger, less-experienced leaders can—and are with increasing frequency—really unloading inappropriately on people below them, around them and even above them in the corporate food chain. It is not clear exactly how a cooler, more laid-back generation is capable of going ugly on others in a very bully-like manner but, unfortunately, it is happening and corrective coaching, which was traditionally reserved for cantankerous and curmudgeonly established leaders, is being called in to calm the wild horses, fiery tempers and impatience of the new movers and shakers. It is not surprising to see that young and brilliant people do not suffer fools kindly, especially older, slower ones, but it is surprising that the young masters of the universe do not think better of lashing out.

Obviously, organizations everywhere are not out of the pain game and coaching will continue to be a good thing as long as the leaders being coached (regardless of age) can see the benefit to themselves and to their organizations of finding a kinder, gentler, more mindful way of expressing themselves. Somehow that message did not make it into the MBA curriculum everywhere. Indeed, coaching skills, which had in recent years been imbedded in the MBA curriculum of a New England University with a marquee pedigree, have been dropped from the programme. One of those things that makes one say, 'Hm-m-m'. Perhaps they were assumed to be engrained in young personalities rendering the teaching unnecessary or, worse, coaching skills were no longer felt to be necessary for executive success.

The word, benefit, can also be defined as well-being. It should come as no wonder that an organizational coaching engagement is designed to preserve or improve the well-being of emerging or established leaders. But a contextual coaching framework and process around and through the coaching engagement will ensure the preservation or improvement in the well-being of emerging or established leaders *and* the organizations they work for. It is only right that emerging or established leaders and the organizations they work for are co-beneficiaries and get and stay well together.

Another synonym for benefit is 'advantage'. In the case of executive coaching becoming true contextual coaching, the term 'advantage' is the opposite of how it is used in tennis or anywhere that saying someone has an advantage means being one up, slightly or much better, or is somehow in competition with one another. In the case of a leader receiving contextual coaching, the leader and the organization he or she works for are not in competition with each other as in against one another; they are in competition with each other as in competition, shoulder-to-shoulder, *together* against a common opponent.

If coaching in an organizational context has been designed and is being executed in such a way as to align what the emerging or established leader does best with what the organization needs most, then the interests of both leader and organization will be aligned. When was the last time you either consciously thought about or studied the leadership population in your organization to purposefully determine whether or not your organization's most intense interests were truly shared by the emerging and established leaders enterprise-wide?

Reward is another common synonym for benefit. In the world of ordinary executive coaching, the reward for the individual leader being coached is the opportunity to self-actualize and become a more fully authentic and, oftentimes, less abrasive leader. The reward for the organization is a more fully authentic and, oftentimes, less abrasive leader. That's great, except that it's not well defined nor in any way ensured that the more fully authentic and, oftentimes, less abrasive leader is any better aligned with the organization's cultural context or strategic agenda.

In a contextual coaching scenario, the reward is deliberately made equal for the organization and the emerging or established leader being coached. The individual coaching goals and desired individual outcomes for the engagement remain front and centre for the leader being coached. But the reward for the organization and the emerging or established leader being coached is a better aligned leader and better resonance, harmony and simpatico between the executive and the organization. Rewards all around.

The synonyms seem obvious enough and how the emerging or established leader being coached can share the benefits of a contextual coaching engagement aren't difficult to piece together. But think of an antonym like 'suffer'. In the ordinary course of business, when the stock prices take a hit or the margins narrow for a time, do many of the leaders in the organization take a corresponding hit? Probably not. Of course, if the margins shrink beyond recognition, profits diminish significantly enough or the stock prices nosedive, heads might roll and select executives and their minions might disappear without a shot at coaching of any kind.

But such punishment does not come often and is usually meted out to innocent hard workers who have their noses too close to the grindstone to see the proverbial, political axe swinging in their direction until it is too late. Executive coaching is often the solution of choice for times in which the organization is or powerful people in the organization are suffering from too much noise, too much upheaval or too much negative energy. That suffering usually begins with an emerging or established leader. The leader brings everyone within his or her span of control to the pity party, and a coach is called in to exorcize the demons.

Usually, the coach is called so late in the cycle that it is difficult to ascertain if the problem was started by the chicken or the egg. By the time the coach shows up, it really is a moot point anyway. The suffering leader is eagerly and freely sharing his or her suffering with the organization and the organization is looking for ways to push back or escape. It is co-suffering. When many people around the generous-with-his-suffering leader are pointing guns to their own heads or stringing themselves up from the fluorescents, the situation is clearly out of control. When others are pointing guns at the suffering leader and/or walking towards him or her carrying nooses, the coach needs to find a fast-acting intervention that will put the larger population out of the leader's misery.

Putting me out of your misery is something that many hard-working people need to deal with daily when similar situations are not dealt with swiftly by management, HR or talent development. Confronting serious issues sooner than later is fundamental to decreasing conflict and increasing accountability.[1] In a true contextual coaching fashion, it is wisest to engage skilled coaches who can align relief from the individual coaching client's suffering with relief for the organization at large. Stop the individual pain— stop the organizational pain. The symbiotic relationship between emerging or established leaders and the organizations that employ them remains the same. In perfect alignment, what is good for one is good for the whole and what is bad for one is bad for the whole. Contextual coaching was created to help everyone get better *together*, whether everyone is a direct recipient of coaching or not.

CONTEXTUAL COACHING COMMANDMENT 9: CONCLUSION

Contextual Coaching Commandment 9 promised to twist the lens on the notion of the leader being coached and the organization sharing co-client status. Coaching coalitions must discuss how much of a benefit the organization and the emerging or established leaders being coached will derive from the expensive engagement. That is, how much profit can a coaching engagement drive and can it be enjoyed equally between the coaching client and the organization?

---

[1] See Hoover and DiSilvestro, *The Art of Constructive Confrontation*.

Is the emerging or established leader receiving the coaching being served in equal measure to the organization and vice versa? Are both being equally helped, aided, assisted, improved, strengthened and/or advanced? In the best application of contextual coaching, the individual agenda of the leader being coached *and* the organization's overarching strategic agenda are being furthered together and as equitably as possible. This is how co-beneficiaries are born.

Contextual Coaching Commandment

No Data Left Behind

Coaching is heuristic at its very core. As a problem-solving solution, coaching (especially in executive environments) employs self-awareness and self-discovery. If the problem is that someone in institutional authority needs to correct counter-productive, sub-optimal executive behaviour and/or simply needs a coach to help develop undeveloped potential, thus preparing the emerging or established leader for expanded responsibilities, much of the growth will leverage general assumptions, rules of thumb, educated guesswork, intuitive judgment and common sense. The behaviours coaches help leaders develop are largely axiomatic in that they seem obviously beneficial.

In examining the contextual coaching commandments, it should be obvious by now that, if executive coaching is truly conducted through an organizational lens and is enterprise-*wide* and enterprise-*wise*, a great many conversations occur in the course of an engagement. That could be said of any coaching engagement to a point (the part about many conversations). Although the coaching client or leader being coached 'owns' the data gathered in 360-degree-structured interviews, in coaching sessions and other coaching conversations, this information is the substance and basis for reports that the coach and emerging or established leader being coached jointly prepare for the purpose of sharing with the stakeholders in the coaching coalition (see Commandments 3 and 4).

The expectation is established early on in a contextual coaching engagement that this data will be shared in a format and with the specificity that is approved for distribution by the leader being coached. If the person or department managing the coaching function in the organization has studied how to manage the coaching function in organizations or managed themselves to piece together processes and protocols in which data across all coaching engagements can be captured, compiled and analysed to identify enterprise-wide leadership trends and patterns—*without compromising confidentiality*—the organization will save millions paid out to Big Five consulting firms to conduct focus groups, generic interviews and distribute surveys to reveal insights that are already more freely and honestly articulated in executive coaching conversations. In short, that data (richer data, in fact) is already being gathered more reliably through intimate coaching engagements.

Quickly review the ten commandments of contextual coaching with an eye for what type of information will surface in the course of the coaching work.

1. *Coach in the context of the organization.* Alignment between leaders and corporate strategy is critical to successful executive development. (Is there alignment or not? All stakeholders in the coaching coalition should know. How can the organizational sponsor be sure?)
2. *Coach with the art of alignment. People, performance and profitability.* Align what your people do best with what your organization needs most. (How much do people in the organization routinely talk about what people do best or what your organization needs most? Much less, how do they align the two? In contextual coaching engagements, there are things that get chatted up a lot. Capture the conversations.)
3. *Keep the voice of the organization present and alive.* Make sure the organization's vocal chords are well exercised throughout

coaching engagements. (Does the organization have a deliberate, methodological practice of seeking and giving volume to its own voice as it speaks through its senior executives and the variety of internal and external stakeholders inside and outside of the coaching client's span of control?)

4. *Coach through an organizational lens.* Establish the coaching coalition—coach, coaching client, coaching client's manager and organizational sponsor. (In organizations with true coaching cultures and/or high-communication and participation cultures, this is easily done. The coaching engagement will expose if and where more organizational awareness and conversations are needed.)

5. *Co-create the engagement.* The Macro Perspective—set the expectations between the coach, coaching client and the organization. (It is amazing how many leaders were never told about the things their coaches have been hired to help them learn and/or change. Even if they are clearly told, clarifying expectations and what they mean is fundamental to meeting or exceeding them on an individual or enterprise level. Coaching engagement data will tell a huge story here.)

6. *Co-create the coaching session.* The Micro Perspective—set the expectations between the coach, coaching client and the coaching client's manager. (As with Commandment 5, expectation setting at the local or interpersonal level must be aligned with the broader, overarching cultural expectations in the organization. Commandments 5 and 6 create two points in the organizational universe that can be compared.)

7. *Establish and maintain a coaching culture.* Articulate the shared values, beliefs and expectations across the enterprise and then consistently coach them around the world. (In a true coaching culture, coaching is for everyone and everyone is for coaching. Enterprise-wide encouragement of coaching is enterprise-wise.)

8. *Keep the leader and the organization as co-clients at all times.* Coach the individual and the organization simultaneously by coaching the real client—the *relationship* between the individual and the organization. (Success for a leader, or any employee for that matter, cannot be determined without a full understanding of the organizational context. It is the health of the leader/organization relationship that matters most. A leader being coached without the voice of the organization at the table will be the proverbial one-hand clapping. Data capture through coaching engagement reports keeps all members of the coaching coalition honest on this matter.)

9. *Establish co-beneficiaries.* Derive maximum value from the coaching spend as the organization and the leader mutually benefit from every coaching conversation. (Do not forget that knowing and accepting what is in it for them is a fundamental component of human motivation. Capturing, compiling and analysing executive coaching data will reveal what motivates organizational leaders individually and collectively—priceless information you do not want to lose.)

10. *No data left behind.* Capture data from coaching conversations in coaching reports for organizational analysis and talent development planning without compromising confidentiality. (The capture compilation and analysis of data from coaching engagement conversations will inform not only what the leadership challenges are that coaching will address but also how effective executive coaching is as a leadership development tool. All data points tell a story when subjected to comparative analysis. Confidentiality is often protected by blind compilation and paraphrase of data points.)

Unlike most focus groups and surveys, data collected during an executive coaching engagement is truly action research in that it is a real-time and real-world study of real people engaged in the course and in the organizational context of their work. People filling out employee engagement surveys might make judgments about whether or not the organization and/or those reviewing and analysing the data can handle the truth and, thereby, soften or withhold authentic responses. Unlike static, self-reporting data gathering, coaching conversations are conducted live and/or in person. Information gathered face-to-face by a skilled interviewer from a feedback provider about a real person, in real time, is far more reliable.

How much real money and vast organizational value is being lost by not capturing, compiling and analysing executive coaching engagement data? Ask McKinsey & Company what they will charge to come in and replicate it, which they really cannot do completely because your data is being gathered by seasoned executive coaches in intimate conversations pinned directly to the leadership growth and development challenges of real emerging and/or established executives in your organization. However, McKinsey will come in and provide you with the next best thing—for a best-thing price.

If organizations are conducting coaching engagements (and thereby coaching conversations) all over the world and yet are not capturing, compiling and analysing the information, priceless organizational data is flowing into the gutter and washing out to sea and/or evaporating into the ether. That is enterprise-wastefulness. It is inconceivable if you stop to ponder it. If for no other reason, the vast amounts of highly critical and valuable data points that surface in coaching conversations and 360-degree assessments across the enterprise must be captured, compiled and analysed to inform the creation of gap analyses and leadership development strategies—strategies that include coaching.

CONTEXTUAL COACHING COMMANDMENT 10: CONCLUSION

One rule of data, big or small: if you lose it, you cannot use it. If indeed contextual coaching propels your coaching clients towards reaching their full potential within the context of the organization sponsoring the coaching—if indeed contextual coaching engenders a strong partnership between the coached leader's immediate needs, long-term career strategy and the organization's immediate needs and long-term success strategy— why would an organization conduct a coaching engagement outside of this essential framework?

Why indeed would anyone conduct any coaching engagement for emerging, high-potential or senior executives in an ad hoc, one-off or disconnected manner? Contextual coaching can transform a potential individual/organizational disconnect or an actual disconnect into a thriving partnership. Coaching in the context of the organization or through an organizational lens can transform dissonance into resonance, contradiction into cultural compatibility and mutual exclusivity into mutual interest.

But remember, no amount of coaching, under any given methodology, will produce co-benefits for co-clients if only one client is engaged in the process. Coaching in the context of the organization not only brings consistency, continuity and quality assurance to enterprise-wide coaching engagements, but also brings consistency and uniform standards of practice to HR and talent partners across the globe. Imagine if all executive coaching engagements in your organization, regardless of the desired individual coaching outcomes, were uniformly framed in your organization's established leadership principles, values and competencies.

What better way to unify enterprise-wide expectations and perceptions of leadership? What better way to gather continuous, enterprise-wide action research data? What better way to ensure that you are receiving full value for the dollars you spend on executive coaching? That is truly the power of making a complete coaching connection between the individual and the organization. This is the power of coaching that is enterprise-*wide* and enterprise-*wise*.

Part II

ENTERPRISE-WIDE COACHING

Resource Guide for Overutilized, Underutilized and Optimally Utilized Leadership Behaviours in Contextual Coaching

As promised in Commandment 1, in the absence of specific organizational leadership competencies, values, priorities, disciplines or characteristics like the ones you might have created for your organization, the 10 dimensions of organization re-posted ahead from Commandment 1 constitute the generic framework of the coaching engagements discussed throughout this book. What has been added is a reference guide of leadership behaviours and issues to be addressed through contextual coaching—framed in under, over and optimally used leadership behaviours. What you will see here are suggested leadership behaviours and what you can coach to when those leadership behaviours are under, over or optimally used.

Leadership topics that correlate to the 10 generic dimensions of organization that form the framework of contextual coaching engagements and reports are given ahead. Organizations that have established their own enterprise-wide leadership attributes, competencies, values, principles or disciplines should use those as the basis for drafting their own over, under and optimally used leadership behaviours to create maximum enterprise-wisdom to ensure consistency and continuity in enterprise-wide executive coaching.

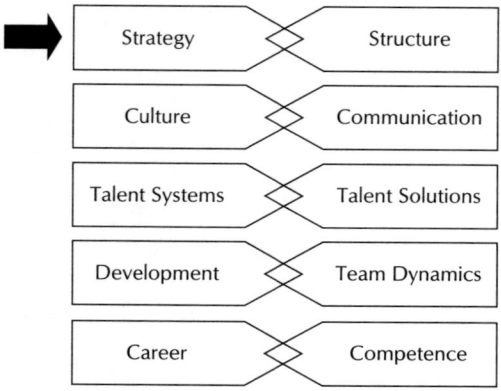

Strategy Behaviour 1: Successfully Manages Resistance to New Ideas—Example One

What It Looks Like When Underutilized	What It Looks Like When Optimally Utilized	What It Looks Like When Overutilized
Team members take advantage of uncertainty when ideas are challenging or uncomfortable and do nothing.	Team members feel heard even if their ideas cannot be utilized at the moment. They know new ideas are not threatening and can be discussed.	Team members might feel that too much time is spent on debate. It might feel as if new ideas are forced down everyone's throats.

Strategy Behaviour 1: Development Suggestions—Example One

Underutilization	Optimal Utilization	Overutilization
Urge your client not to take challenges personally. Learn how to diagnose resistance to determine where it is coming from and then how to work through it.	Seek outside, objective input regarding steps to take to keep communication channels open and active. Keep up the things that overcome the reasons people resist new ideas.	Balance the need for open voices with the activities required for implementation. Call on responsible team members to step up and show support for the new ideas.

Strategy Behaviour 1: Successfully Manages
Resistance to New Ideas—Example Two

What It Looks Like When Underutilized	What It Looks Like When Optimally Utilized	What It Looks Like When Overutilized
Team members feel shut down when they start to raise questions, offer feedback or simply try to provide input.	Team members find the leader is able to bounce back from setbacks and to push back and move the change process forward.	Team members might want a more decisive leadership style from you with clear direction that engenders more confidence in new ideas.

Strategy Behaviour 1: Development
Suggestions—Example Two

Underutilization	Optimal Utilization	Overutilization
Allow and even encourage your team members to raise their issues, and promote constructive confrontation. Reward the honest exchange of ideas.	If free space for objections to be heard is allowed and dealt with, make sure that natural levels of resistance and scepticism are encouraged to strengthen and make new ideas more sustainable.	While allowing discussion and input, encourage willingness to make final decisions that require commitment from all involved.

Strategy Behaviour 1: Successfully Manages Resistance to New Ideas—Example Three

What It Looks Like When Underutilized	What It Looks Like When Optimally Utilized	What It Looks Like When Overutilized
Team members triangulate in order to block progress.	Team members are encouraged to get issues out on the table and express resistance out in the open.	Team members might feel 'negative voices' are given too much time to speak.

Strategy Behaviour 1: Development Suggestions—Example Three

Underutilization	Optimal Utilization	Overutilization
Acknowledge your team members' objections, but finalize decisions and ask individuals to commit to staying on the same page.	Always pay attention to who the most influential people are among resistant team members and sell them on the new ideas first. The others will follow.	Balance allowing people to raise issues with input from individuals who are more open to change.

Strategy Behaviour 2: Formulates a Strategy Related to Business Goals—Example One

What It Looks Like When Underutilized	What It Looks Like When Optimally Utilized	What It Looks Like When Overutilized
Team members may feel that decisions are made in a haphazard manner and do not support stated business goals.	Team members understand that leadership decisions are well planned, systematic and consider the impact they will have.	Team members feel decisions are delayed because of the strategic process. Opportunities are lost and problems requiring a fast response are not being met.

Strategy Behaviour 2: Development Suggestions—Example One

Underutilization	Optimal Utilization	Overutilization
Make a point to discuss, document and demonstrate how decisions are made based on strategy.	Continue to keep the team's goals posted, publicized and otherwise adequately promoted to keep everyone focused.	Balance planning with the team's sense of urgency. Never forget to ask, 'When does this need to be done?'

Strategy Behaviour 2: Formulates a Strategy Related to Business Goals—Example Two

What It Looks Like When Underutilized	What It Looks Like When Optimally Utilized	What It Looks Like When Overutilized
Team members don't believe there is a well-developed and intelligent plan to support decisions.	Team members accept change respecting that carefully formulated and analysed decisions have been made that consider potential impact.	Team members might feel more time is spent on strategizing than on executing.

Strategy Behaviour 2: Development Suggestions—Example Two

Underutilization	Optimal Utilization	Overutilization
Suggest spending time on strategic planning and involving other members of the team who bring different skill sets to the process.	Support continuously seeking out new and better ways to involve as many interested parties as possible in goal setting and strategy alignment with goals.	Advocate a focus on executing plans in a careful and diligent way, and delegate the monitoring of it to ensure progress towards goals.

Strategy Behaviour 2: Formulates a Strategy Related to Business Goals—Example Three

What It Looks Like When Underutilized	What It Looks Like When Optimally Utilized	What It Looks Like When Overutilized
Team members may grow less confident in leadership's ability to take the organization into a positive direction.	Team members demonstrate confidence in the decisions of the leadership group and are willing to participate in the decisions wholeheartedly.	Team members desire more concrete, actionable items that can be observed, measured and monitored over time.

Strategy Behaviour 2: Development Suggestions—Example Three

Underutilization	Optimal Utilization	Overutilization
Involve everyone possible in studying how the leader's decisions as well as the group decisions propel the organization in the right direction.	Be aware of how key constituents are responding to goal orientation and strategic alignment. Use 360-degree feedback to find and monitor the pulse of all key constituencies.	Assign tasks that empower individuals to design and enact strategy, specifically in reference to organizational goals.

Strategy Behaviour 3: Articulates the Strategic Vision of the Organization—Example One

What It Looks Like When Underutilized	What It Looks Like When Optimally Utilized	What It Looks Like When Overutilized
Team members may be uncertain about the organization's direction or how what they do is plugged into or potentially irrelevant to the company's agenda.	Team members are clear on the direction of the company and how it impacts the local team and each team member. Expectations are clear.	Team members might feel as if the leader underestimates their ability to understand the larger strategy. At some point, you need to execute.

Strategy Behaviour 3: Development Suggestions—Example One

Underutilization	Optimal Utilization	Overutilization
Deliberately schedule time on a regular basis to discuss organizational strategy with direct reports and peers.	Continue seeking new and better ways to inform others who will be affected about organizational strategy. Emphasize how they will benefit from it.	Address team members in such a way that they feel they are in dialogue, not being talked down to.

Strategy Behaviour 3: Articulates the Strategic Vision of the Organization—Example Two

What It Looks Like When Underutilized	What It Looks Like When Optimally Utilized	What It Looks Like When Overutilized
Team members may question the motivations and philosophies behind decisions that affect them.	Team members better understand how tactical decisions relate to larger goals.	Team members are concerned that the leader remains too strategic and doesn't appreciate the hard, tactical work they do.

Strategy Behaviour 3: Development
Suggestions—Example Two

Underutilization	Optimal Utilization	Overutilization
Discuss organizational philosophies and rationale behind day-to-day decisions. Include discussions of how your people contribute.	Continue seeking new and better ways to keep team members and other constituents engaged in dialogue about strategy.	Make sure that you recognize and reward tactical contributions that support the overall strategy.

Strategy Behaviour 3: Articulates the Strategic
Vision of the Organization—Example Three

What It Looks Like When Underutilized	What It Looks Like When Optimally Utilized	What It Looks Like When Overutilized
Team members may become cynical about the reasons decisions are made. This is especially true when they are not consulted.	Team members can see the leader as a champion for the organization's messages ... yet ties the organization's needs to the team members' needs.	Team members might feel the leader has no individual voice but is merely a puppet of the corporate mantra. Their needs are never mentioned, much less considered.

Strategy Behaviour 3: Development
Suggestions—Example Three

Underutilization	Optimal Utilization	Overutilization
Allow team members the opportunity to ask questions about decisions that are made as well as to challenge the logic and reasoning behind them.	Regularly solicit input from a balanced population of direct reports, peers and other constituents to remain current and allow everyone to participate.	Avoid giving too much 'company speak' about strategy—translate the company message into an authentic voice.

Strategy Behaviour 4: Applies Organizational
Strategy to Area of Responsibility—Example One

What It Looks Like When Underutilized	What It Looks Like When Optimally Utilized	What It Looks Like When Overutilized
Team members may note disconnects between company strategy and the local responsibilities of the team.	Team members see how their work helps drive organizational strategy forward. Seeing and appreciating this increases their energy and buy-in.	Team members might feel that their local work and decisions are completely absorbed by corporate decisions and influence.

Strategy Behaviour 4: Development
Suggestions—Example One

Underutilization	Optimal Utilization	Overutilization
Regularly tie company strategy to local responsibilities, especially at times when you delegate tasks.	Continually seek ways to help team members and other constituents identify connections between company strategies and their individual or collective responsibilities.	Emphasize the importance of local decision-making and individual commitment to job roles as they impact company strategy.

Strategy Behaviour 4: Applies Organizational
Strategy to Area of Responsibility—Example Two

What It Looks Like When Underutilized	What It Looks Like When Optimally Utilized	What It Looks Like When Overutilized
Team members may be confused about why the larger strategy matters to them.	Team members begin to think more strategically and make connections between company direction and their individual and team work.	Team members might grow tired of constant reminders of the connection to strategy and feel as if they're not respected for making the connections on their own.

Strategy Behaviour 4: Development
Suggestions—Example Two

Underutilization	Optimal Utilization	Overutilization
Help communicate how the business strategy impacts team members in the way they perform their roles.	Continuously anticipate the type of confusion that results if the connection between organizational strategy and local responsibility is not made.	Ask team members to describe the connection between strategy and tactics in their own words instead of dictating it to them.

Strategy Behaviour 4: Applies Organizational Strategy to Area of Responsibility—Example Three

What It Looks Like When Underutilized	What It Looks Like When Optimally Utilized	What It Looks Like When Overutilized
Team members may disregard the strategy as purely philosophical and irrelevant to their day-to-day operation of the business.	Team members will be open to changes in strategy and going in new directions since they have seen its successful implementation in the past.	Team members might feel paralyzed when they don't see concrete connections with the larger strategic direction.

Strategy Behaviour 4: Development Suggestions—Example Three

Underutilization	Optimal Utilization	Overutilization
Relate the strategy to real and tangible decisions that occur in the job on an operational level.	Seek out innovative ways to regularly illustrate the real-time connection between strategy and local activity.	Balance communications to avoid overemphasizing strategic importance of every task.

Strategy Behaviour 5: Manages Strategic Planning Process Within Area of Responsibility—Example One

What It Looks Like When Underutilized	What It Looks Like When Optimally Utilized	What It Looks Like When Overutilized
Team members do not understand the strategy and related goals as they pertain to the local business unit.	Team members understand the process developed by the leader that will need to be enacted to achieve business unit goals.	Team members might feel the plan over-orchestrates their work, impinging on their individual decisions.

Strategy Behaviour 5: Development Suggestion—Example One

Underutilization	Optimal Utilization	Overutilization
Involve team members and other interested constituents in the planning process in a meaningful way from the beginning.	Keep the time issue alive when making strategic plans a part of ongoing team and/ or departmental activities. Take a strategic planning approach to everything.	Balance the planning process with the appropriate sense of urgency and autonomy for the individual, for the team and for the organization.

Strategy Behaviour 5: Manages Strategic Planning Process Within Area of Responsibility—Example Two

What It Looks Like When Underutilized	What It Looks Like When Optimally Utilized	What It Looks Like When Overutilized
Team members do not see the steps involved in the process of achieving the overall goal.	Team members understand the achievable goals as outlined in the plan and see how their area of responsibility ties to each.	Team members might feel the process takes too much time and energy to be useful over time.

Strategy Behaviour 5: Development Suggestion—Example Two

Underutilization	Optimal Utilization	Overutilization
Spend time training on strategic planning and involve other members of the team who bring different skill sets to the process.	Always look for opportunities to engage real-time, real-world action learning around strategic planning.	Focus on execution in a careful and diligent way, and/or delegate the monitoring process to ensure progress is being made.

Strategy Behaviour 5: Manages Strategic Planning Process Within Area of Responsibility—Example Three

What It Looks Like When Underutilized	What It Looks Like When Optimally Utilized	What It Looks Like When Overutilized
Team members do not have time frames in mind for implementing the strategy and may be concerned about the realistic nature of the strategy.	Team members demonstrate confidence in the plan being realistic and achievable. They regularly speak in time reference terms when describing progress or lack thereof.	Team members might look to the plan too often and become mired in details, thereby delaying actions.

Strategy Behaviour 5: Development Suggestion—Example Three

Underutilization	Optimal Utilization	Overutilization
Communicate the time parameters for strategic plans. Clearly articulate the purpose behind decisions and the need to work the planning process.	Teach time management. If the planning process is being managed well, examine what people are doing right and challenge them to do even better. Celebrate success.	Assign tasks that empower individuals to participate more fully in keeping the planning and execution process on a schedule.

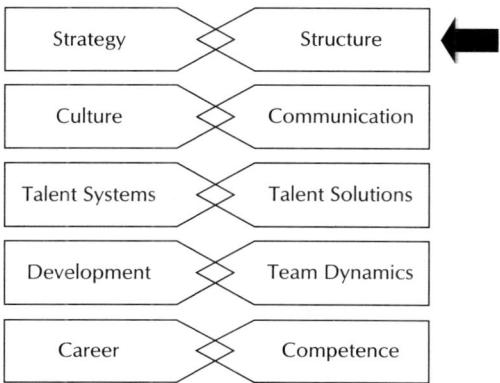

Structure Behaviour 1: Uses Power for the Benefit of the Organization—Example One

What It Looks Like When Underutilized	What It Looks Like When Optimally Utilized	What It Looks Like When Overutilized
Chaos is the order of the day as your client avoids dealing directly with people and issues that cause anxiety or uncertainty.	Your client uses appropriate structural relationships to promote continuous learning and to build and maintain flexible work practices and processes that make the most sense.	Your client creates rigid structures and processes to the point that the wheels of progress slow down or come to a complete and grinding halt.

Structure Behaviour 1: Development Suggestions—Example One

Underutilization	Optimal Utilization	Overutilization
Help your client learn to work more harmoniously across structural divides and organize others when possible to work in ordered ways.	Explore new ways to maximize power and influence so that the organization can benefit even more from your client's structural knowledge.	Help your client study productivity and work process design—and to let go of antiquated and self-serving notions of command and control.

Structure Behaviour 1: Uses Power for the Benefit of the Organization—Example Two

What It Looks Like When Underutilized	What It Looks Like When Optimally Utilized	What It Looks Like When Overutilized
Your client uses institutional authority and structure to promote a personal agenda at the expense of team members' work–life balance, stability and cohesiveness.	Your client champions the cause of work–life balance by creating and enforcing structural policies that make it possible to maintain a healthy balance between work and home.	People around your client experience a level of fear and imprisonment that can negatively impact work–life balance.

Structure Behaviour 1: Development Suggestions—Example Two

Underutilization	Optimal Utilization	Overutilization
Use 360-degree feedback and other objective analysis of power and structure usage to determine where your client can become more organizationally balanced.	Continue to study and put into practice methods, techniques and structural design to increase shared responsibility and distribute power to increase organizational effectiveness.	Begin to accept that people need structural balance in their lives and work, and the more balanced you help them to be, the more the organization will benefit.

Structure Behaviour 1: Uses Power for the Benefit of the Organization—Example Three

What It Looks Like When Underutilized	What It Looks Like When Optimally Utilized	What It Looks Like When Overutilized
People above, below and lateral to your client in the organization are confused as to what role your client should be playing in the organization's success and their own.	The policies and procedures within a jurisdiction are designed and executed to benefit the organization and its internal and external customers. Beyond the jurisdiction, your client supports similar policies and processes.	Your client uses institutional authority to clamp down on everything that does not have prior approval and even oversteps the boundaries of authority causing territorial disputes in the organization.

Structure Behaviour 1: Development Suggestions—Example Three

Underutilization	Optimal Utilization	Overutilization
Get help from HR and the manager to accurately define a role from their point of view. Then express this authority consistently across the board.	Become familiar with the concept of organization development to expand awareness of power and position, and to become more skilled around applications of power and structure.	Learn how to express respect for other people's roles in the organization and maintain appropriate boundaries to protect one's own sphere of influence.

Structure Behaviour 2: Demonstrates Political Savvy in Getting Things Done—Example One

What It Looks Like When Underutilized	What It Looks Like When Optimally Utilized	What It Looks Like When Overutilized
Your client is blindsided and derailed by influences and agendas that were unknown.	Your client acknowledges that all sides of and perspectives on an issue have a legitimate claim to truth and relevance.	Your client is so consumed with politics and Machiavellian intrigue that any real, tangible or helpful results remain unaccomplished.

Structure Behaviour 2: Development Suggestions—Example One

Underutilization	Optimal Utilization	Overutilization
Seek out a skilled mentor, wise in the ways of office politics and open to seeing the workplace in a new way.	Beware of becoming complacent or believing that politics have ceased to exist or don't influence anything or anyone anymore. There will always be politics.	Adjust any overactive competitive throttles to become more accepting of win/win solutions.

Structure Behaviour 2: Demonstrates Political Savvy in Getting Things Done—Example Two

What It Looks Like When Underutilized	What It Looks Like When Optimally Utilized	What It Looks Like When Overutilized
Your client builds a reputation for political clumsiness that is less than helpful to career aspirations.	Your client builds a reputation for being knowledgeable-yet-fair regarding the political realities of organizational life.	Your client builds a reputation for political savagery that is less than helpful to the ability to work effectively with others.

Structure Behaviour 2: Development
Suggestions—Example Two

Underutilization	Optimal Utilization	Overutilization
Embark on a process of demonstrating political awareness (not prejudice) in acknowledging other people's ideas and agendas (i.e., 'I see how this will promote your cause in a good way').	A reputation for being fair-minded and politically neutral needs to be emphasized. People need to feel it is safe to approach your client and that sensitive information will be safe because of the ability to rise above political forces.	Use 360-degree feedback to better understand how others perceive the intentions behind actions. Learn and practise new ways to promote principles more than personal and political gain.

Structure Behaviour 2: Demonstrates Political
Savvy in Getting Things Done—Example Three

What It Looks Like When Underutilized	What It Looks Like When Optimally Utilized	What It Looks Like When Overutilized
Your client fails to develop any sort of capacity for positive influence in and around the organization.	By making all sides of an issue feel acknowledged and respected, your client becomes a peacemaker and coalition builder.	Your client can become better known as a political animal than as a trustworthy colleague, so that everything done is greeted and bracketed with suspicion.

Structure Behaviour 2: Development
Suggestions—Example Three

Underutilization	Optimal Utilization	Overutilization
Expand the capacity for influence to test the waters and experience small victories in getting suggestions heard and acknowledged.	Extend the hand of neutrality whenever possible and offer to help mediate problems to find the most equitable solutions for all concerned. Never forget that a healthy and successful organization is a fertile ground for healthy and successful team members.	Begin building trust among colleagues by vocally placing the needs of the organization above one's own. Visibly seek out the best solutions for most people.

Structure Behaviour 3: Provides Framework for
Achieving Organizational Objectives—Example One

What It Looks Like When Underutilized	What It Looks Like When Optimally Utilized	What It Looks Like When Overutilized
People have no idea whether or not any of their efforts are helping achieve organizational goals.	People's efforts, energies and resources are aligned with the achievement of organizational goals and objectives.	Your client is obsessed with details and immobilized in the minutia of putting together a plan to reach objectives.

Structure Behaviour 3: Development Suggestions—Example One

Underutilization	Optimal Utilization	Overutilization
Increase knowledge of how efforts can be tracked and measured to identify if goals are being reached within the structure of the business.	Keep monitoring progress in the planning and execution process by setting benchmarks and milestones with the help of peers and training professionals.	Learn how to balance action and contemplation—between pure planning and executing the plans with the people and resources that are in place.

Structure Behaviour 3: Provides Framework for Achieving Organizational Objectives—Example Two

What It Looks Like When Underutilized	What It Looks Like When Optimally Utilized	What It Looks Like When Overutilized
Your client's direct reports have no way to focus their efforts towards achievement of organizational goals and/or objectives.	Everyone on your client's team has a clear picture of how they can most effectively spend their time, talents and available resources to achieve organizational objectives.	Your client manages to immobilize team members by immersing them in minute details of an over-engineered execution plan.

Structure Behaviour 3: Development Suggestions—Example Two

Underutilization	Optimal Utilization	Overutilization
Provide training and development opportunities for the team to identify goals and plan for effective execution.	Make sure to pass forward to colleagues and the team any new knowledge and skills that emerge so that team members become even better at execution.	Lead the team in executing a plan. This can involve team development activities like action learning and sharing goal-attainment responsibility with team members.

Structure Behaviour 3: Provides Framework for Achieving Organizational Objectives—Example Three

What It Looks Like When Underutilized	What It Looks Like When Optimally Utilized	What It Looks Like When Overutilized
Your client's team members hear about organizational goals elsewhere and are confused as to why they are not led towards achieving them.	Your client's team members respect and respond to their leader as they see consistency between how policies, procedures and work processes are structured and aligned to stated organizational goals and objectives.	Team members are capable of engineering an efficient and cost-effective plan for reaching organizational objectives, yet your coaching client blocks them.

Structure Behaviour 3: Development Suggestions—Example Three

Underutilization	Optimal Utilization	Overutilization
Make attainment of organizational goals and objectives a top priority and design reward systems to support it.	Build a skill set around reward and recognition. Check out authors who write about motivation and recognition. One can never be too good at motivating for enthusiastic and effective execution.	Go beyond training for executing plans and leadership to include prioritizing and reward systems that truly inspire people to go after timely and meaningful results.

Structure Behaviour 4: Creates Relationship with Manager to Support Initiatives and Reach Goals—Example One

What It Looks Like When Underutilized	What It Looks Like When Optimally Utilized	What It Looks Like When Overutilized
Your client avoids contact with the manager because the working relationship is difficult or unpleasant. The manager is not supportive of his or her career growth.	Your client communicates clearly with the manager and seeks out his or her best thinking on initiatives and goals that have been set forth for the department.	Your client makes too much gratuitous contact with the manager to the point that appropriate professional boundaries are erased.

Structure Behaviour 4: Development Suggestions—Example One

Underutilization	Optimal Utilization	Overutilization
Begin by making respectful but limited contact with management to hear what the agenda is for the department.	Continue to study what management wants and needs in terms of performance in order to execute the initiatives and reach the goals set forth.	Limit interaction with management to productive time that provides new information and moves the initiatives for the department forward.

Structure Behaviour 4: Creates Relationship with Manager to Support Initiatives and Reach Goals—Example Two

What It Looks Like When Underutilized	What It Looks Like When Optimally Utilized	What It Looks Like When Overutilized
Your client disagrees with the initiatives and goals the manager puts forth and sabotages them. As a result, the manager is understandably not supportive of your client's career growth.	Your client values the relationship with the manager and is willing to respectfully engage in discussions and feedback about the merits of his or her initiatives and goals.	Your client agrees with the manager's initiatives and goals too easily and without question. Hence, allowing him or her to damage the department and/or organization.

Structure Behaviour 4: Development Suggestions—Example Two

Underutilization	Optimal Utilization	Overutilization
Learn respectful and effective ways to express professional opinions about initiatives and goals management sets forth. Use terms and phrase familiar to the audience you are addressing.	Help others learn about critical thinking and effective ways to initiate and facilitate conversations and constructive confrontations about the merits of initiatives and goals management establishes. Seek fairness always.	Learn to seek the opinions and perspectives of respected and objective parties that might help with insight and appreciation for management's initiative and goal selection.

Structure Behaviour 4: Creates Relationship with Manager to Support Initiatives and Reach Goals—Example Three

What It Looks Like When Underutilized	What It Looks Like When Optimally Utilized	What It Looks Like When Overutilized
Your client agrees to support the manager's initiatives and goals yet provides little visible support for the manager among circles of peers.	Your client is a visible and vocal proponent of the manager and the initiatives and goals he or she sets forth, reasonably defending their merits when assaulted by peers or others in the organization.	Your client supports the manager so enthusiastically in the organization that this attitude actually reflects badly on the manager and the initiatives and goals he or she seeks to realize.

Structure Behaviour 4: Development Suggestions—Example Three

Underutilization	Optimal Utilization	Overutilization
Using written communications and verbal presentations, give management due credit for the initiatives and goals set forth.	Explore ways to become an advocate for management to promote an atmosphere of collaboration and cooperation between departments and business verticals across the organization.	Understand how management is perceived and then show support in culturally appropriate ways that will engender a quality professional working relationship.

Structure Behaviour 5: Participates in Cross-functional Task Forces that Build Organizational Alliances—Example One

What It Looks Like When Underutilized	What It Looks Like When Optimally Utilized	What It Looks Like When Overutilized
Your client does not reach out to other business verticals or disciplines within the organization for assistance or to share information.	Your client reaches out to peers and even to those superior in the organization to initiate cross-functional alliances that foster quality enterprise-wide communication.	Your client reaches out to peers and others in the organization to excess and dilutes the spirit of true collaboration and cooperation.

Structure Behaviour 5: Development Suggestions—Example One

Underutilization	Optimal Utilization	Overutilization
Make a conscious effort to initiate contact with others in the organization to share information and lessons learned.	Promote interdisciplinary efforts to increase visibility for the department and for the principles of information sharing and group problem-solving process.	Maintain appropriate boundaries when engaging with other departments or factions in the organization. Do not overdo.

Structure Behaviour 5: Participates in Cross-functional Task Forces that Build Organizational Alliances—Example Two

What It Looks Like When Underutilized	What It Looks Like When Optimally Utilized	What It Looks Like When Overutilized
Your client resists the encouragement of upper management to join team's problem-solving efforts involving those from other departments and disciplines.	Your client readily accepts the invitation from peers or those superior in the organization to cross business verticals in search of more collaborative ways to work more efficiently.	Your client pushes those superior in the organization to smudge or erase lines between business disciplines to the point that reporting accountability becomes blurred and fuzzy.

Structure Behaviour 5: Development Suggestions—Example Two

Underutilization	Optimal Utilization	Overutilization
Pay particular attention to the sorts of interdepartmental alliances upper management is trying to encourage, and make it a priority to participate.	Make sure that upper management sees what is being done effectively by reporting on task force activities. Successful task force activities should be shared.	Work to identify when the focus of an effort should be external to the department and when the focus should be on building a stronger team inside.

Structure Behaviour 5: Participates in Cross-functional Task Forces that Build Organizational Alliances—Example Three

What It Looks Like When Underutilized	What It Looks Like When Optimally Utilized	What It Looks Like When Overutilized
Your client tends to be isolated and to also isolate subordinates and thereby rob them of growth and expansion opportunities.	Your client is always on the lookout for opportunities to team subordinates with their peers across business verticals in order to bring fresh ideas into the workspace and to expose people to new opportunities.	Your client encourages the team members to rely more on their peers and others in the organization for the guidance he or she should be providing as a leader.

Structure Behaviour 5: Development Suggestions—Example Three

Underutilization	Optimal Utilization	Overutilization
Give team members the option of choosing what task forces to join or encourage them to start their own.	Work across business verticals with peers to help facilitate the cross-functional integration of team members reporting to this level of peers.	Allow team members to be exposed to the leadership of other teams in a variety of verticals on a reciprocal basis.

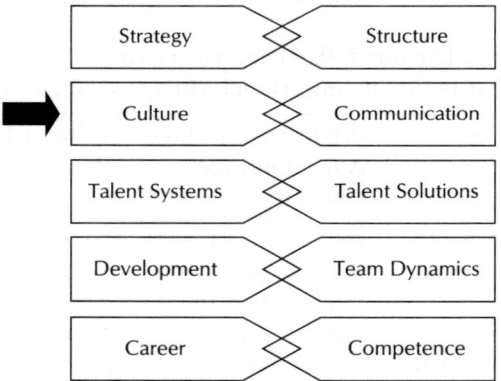

Culture Behaviour 1: Values the Differences of Others—Example One

What It Looks Like When Underutilized	What It Looks Like When Optimally Utilized	What It Looks Like When Overutilized
Your clients might be annoyed by the differences that people with other backgrounds and perspectives bring to the team.	Your clients appreciate that brilliant and resilient ideas can come from many diverse perspectives and opinions.	Your client reaches too far and tries to make everything the exception, not the rule, tolerating nothing 'normal'.

Culture Behaviour 1: Development Suggestions—Example One

Underutilization	Optimal Utilization	Overutilization
Help your client begin to see the resistance to diversity as one's own issue rather than an issue thrust upon them by others.	Help your client to never stop stretching personal boundaries around issues of diversity and differences of perspective.	Urge your client to seek objective feedback from others that can help create better insight into oneself.

Culture Behaviour 1: Values the Differences of Others—Example Two

What It Looks Like When Underutilized	What It Looks Like When Optimally Utilized	What It Looks Like When Overutilized
Your clients might not treat certain members of the team as equals or as peers.	Your clients can see how diversity creates a strong basis for idea and strategy formation with many different perspectives present.	If something, an idea or opinion, seems too mainstream, your clients might reject it out of hand.

Culture Behaviour 1: Development Suggestions—Example Two

Underutilization	Optimal Utilization	Overutilization
Help your clients learn from other team members how to appreciate one another, especially if they are a more diverse group of thinkers.	Help your client recognize the potential for blind spots in oneself and recognize that others may experience them as well.	Help your client avoid being overly provocative. Do not force people to accept each other. Give them rich opportunities to do so on their own.

Culture Behaviour 1: Values the Differences of Others—Example Three

What It Looks Like When Underutilized	What It Looks Like When Optimally Utilized	What It Looks Like When Overutilized
Your clients might be afraid that senior management sees diversity among team members as confusing and threatening.	Your clients make it a point to comply with organizational diversity policies and ensure that the team looks like the entire population being served.	Your clients' decision-making is stilted by overcompensation, and even the members of the team are uncomfortable with the extremism.

Culture Behaviour 1: Development Suggestions—Example Three

Underutilization	Optimal Utilization	Overutilization
Urge your client to discuss diversity policy with senior management and leave nothing to assumption.	Have your client study the history of diversity in the organization and situate the team and its members into that evolving history.	Caution your client not to swing the pendulum too far in the opposite direction when correcting for overcompensation and observe-moderation.

Culture Behaviour 2: Acts as a Change Agent at Appropriate Times—Example One

What It Looks Like When Underutilized	What It Looks Like When Optimally Utilized	What It Looks Like When Overutilized
When the organization needs change the most, your client does not participate or, worse, stands in the way of progress.	Your client recognizes the need for change, not for the sake of change, but because the organization needs to move forward.	Your clients are change junkies and lobby hard to change everything they encounter, whether or not the change is needed.

Culture Behaviour 2: Development Suggestions—Example One

Underutilization	Optimal Utilization	Overutilization
Help your client to understand more deeply how resistance to change is a personal issue causing push back most of the time.	Help your client understand the dynamics of change and that change can be a blind spot for people and cause tremendous anxiety.	Help your client maintain a more balanced perspective on change.

Culture Behaviour 2: Acts as a Change Agent at Appropriate Times—Example Two

What It Looks Like When Underutilized	What It Looks Like When Optimally Utilized	What It Looks Like When Overutilized
Team members know that change is needed, but for some reason your client does not step up to the challenge.	Your client is the one championing change among team members, not the other way around, as well as advocating for the change.	Your client tries to recruit team members to champion an ill-advised change even though they know better.

Culture Behaviour 2: Development Suggestions—Example Two

Underutilization	Optimal Utilization	Overutilization
Have your client attend change management workshops with other team members to learn about change and stop fearing it.	Help your client, as a leader, take the responsibility to support organizational change even when there is some uncertainty about it.	Help your client consult with team members about the relative benefits or possible liabilities of change.

Culture Behaviour 2: Acts as a Change Agent at Appropriate Times—Example Three

What It Looks Like When Underutilized	What It Looks Like When Optimally Utilized	What It Looks Like When Overutilized
Your client fails to communicate the need for change to others even after senior management expects everyone to support the change.	Your client becomes a spokesperson for change and carries senior management's message out to the extent of his or her credibility.	Your clients develop a reputation among senior management that they lack a full understanding of change and why it is necessary.

Culture Behaviour 2: Development Suggestions—Example Three

Underutilization	Optimal Utilization	Overutilization
Help your client to listen more closely to how senior management justifies the need for change.	Suggest that your client become the change champion to help the organization grow and prosper, especially in uncertain times.	Help your clients articulate a clear and concise case for supporting change so they sound credible and everyone understands.

Culture Behaviour 3: Negotiates in a Manner that Builds Consensus—Example One

What It Looks Like When Underutilized	What It Looks Like When Optimally Utilized	What It Looks Like When Overutilized
Your client sees no need to negotiate, relying instead purely on institutional authority to control others and boss them around.	Your client reaches out to all constituencies to ensure their voices are heard and validated in the negotiating process.	Your client seeks consensus and accepts nothing less and, consequently, winds up frustrated and disappointed.

Culture Behaviour 3: Development Suggestions—Example One

Underutilization	Optimal Utilization	Overutilization
Give your clients objective assistance to help them learn to be consensus builders instead of autocrats.	Complete consensus might be too much to ask for all at once. It is sometimes helpful to seek collaboration as a first step towards achieving genuine consensus.	Help your client learn to appreciate the diversity of opinion that might preclude consensus.

Culture Behaviour 3: Negotiates in a Manner that Builds Consensus—Example Two

What It Looks Like When Underutilized	What It Looks Like When Optimally Utilized	What It Looks Like When Overutilized
Your clients gravitate towards those members of the team who agree with them and disregard the rest.	Your clients anticipate the need and make the time for various opinions to be expressed in a search for consensus.	Your clients mistakenly expect everyone on the team to automatically agree on everything.

Culture Behaviour 3: Development Suggestions—Example Two

Underutilization	Optimal Utilization	Overutilization
Help your client begin to see the team as a means of seeking and testing consensus.	People can work together, even when they do not fully agree. Achieving a working coalition is a victory in itself.	Help your client learn, if the team is viewed as a whole identity, there will likely be a level or a point at which they all can agree to agree.

Culture Behaviour 3: Negotiates in a Manner that Builds Consensus—Example Three

What It Looks Like When Underutilized	What It Looks Like When Optimally Utilized	What It Looks Like When Overutilized
Your clients seek to supplement their own authority by borrowing authority from senior management.	Your clients accept that the more one can bring consensus to senior management, the more valuable one will be in the process.	Your clients can appreciate and reflect back to everyone the diversity of their opinion but discount it if it is not consensual.

Culture Behaviour 3: Development Suggestions—Example Three

Underutilization	Optimal Utilization	Overutilization
Help your client study closely how senior management manages to reach consensus when possible.	Help your client understand and appreciate that consensus is not always possible and that it is important to always seek collaboration.	Help your client learn to not discount any opinion while moving people to the point where consensus exists.

Culture Behaviour 4: Exemplifies the Norms and Values of the Organization—Example One

What It Looks Like When Underutilized	What It Looks Like When Optimally Utilized	What It Looks Like When Overutilized
In many ways, your clients represent the opposite of what the organization, as a whole, values.	Your clients dress and present in a way that is consistent with the organization's brand and image in the community and marketplace.	Your clients are complete company people, never questioning anyone, any policy or anything else.

Culture Behaviour 4: Development Suggestions—Example One

Underutilization	Optimal Utilization	Overutilization
If your client is a rebel, help him or her explore what it is like to be a conformist to see how it feels to take on that role.	Help your client accept, at a deep level, the imperfect nature of organizations and how inconsistent they can be, even in the best of times.	Help your client learn the value of questioning, researching and coming to one's own conclusions.

Culture Behaviour 4: Exemplifies the Norms and Values of the Organization—Example Two

What It Looks Like When Underutilized	What It Looks Like When Optimally Utilized	What It Looks Like When Overutilized
Your clients preach (perhaps whisper) to the team that they should reject or rebel against organizational values.	Your clients appreciate the organization for what it truly stands for and attempt to carry that message to internal and external customers.	Your clients lose credibility as they try to convince team members that the organization is the answer to all of their problems.

Culture Behaviour 4: Development Suggestions—Example Two

Underutilization	Optimal Utilization	Overutilization
Help your client learn to give the team and peers quality, balanced information and not to recruit them to a specific cause.	Help your client make a good faith effort to influence the norms and values of the organization to help make the organization stronger.	Help your client try to give team members every opportunity to form their own opinions about the organization and its culture.

Culture Behaviour 4: Exemplifies the Norms and Values of the Organization—Example Three

What It Looks Like When Underutilized	What It Looks Like When Optimally Utilized	What It Looks Like When Overutilized
Senior management sees your clients as a threat and a disruption to the agenda they want to advance.	Your clients pay close attention to what senior management says and does and give them the benefit of the doubt in their execution.	Your clients set senior management upon a pedestal from which they can neither do any wrong nor make a mistake.

Culture Behaviour 4: Development
Suggestions—Example Three

Underutilization	Optimal Utilization	Overutilization
Help your clients to demonstrate for senior management the behaviour that shows support for the organizational agenda.	Your clients can respectfully speak truth to authority and let senior management know when there is something that needs their attention.	Encourage your clients to engage in as much interaction as possible with different levels of management to get a realistic picture.

Culture Behaviour 5: Demonstrates Concern for
How the Culture Impacts the Business—Example One

What It Looks Like When Underutilized	What It Looks Like When Optimally Utilized	What It Looks Like When Overutilized
Your clients do not connect the shared values and beliefs of the organization and the team with the business they do.	Your clients fully understand that a culture is the true collective of beliefs and values of the organizational population.	Your clients believe in the culture so strongly they think that even the customers should adopt it.

Culture Behaviour 5: Development
Suggestions—Example One

Underutilization	Optimal Utilization	Overutilization
Help your clients analyse what the organization believes and what it does so they will feel better about supporting a positive culture.	Do everything possible to achieve true alignment between what the organizational population believes and what the organization does in the marketplace.	Help your clients seek out objective data that reveals how well the organization's culture is aligned with its customers' needs. Be realistic.

Culture Behaviour 5: Demonstrates Concern
for How the Culture Impacts the Business—Example Two

What It Looks Like When Underutilized	What It Looks Like When Optimally Utilized	What It Looks Like When Overutilized
Your clients' communication of key cultural principles has little effect on others. The support for cultural principles is lukewarm.	Your clients know that the people working for an organization might believe something different from what the public face of the organization professes, they seek alignment.	Your clients will not accept that there might be a rift between the organization's culture and its professed mission statement.

Culture Behaviour 5: Development
Suggestions—Example Two

Underutilization	Optimal Utilization	Overutilization
Help team members to have a voice in how the culture is shaped and maintained to increase their sense of ownership.	Help your clients to promote the virtues and values most helpful to the organization and the various constituencies the organization serves.	Help your clients close the gaps where there are differences in the organization's mission statement and actual practices.

Culture Behaviour 5: Demonstrates Concern for How the Culture Impacts the Business—Example Three

What It Looks Like When Underutilized	What It Looks Like When Optimally Utilized	What It Looks Like When Overutilized
Your clients say one thing and do another. They agree to support the organizational agenda and then don't follow through.	Your clients are aware of and accept the awesome power of an undefined culture to take apart everything well-intentioned team members and senior management try to do.	Your clients take the words and actions of senior management as gospel and accept them as the culture for the whole organization.

Culture Behaviour 5: Development Suggestions—Example Three

Underutilization	Optimal Utilization	Overutilization
Help your clients to adopt a structured policy of following through. Help them learn consistency and the value of supporting organizational needs.	Try to make everyone more aware of the role they play in establishing a culture of choice and benefit to everyone in the organization.	Help your clients seek collaborations among factions within the organization to come up with solutions to secure a more customer-centric culture.

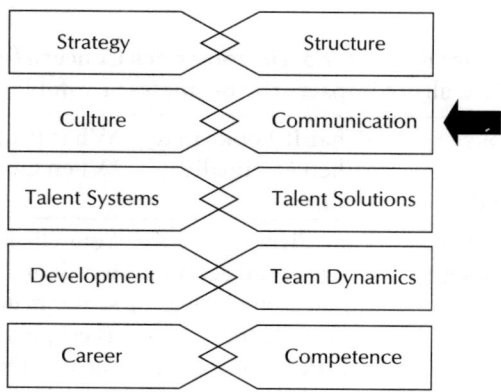

Communication Behaviour 1: Persuades Others to Make Commitments—Example One

What It Looks Like When Underutilized	What It Looks Like When Optimally Utilized	What It Looks Like When Overutilized
Your client invests no time or energy attempting to secure commitment from anyone.	Your client begins by assessing personal commitment to the organization and quickly realizes how it affects one's performance.	Your client can come off as needy and insecure begging everybody to pledge their lives, their fortunes, their children, etc. to the cause.

**Communication Behaviour 1: Development
Suggestions—Example One**

Underutilization	Optimal Utilization	Overutilization
Help your client understand that commitment is very important to the health and well-being of the organization.	Help your client identify and appreciate the many ways in which the organization provides support through commitment to compensation, benefits, a comfortable working environment, etc.	Help your client make the case for why making and keeping commitments is essential to organizational success.

**Communication Behaviour 1: Persuades Others
to Make Commitments—Example Two**

What It Looks Like When Underutilized	What It Looks Like When Optimally Utilized	What It Looks Like When Overutilized
Any commitment from your client's team members comes from their own initiative and loyalty.	Your client appreciates the significance of having people committed to the organization as well as the substantial value their commitment adds.	Team members feel like your client does not recognize their current level of commitment.

Communication Behaviour 1: Development Suggestions—Example Two

Underutilization	Optimal Utilization	Overutilization
By learning to communicate better with team members, it will become apparent how eager they are to commit to the organization.	Help your client realize the degree to which the organization commits to supporting the lives and lifestyles of every team member, every day.	Help your client learn to recognize team members for their loyalties and parlay that recognition into new commitments.

Communication Behaviour 1: Persuades Others to Make Commitments—Example Three

What It Looks Like When Underutilized	What It Looks Like When Optimally Utilized	What It Looks Like When Overutilized
Your client does not approach superiors in the organization to commit support for initiatives.	As a leader, your client knows how important one's own commitment is to the success of those who are direct reports.	Your client over-negotiates the work with others to secure buy-in.

Communication Behaviour 1: Development
Suggestions—Example Three

Underutilization	Optimal Utilization	Overutilization
Help your client become willing to approach others to make judicious and voluntary commitments and to own their commitments.	Help your client express sincere gratitude for the many ways the organization commits to its employees when carrying the message from senior executives back to the team.	Help your client take advantage of opportunities for gratitude to secure future commitments from senior management to support initiatives.

Communication Behaviour 2: Demonstrates Empathy
in Communications—Example One

What It Looks Like When Underutilized	What It Looks Like When Optimally Utilized	What It Looks Like When Overutilized
In the absence of expressed empathy, people do not believe that your client cares about how they feel.	People with whom your client communicates truly feel appreciated for the full depth of what they are experiencing in the moment.	It is difficult to over-empathize, but people tend to feel emotionally invaded when your client is too curious and crawls into their space.

Communication Behaviour 2: Development Suggestions—Example One

Underutilization	Optimal Utilization	Overutilization
Help your client practise the techniques of active and empathetic listening.	More than words, the demonstration of empathy shows up most in eye contact and body language that reflects the other person's emotional state.	Help your clients pay attention to how someone responds to their emotional connection and adjust behaviour to match the response.

Communication Behaviour 2: Demonstrates Empathy in Communications—Example Two

What It Looks Like When Underutilized	What It Looks Like When Optimally Utilized	What It Looks Like When Overutilized
Your client's team members begin to feel as if they are mechanical robots being remotely controlled by their leader.	Your client knows better than to over-intellectualize when someone is sharing emotionally. People do not care how much someone knows until they know how much someone cares.	Your client's team members experience being held hostage in an 'emotional check in' for too long. As a result, they get nervous and pull back inside.

Communication Behaviour 2: Development Suggestions—Example Two

Underutilization	Optimal Utilization	Overutilization
Help your client take genuine interest in others by asking questions and listening to the answers.	Help your client acknowledge verbally, when addressing a group, what is known to be true about the emotional state of the environment at the time.	Help your client study the temperament of a group that has worked together for a long time, and never take their individual or collective emotions for granted.

Communication Behaviour 2: Demonstrates Empathy in Communications—Example Three

What It Looks Like When Underutilized	What It Looks Like When Optimally Utilized	What It Looks Like When Overutilized
Senior executives often have difficulty processing or expressing emotions. Yet, they do not want their own emotions discounted when dealing with others.	People's underlying emotional states are often where your client can find enough common ground to transcend political differences and begin consensus and coalition building.	Your client allows empathy to become sympathy. People begin to resent being pitied, and relationships become cold and brittle.

Communication Behaviour 2: Development Suggestions—Example Three

Underutilization	Optimal Utilization	Overutilization
Help your client practise repeating back what someone has said to ensure that understanding is complete.	Help your clients understand that meetings can be emotionally charged, but their body language should show controlled alertness and focus.	People, especially senior people, will hint at how they feel long before they will cop to it. Do not comment on what they appear to be feeling. Let them reveal it.

Communication Behaviour 3: Consistently Communicates Essential Information—Example One

What It Looks Like When Underutilized	What It Looks Like When Optimally Utilized	What It Looks Like When Overutilized
Your client leaves essential information out of conversations. Consequently, people are under-informed as they move ahead.	Your clients show balance in the amount and type of information shared. They never assume someone does not need or want to know.	Your client overinforms and tends to annoy others and diminish good communications.

Communication Behaviour 3: Development Suggestions—Example One

Underutilization	Optimal Utilization	Overutilization
Help your client learn to check in with people for their questions in case something has been left out.	Help your client cascade information to appropriate listeners. Cover every topic that could be considered essential information and add a couple more items.	Help your client understand that cascading information is vastly different from dumping. Imagine a stream skipping over stones in the creek bed versus a mudslide.

Communication Behaviour 3: Consistently Communicates Essential Information—Example Two

What It Looks Like When Underutilized	What It Looks Like When Optimally Utilized	What It Looks Like When Overutilized
Peers, team members and others become suspicious of your client as essential information is consistently absent from conversations.	Your client is aware that the structure and sequence used to communicate will lend more weight to certain pieces of information and less to others.	Your client attempts to make everything a critical piece of information, thus diminishing the importance of everything.

Communication Behaviour 3: Development Suggestions—Example Two

Underutilization	Optimal Utilization	Overutilization
Help your client avoid the appearance of hiding or withholding information intentionally. Teach them to use phrases like, 'In the interest of full disclosure....'	Teach your client to speak in headlines. By giving the high points and letting listeners request a drill down, more information will be covered quickly without boring people with details they don't want or need.	Teach your clients to adjust rate of speech, and pitch—upward and downward dynamics can help emphasize essential information. Visual structure of the page helps increase retention when writing.

Communication Behaviour 3: Consistently Communicates Essential Information—Example Three

What It Looks Like When Underutilized	What It Looks Like When Optimally Utilized	What It Looks Like When Overutilized
Your client too often treats senior executives on a need to know basis. Executives don't want too much detail, but being left out of the loop really annoys them.	What is essential information to one person might not be considered essential to another. That is why your client puts the heavy stuff out first but skilfully leaves the final judging up to the listener.	Your client pushes essential information on senior executives too hard and ad nauseam, making them feel uncomfortable and as if they are being demanded to do something.

Communication Behaviour 3: Development Suggestions—Example Three

Underutilization	Optimal Utilization	Overutilization
Help your client not to share information at high levels that they might not want to acknowledge as known and being discussed.	Teach your clients: When essential information is shared, ask key people for whom the information is important to send an email with a recap to ensure they received and understood it.	Teach your clients: If it is important for someone to act on what is being said, then ask for action. Do not just put out information and assume the person will feel compelled to act.

Communication Behaviour 4: Clear Direction Regarding Roles and Responsibilities—Example One

What It Looks Like When Underutilized	What It Looks Like When Optimally Utilized	What It Looks Like When Overutilized
People are confused and do not know what your client expects of them. As a result, they do nothing.	Your client delivers understandable instructions regarding who, what, when, why, where and how that establishes clear expectations.	Your client can delve into such detail that people will wind up more confused and annoyed after the conversation than before.

Communication Behaviour 4: Development Suggestions—Example One

Underutilization	Optimal Utilization	Overutilization
Help your client understand that it is unreasonable to assume that people will know the complexity of their roles and responsibilities. They must be discussed.	Help your client keep the conversation about roles and responsibilities free-flowing, staying mindful that there are roles and responsibilities to be assigned before the conversation ends, even if they change throughout.	Help your client learn to constantly monitor body language, eye contact and direct questions from team members to gauge the level of detail for roles and responsibilities.

Communication Behaviour 4: Clear Direction Regarding Roles and Responsibilities—Example Two

What It Looks Like When Underutilized	What It Looks Like When Optimally Utilized	What It Looks Like When Overutilized
Your client's team members not only do not know what is expected of them, but they do not even know what to expect from one another.	The instruction conversation given by your client leaves absolutely no ambiguity as to who is responsible for what role. The final instruction given is: 'If in doubt, ask'.	Your client can cast people in the wrong roles without knowing it and thereby generate resentment as people disconnect from the spirit of what is being requested of them.

Communication Behaviour 4: Development Suggestions—Example Two

Underutilization	Optimal Utilization	Overutilization
Teach your clients to use a check-in process while assigning roles and responsibilities to team members—then ask team members to feed back what has been said to them.	Make sure your clients know that the roles and responsibilities conversation includes feedback on expectations for the team leader and team members, plus feedback on what is expected.	Teach your clients to take notes about what each person's area of contribution is and monitor their performance to ensure it is what it should be.

Communication Behaviour 4: Clear Direction Regarding Roles and Responsibilities—Example Three

What It Looks Like When Underutilized	What It Looks Like When Optimally Utilized	What It Looks Like When Overutilized
Because they have not been given clear roles and responsibilities, people do not know what to expect from your client.	The roles and responsibilities conversation allows team members to give feedback and challenge their assignments since they know best about their respective capabilities and capacity.	Your client may take instruction-giving to a higher level than is necessary or appropriate. Senior executives typically do not appreciate being managed by subordinates.

Communication Behaviour 4: Development Suggestions—Example Three

Underutilization	Optimal Utilization	Overutilization
To ensure understanding of team members' expectations, your client must be able to repeat back to them what they have expressed.	Your clients must solicit feedback from their team members during and after the work to establish benchmarks, to establish best practices and to close the loop.	Have your client ask people Starbucks style if they are willing to accept roles and responsibilities designated for them.

Communication Behaviour 5: Fosters Open Communication Throughout the Organization—Example One

What It Looks Like When Underutilized	What It Looks Like When Optimally Utilized	What It Looks Like When Overutilized
The people who need to know or could benefit greatly from the information your client has, do not get the information they need.	Your clients make it a point to solicit input from other departments about the activities they are engaged in, not just those efforts that involve your clients' own department.	Your clients might develop a reputation for being busy-bodies, asking too many questions and making people suspicious of their motives.

Communication Behaviour 5: Development Suggestions—Example One

Underutilization	Optimal Utilization	Overutilization
Urge your clients to publish regularly on every forum available because many people can benefit from knowing what their departments and teams are doing.	Have your clients become strategic about who is targeted with essential information. If it is possible to reach only a limited number of people, make sure they are the right people.	Help your clients to read signals from others when they are getting nervous and uncomfortable with their level of curiosity and information sharing.

Communication Behaviour 5: Fosters Open Communication Throughout the Organization—Example Two

What It Looks Like When Underutilized	What It Looks Like When Optimally Utilized	What It Looks Like When Overutilized
Your clients' team members are well informed but get stonewalled when they deal with other sectors of the organization.	Your client shares third-party compliments whenever possible, reporting good things that were said by party #2 about party #1 back to party #1. Party #1 then opens up favourably about party #2.	Your client runs the risk of becoming an overzealous self-promoter, unloading information of the department's doings way beyond anyone else's interests.

Communication Behaviour 5: Development Suggestions—Example Two

Underutilization	Optimal Utilization	Overutilization
Have your client train team members to converse with people outside of their regular network with an overview of what the department is doing.	Help your clients find clever and entertaining ways to disseminate information that will be a welcome relief and help break up the tedium of some people's workdays.	Have your clients study people's reactions when disseminating information to them. It will become apparent when enough is enough.

Communication Behaviour 5: Fosters Open Communication Throughout the Organization—Example Three

What It Looks Like When Underutilized	What It Looks Like When Optimally Utilized	What It Looks Like When Overutilized
Senior executives don't know what it is your client is trying to do and get the blanks filled in by other people ... usually incorrectly.	Your client does not leave gaps in the story when communicating information that others then tend to complete with their own imaginations.	Your client could make known some information that senior executives don't want broadcast far and wide and then be called on the carpet for the lack of discretion.

Communication Behaviour 5: Development Suggestions—Example Three

Underutilization	Optimal Utilization	Overutilization
Help your clients become role models for good communication by completing the story and giving thought to what information is necessary to present and to whom it should be presented.	Urge your clients to tell their teams' stories on every available platform in order to keep people from jumping to their own conclusions and possibly selling their accomplishments short.	Help your clients learn to exercise discretion when it comes to who is providing information and whom to pass it on to. When in doubt, less is more. Better to be safe.

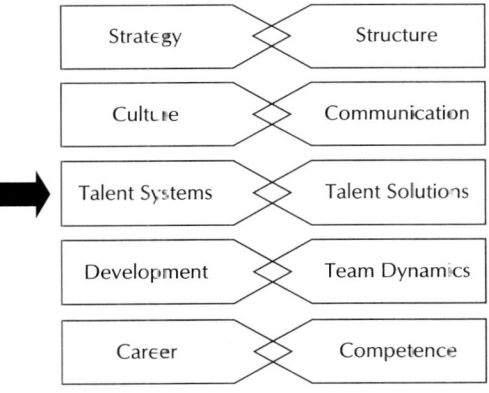

Talent Systems Behaviour 1: Sets Standards for Performance—Example One

What It Looks Like When Underutilized	What It Looks Like When Optimally Utilized	What It Looks Like When Overutilized
Your client's team members are unclear about how to reach successful goals.	Your client's team members have a clear sense of performance and development goals going forward.	Your client's team members feel that work is overly regimented leaving little room for creativity.

Talent Systems Behaviour 1: Development Suggestions—Example One

Underutilization	Optimal Utilization	Overutilization
Be more willing to lead direct reports in setting goals that impact the business.	Continually gauge the team on meeting the goals and fulfilling the standards.	Avoid rules-oriented approaches to setting performance goals.

Talent Systems Behaviour 1: Sets Standards for Performance—Example Two

What It Looks Like When Underutilized	What It Looks Like When Optimally Utilized	What It Looks Like When Overutilized
Your client has difficulty with focused performance management conversations.	Your client's conversations on performance management topics have clarity and baseline definitions.	Your client's team members feel that conversations become negotiations instead of developmental opportunities.

Talent Systems Behaviour 1: Development Suggestions—Example Two

Underutilization	Optimal Utilization	Overutilization
Be clear on what is expected from the team.	Continue to communicate the goal perspective when it comes to performance.	Be willing to receive input from the team on the standards.

Talent Systems Behaviour 1: Sets Standards for Performance—Example Three

What It Looks Like When Underutilized	What It Looks Like When Optimally Utilized	What It Looks Like When Overutilized
Performance evaluations with your client become a potential point of conflict.	Your client presents expectations clearly which helps to put people on the same page when it comes to what is expected of them.	Your client needs to understand that flexibility in expectations may be required if business context changes.

Talent Systems Behaviour 1: Development Suggestions—Example Three

Underutilization	Optimal Utilization	Overutilization
Have good reasons that support the standards being set in expectations.	At performance review, remind the team about the standards that were communicated.	Be willing to adjust the expectations in a reasonable way if circumstances change

Talent Systems Behaviour 2: Reward Performance Appropriately—Example One

What It Looks Like When Underutilized	What It Looks Like When Optimally Utilized	What It Looks Like When Overutilized
Your client's team members do not feel valued for their contribution.	Your client's team members feel valued for their contribution.	Your client's team members do not understand the real relationship between contribution and reward.

Talent Systems Behaviour 2: Development Suggestions—Example One

Underutilization	Optimal Utilization	Overutilization
Consider enhancing the reward process for stellar performance.	Continue rewarding performance and achievement in proper measure, commensurate with accomplishment.	Consider educating team members on a reward process that balances proper reward and performance.

Talent Systems Behaviour 2: Reward Performance Appropriately—Example Two

What It Looks Like When Underutilized	What It Looks Like When Optimally Utilized	What It Looks Like When Overutilized
Key performers on your client's team may look outside the organization for better rewards.	Key performers on your client's team find rewards inside the organization that motivate them.	Key performers expect too much opportunity and reward for too little effort and underperformance.

Talent Systems Behaviour 2: Development Suggestions—Example Two

Underutilization	Optimal Utilization	Overutilization
Focus on key talent and ensure adequate focus on retention.	Do not stop focusing on key talent and focus on retention-driven decisions.	Balance positive expectations with realistic consequences for underperformance.

Talent Systems Behaviour 2: Reward Performance Appropriately—Example Three

What It Looks Like When Underutilized	What It Looks Like When Optimally Utilized	What It Looks Like When Overutilized
Your client could promote a feeling that the organization does not value performance and is not fair.	Your client promotes a feeling that the organization values performance in a fair and balanced way.	Your client promotes a feeling that the organization over rewards less-than-stellar performance.

Talent Systems Behaviour 2: Development Suggestions—Example Three

Underutilization	Optimal Utilization	Overutilization
Create a performance culture within the team by demonstrating a willingness to reward.	Sustain the performance culture within the team by rewarding in new and creative ways.	Create a performance culture with deliberately balanced reward systems that promote equity and fairness.

Talent Systems Behaviour 3: Gives Specific
and Accurate Feedback—Example One

What It Looks Like When Underutilized	What It Looks Like When Optimally Utilized	What It Looks Like When Overutilized
Team members do not have a sense of where they stand with your client.	Team members have sense of your client's position and can take action.	Your client's team members could feel overwhelmed if feedback is given too constantly.

Talent Systems Behaviour 3: Development
Suggestions—Example One

Underutilization	Optimal Utilization	Overutilization
Be consistent in giving feedback that could have an impact on the work of individual team members.	Continue to engage team members in robust conversations that explain positions and the reasons behind them.	Balance positive and negative feedback.

Talent Systems Behaviour 3: Gives Specific
and Accurate Feedback—Example Two

What It Looks Like When Underutilized	What It Looks Like When Optimally Utilized	What It Looks Like When Overutilized
Your client's team members have to make the connection themselves between generic feedback and specific circumstances.	Your client's direct reports will be able to learn on the job about how they can grow by receiving specific feedback and then discussing it.	Your client's direct reports may become overly sensitive about taking action if they worry that they will be judged for their every move.

Talent Systems Behaviour 3: Development Suggestions—Example Two

Underutilization	Optimal Utilization	Overutilization
Give examples that help articulate a goal-oriented perspective.	Use the feedback process as a developmental tool that builds career potential.	Provide feedback without removing autonomy or instilling fear.

Talent Systems Behaviour 3: Gives Specific and Accurate Feedback—Example Three

What It Looks Like When Underutilized	What It Looks Like When Optimally Utilized	What It Looks Like When Overutilized
People can develop mistrust if the performance feedback from the individual does not reflect the real situation.	Your client provides a feedback process that is continual so that team members feel that the work they do accurately reflects what is occurring in their roles.	Your client's team can feel overly managed and wonder if they are being watched over their shoulder.

Talent Systems Behaviour 3: Development Suggestions—Example Three

Underutilization	Optimal Utilization	Overutilization
Verify with the team members that information is accurate, timely and useful.	Stay close to the work that team members do so that the current conversation connects to a former conversation.	Try not to make each conversation a 'teachable moment' but provide insights at pertinent times.

Talent Systems Behaviour 4: Identifies Top Talent Against Succession Plan—Example One

What It Looks Like When Underutilized	What It Looks Like When Optimally Utilized	What It Looks Like When Overutilized
Your client is unprepared for staffing changes that could affect the performance of the team.	Your client is ready to make adjustments when staffing needs arise.	Your client is overly focused on potential of talent and not the current performance of talent.

Talent Systems Behaviour 4: Development Suggestions—Example One

Underutilization	Optimal Utilization	Overutilization
Identify the potential of key members of the team in order to align them with organizational needs.	Continue to enhance the team's working experience by having talent development conversations.	Balance the need for day-to-day success with potential future roles for individuals.

Talent Systems Behaviour 4: Identifies Top Talent Against Succession Plan—Example Two

What It Looks Like When Underutilized	What It Looks Like When Optimally Utilized	What It Looks Like When Overutilized
Top talent could leave the organization if your client gives them no sense of advancement in the future.	Your client provides motivation for top talent who show potential for future roles.	Your client's indiscriminate focus on talent development could lead to a sense that everyone deserves promotions instead of a more selective approach.

Talent Systems Behaviour 4: Development Suggestions—Example Two

Underutilization	Optimal Utilization	Overutilization
Engage in talent conversations with high potentials to prepare them for future roles.	Maintain a readiness to replace top talent with internal candidates.	Be selective about who has potential for next level roles and who does not.

Talent Systems Behaviour 4: Identifies Top Talent Against Succession Plan—Example Three

What It Looks Like When Underutilized	What It Looks Like When Optimally Utilized	What It Looks Like When Overutilized
Your client demonstrates failure to take an enterprise approach to leadership role and is too insular.	Your client maintains a proper balance between the organization's needs and the needs of your client s own team.	Your client has too much focus on the enterprise and not enough concern for advancement of the team's goals.

Talent Systems Behaviour 4: Development Suggestions—Example Three

Underutilization	Optimal Utilization	Overutilization
Do not allow a concern for losing a talented team member to another department stand in the way of setting up team stars for future roles.	Consider the succession plan for the team and attempt to prepare the replacements for all the individuals.	Move from identifying individuals to building a career plan for them, balanced with the need to perform in the here and now.

Talent Systems Behaviour 5: Uses Effective
Hiring Process to Engage Top Talent—Example One

What It Looks Like When Underutilized	What It Looks Like When Optimally Utilized	What It Looks Like When Overutilized
Your client's failure to hire the right people in a consistent way distracts the team, wastes time and hurts overall performance	Your client hires employees who meet or exceed job expectations.	Your client may be overly rigid in expectations for candidates, leading to inaction.

Talent Systems Behaviour 5: Development
Suggestions—Example One

Underutilization	Optimal Utilization	Overutilization
Develop a deeper understanding of the qualities necessary for success in a particular role.	Stay focused on the right talent and do not give into impatience when trying to fill a role.	Be prepared to compromise when it is appropriate.

Talent Systems Behaviour 5: Uses Effective Hiring
Process to Engage Top Talent—Example Two

What It Looks Like When Underutilized	What It Looks Like When Optimally Utilized	What It Looks Like When Overutilized
The morale of your client's team is lowered if some roles are 'revolving' doors.	Team members trust your client's ability to bring on new talent that can make an impact.	Your client can take too long to fill key roles.

Talent Systems Behaviour 5: Development Suggestions—Example Two

Underutilization	Optimal Utilization	Overutilization
Use behaviour-based interviews that discuss past performance.	Remain clear about job expectations so that candidates can be clear of how the role is structured.	Set personal goals that relate to filling open positions.

Talent Systems Behaviour 5: Uses Effective Hiring Process to Engage Top Talent—Example Three

What It Looks Like When Underutilized	What It Looks Like When Optimally Utilized	What It Looks Like When Overutilized
Your client has a tendency to hire in his or her own image instead of hiring against the job-required tasks.	Your client hires against job criteria to help avoid mistakes and to ensure quality job matching.	Your client may lose the opportunity to bring on stellar talent by being inflexible on job design.

Talent Systems Behaviour 5: Development Suggestions—Example Three

Underutilization	Optimal Utilization	Overutilization
Include others from the team who may be more talented in the area of selection to balance any challenges that arise.	Include team members in the hiring process so that they can learn from it as well.	Partner with others to create balance in following a hiring process.

Talent Systems Behaviour 6: Uses Performance Management Systems to Monitor Performance of Individuals—Example One

What It Looks Like When Underutilized	What It Looks Like When Optimally Utilized	What It Looks Like When Overutilized
Your client lacks verifiable data for important performance discussions.	Your client has the available data for key conversations.	Team members feel overly managed by your client's numbers approach to the jobs.

Talent Systems Behaviour 6: Development Suggestions—Example One

Underutilization	Optimal Utilization	Overutilization
Be sure to use available systems as a tool.	Stay balanced between behavioural observations and performance metrics in conversations with team members.	Be open-minded in the way data is presented as it supports a given position.

Talent Systems Behaviour 6: Uses Performance Management Systems to Monitor Performance of Individuals—Example Two

What It Looks Like When Underutilized	What It Looks Like When Optimally Utilized	What It Looks Like When Overutilized
Your client fails to integrate with the enterprise approach to performance management.	A consistency in managing performance exists between your client's department and other parts of the enterprise.	The individual's overworked approach to performance conversations could come across as rigid and prescriptive.

Talent Systems Behaviour 6: Development
Suggestions—Example Two

Underutilization	Optimal Utilization	Overutilization
Remember the importance of consistent process.	Stay consistent between individuals as well as be aligned to the rest of the organization.	Be flexible in the interpretation of data.

Talent Systems Behaviour 6: Uses Performance Management
Systems to Monitor Performance of Individuals—Example Three

What It Looks Like When Underutilized	What It Looks Like When Optimally Utilized	What It Looks Like When Overutilized
Your client is unable to provide specifics that could help drive performance.	Your client has the ability to tie specific behaviours to expectations and areas identified for growth.	Your client places more focus on the performance management system than on the circumstances of the team member in the role.

Talent Systems Behaviour 6: Development
Suggestions—Example Three

Underutilization	Optimal Utilization	Overutilization
Note the power of specifics for difficult conversations.	Use the specifics wisely in conversations.	Remember the context of the person in the role.

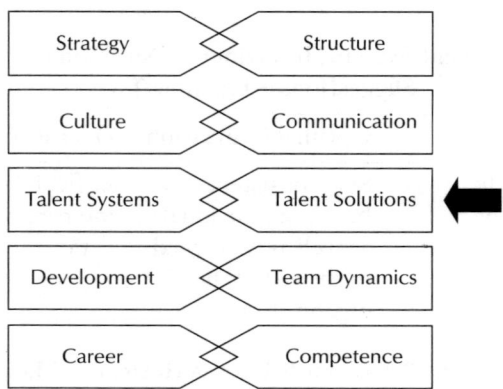

Talent Solutions Behaviour 1: Encourages Others to Learn—Example One

What It Looks Like When Underutilized	What It Looks Like When *Under*-utilized	What It Looks Like When *Under*-utilized
Your client's team members are not aware of how they can develop new skill sets to assist the growth and success of the organization.	Your client has built a learning organization, where everyone is encouraged to grow and develop personally and professionally.	Your client involves team members in excessive amounts of learning activities to the exclusion of their day-to-day activities.

Talent Solutions Behaviour 1: Development Suggestions—Example One

Underutilization	*Under*-utilization	*Under*-utilization
Work together with your internal learning and development professionals to conduct a skills assessment of team members.	Continue to recognize team members' need for continuous reinforcement because the need for learning activities never ends.	Engage team members in real-time action learning that keeps them on the job as they grow and develop.

Talent Solutions Behaviour 1: Encourages
Others to Learn—Example Two

What It Looks Like When Underutilized	What It Looks Like When Optimally Utilized	What It Looks Like When Overutilized
Your client's team members are not aware that their own careers are being held back by their lack of learning and development.	The learning and development your client encourages is tied to career growth in practical and measurable ways.	Your client focuses team members' attention too far out into the future on career matters and leveraging their learning.

Talent Solutions Behaviour 1: Development
Suggestions—Example Two

Underutilization	Optimal Utilization	Overutilization
Expose team members to HR and learning department materials regarding the career benefits of learning and development.	Continue to prepare people for future success.	Provide balanced career guidance to team members and incorporate an optimal dosage of learning and development to keep them active.

Talent Solutions Behaviour 1: Encourages Others to Learn—Example Three

What It Looks Like When Underutilized	What It Looks Like When Optimally Utilized	What It Looks Like When Overutilized
Your client's team members are under-trained and under-skilled in their job functions, costing the organization time, money and lost resources.	Your client has correctly positioned organizational learning and development by tying it to cost savings and enhanced revenue production, as well it should be.	Your client's team members are too immersed in the details of the learning process and procedure to be as effective as they could be in executing their jobs.

Talent Solutions Behaviour 1: Development Suggestions—Example Three

Underutilization	Optimal Utilization	Overutilization
Encourage and support the active involvement by team members enrolling in learning and development programmes, including individual coaching.	The most powerful learning and development agendas are learner-driven. As the champion for learning and development for the team, it is important to let team members make decisions.	Expand upon an Action Learning Model to include work process and efficiency concerns in order to maximize productivity. Become a skilled coach.

Talent Solutions Behaviour 2: Utilizes Company
Resources to Develop Others—Example One

What It Looks Like When Underutilized	What It Looks Like When Optimally Utilized	What It Looks Like When Overutilized
Your client's team members are unaware that funded expectations for their growth and development are not being addressed.	Your client makes wise use of organizational resources to ensure the highest quality and most effective learning possible for team members.	Your client enrols team members in every training programme imaginable and sets unreasonably high expectations for performance improvements.

Talent Solutions Behaviour 2: Development
Suggestions—Example One

Underutilization	Optimal Utilization	Overutilization
Work with the HR and/or learning and development professionals in the organization to make learning expectations and opportunities clear to everyone.	In order to establish and maintain a strong learning and development atmosphere in the department, continue to partner with HR and learning and development professionals on an ongoing basis.	Make careful use of the learning and development professionals at work and coordinate with them to match training programmes to specific needs and to set reasonable expectations for participants.

Talent Solutions Behaviour 2: Utilizes Company
Resources to Develop Others—Example Two

What It Looks Like When Underutilized	What It Looks Like When Optimally Utilized	What It Looks Like When Overutilized
Team members are confused because they know that learning and development funds and resources are available, but your client does not encourage them to use the funding.	Your client lets team members know how much is available in learning and development resources and then includes them in the decisions on how to allocate those resources.	Your client makes full use of allocated learning funds but also urges team members to use those funds indiscriminately without a coordinated plan.

Talent Solutions Behaviour 2: Development
Suggestions—Example Two

Underutilization	Optimal Utilization	Overutilization
Encourage team members to be aware of and to use every organizational learning resource available to them.	Be the champion of organizational learning and development and model enthusiastic participation in learning and development activities, including coaching.	Work with the learning and development professionals to design a well-coordinated learning path for each team member.

Talent Solutions Behaviour 2: Utilizes Company
Resources to Develop Others—Example Three

What It Looks Like When Underutilized	What It Looks Like When Optimally Utilized	What It Looks Like When Overutilized
Your client does not use the allocated funds for learning and development, which are then absorbed back into the general budget of the department or organization causing lost opportunities.	Your client uses allocated learning and development funds wisely and lobbies for even more funding and resources for the years ahead.	Team members are confused because they feel that company resources are being overspent on training far beyond their ability to take it all in.

Talent Solutions Behaviour 2: Development
Suggestions—Example Three

Underutilization	Optimal Utilization	Overutilization
Develop an appreciation for how resources allocated for learning and development return exponentially more to the organization's bottom line when supported by management.	Learning and development activities need to be evaluated by how they impact revenue generation and drive costs from the business. As an advocate for learning and development, take on this job of evaluating, especially regarding the department and team members.	Work with the learning and development professionals to develop a cost-benefit equation that compares the learning and development charges with projected revenue increases and the cost savings that will result.

Talent Solutions Behaviour 3: Understands Strengths
and Weaknesses of Direct Reports—Example One

What It Looks Like When Underutilized	What It Looks Like When Optimally Utilized	What It Looks Like When Overutilized
Your client invariably casts the wrong people in the wrong roles, leading to gross inefficiencies and wasted effort and resources.	Your client's knowledge about team members' strengths and challenges helps to position them properly in the best possible roles to benefit the organization.	Your client is overly attentive to assessment that exceeds practical value.

Talent Solutions Behaviour 3:
Development Suggestions—Example One

Underutilization	Optimal Utilization	Overutilization
Work with HR and the learning and development professionals to learn how to assess team members' strengths in order to align those strengths with their role descriptions.	Expand existing knowledge of assessments and assessment theory by becoming familiar with many instruments in order to stay on top of your team members' talents and abilities.	Make good use of personality profiles and competency assessments to match what team members do best with what the organization needs most.

Talent Systems Behaviour 3: Understands Strengths and Weaknesses of Direct Reports—Example Two

What It Looks Like When Underutilized	What It Looks Like When Optimally Utilized	What It Looks Like When Overutilized
Your client does not provide adequate career guidance to help individual team members fulfil their career destinies or potential.	This same knowledge that helps your client to position people properly makes it possible as well to provide expert career guidance to team members who look to their leader for advice.	Your client focuses on career coaching to the detriment of current roles and responsibilities.

Talent Solutions Behaviour 3: Development Suggestions—Example Two

Underutilization	Optimal Utilization	Overutilization
Become skilled at guiding the careers of team members. Take an active role in their success in order to assure the success of the entire team.	Career guidance for team members is counselling to be provided as well as possible. Remember that HR professionals have expertise and resources available to provide expert career guidance for team members.	Engage team members fully, which means helping them to keep an eye on the future and their growth opportunities inside of the organization and industry.

Talent Systems Behaviour 3: Understands Strengths and
Weaknesses of Direct Reports—Example Three

What It Looks Like When Underutilized	What It Looks Like When Optimally Utilized	What It Looks Like When Overutilized
Your client is unable to align team member's strengths and abilities with the organization's greatest needs, thus leaving the organization talent poor.	Yet another positive and productive use of your client's well-studied knowledge and awareness is the alignment of the team members' best abilities with the organization's greatest needs.	Similarly, in the rare case that your client is over-coaching and over-training, other team members' talents and abilities might be left under-utilized.

Talent Solutions Behaviour 3: Development
Suggestions—Example Three

Underutilization	Optimal Utilization	Overutilization
Work to expand existing knowledge of organization development to align individual strengths and skills with evolving organizational needs.	Knowing the structure and formation of the organization and the various spheres of influence within it will play a major role in available options to manage and develop the available talent.	Using team members' development plans, share with senior executives how the team is being developed to enrich the organization's human capital resource needs.

Talent Solutions Behaviour 4: Invests Time and Energy
in Development Planning Process—Example One

What It Looks Like When Underutilized	What It Looks Like When Optimally Utilized	What It Looks Like When Overutilized
Your client and the team members are unaware of the developmental challenges they face. They make no effort to discover the process of effective learning and development.	Your client makes it clear to the team members that learning and development activities are part of a systemic process. The best learning is a continuous circle.	Your client over-focuses on developmental needs of team members to the point they might feel inadequate as they are.

Talent Solutions Behaviour 4: Development
Suggestions—Example One

Underutilization	Optimal Utilization	Overutilization
Engage the HR and/or learning and development representatives to assess team members' learning and development needs.	Make use of the expertise and experience offered by the HR and learning and development professionals.	Include recognition of team members' skills and abilities in their learning and development planning. Couch new learning requests as 'building upon existing strengths'.

Talent Solutions Behaviour 4: Invests Time and Energy in Development Planning Process—Example Two

What It Looks Like When Underutilized	What It Looks Like When Optimally Utilized	What It Looks Like When Overutilized
The team members are aware of their developmental potential and resent the fact that Your client does not apparently value them enough to invest in their futures.	Your client recognizes the opportunity that talent development represents and positions talent development as a means to recognize the potential that team members have in the industry and organization.	In the rare event that this behaviour is overutilized, team members might again feel as if the natural abilities and prior training they bring to their positions is under appreciated and unrecognized.

Talent Solutions Behaviour 4: Development Suggestions—Example Two

Underutilization	Optimal Utilization	Overutilization
Take the time and effort to match team members' learning and development needs to available resources.	Planning for the most effective use of learning and development resources requires thought. It calls for a dual awareness of the team members' strengths and weaknesses coupled with resources available to them.	Balance enthusiasm for learning and development of team members with their natural abilities and the prior training they bring to their jobs.

Talent Solutions Behaviour 4: Invests Time and Energy in Development Planning Process—Example Three

What It Looks Like When Underutilized	What It Looks Like When Under-utilized	What It Looks Like When Under-utilized
The team members enrol and participate in learning and development activities haphazardly and derive limited benefit for themselves or the organization.	The team members enrol and participate in learning and development activities haphazardly and derive limited benefit for themselves or the organization.	The team members enrol and participate in learning and development activities haphazardly and derive limited benefit for themselves or the organization.

Talent Solutions Behaviour 4: Development Suggestions—Example Three

Underutilization	Under-utilization	Under-utilization
Make it a leadership priority to develop and execute well-designed and adequately funded development plans.	Make it a leadership priority to develop and execute well-designed and adequately funded development plans.	Make it a leadership priority to develop and execute well-designed and adequately funded development plans.

Talent Solutions Behaviour 5: Praise When Individuals and Groups take Appropriate Risks—Example One

What It Looks Like When Underutilized	What It Looks Like When Optimally Utilized	What It Looks Like When Overutilized
Your client's team members do not know when they are doing a good job at extending themselves beyond normal risk parameters to grow the business.	Your client uses praise, recognition and reward as a tremendously powerful trio of tools to amplify and encourage positive behaviour, including risk assessment and risk taking.	Your client describes everything team members are doing in terms of risk. This can make people feel jumpy about doing the normal activities called for in their job descriptions.

Talent Solutions Behaviour 5: Development Suggestions—Example One

Underutilization	Optimal Utilization	Overutilization
Expand the knowledge and comfort level associated with risk taking, and explore the value of risk taking.	The comfort level of the leader with risk taking sets the tone for how much risk the team members will be willing to take. Examine the level of comfort with risk taking as well as the role of risk in the team's success.	In discussing risk with team members, balance the concept of risk with routine and examine the time and appropriateness for both.

Talent Solutions Behaviour 5: Praise When Individuals and Groups take Appropriate Risks—Example Two

What It Looks Like When Underutilized	What It Looks Like When Optimally Utilized	What It Looks Like When Overutilized
Because your client does not give praise for risk taking, the team members probably assume that this silence indicates general disapproval of risk taking.	The client models good risk-taking behaviour by engaging team members in dialogue about risk versus reward regarding specific issues and opportunities available to them.	The client gives so much praise for team members' risk taking that it dilutes the impact praise and recognition can have.

Talent Solutions Behaviour 5: Development Suggestions—Example Two

Underutilization	Optimal Utilization	Overutilization
Engage team members in dialogue about appropriate risk taking that will push the business to excel in new ways.	Remain aware that risk must not be taken lightly. The most important first step is to remain in open and continuous dialogue with team members about it.	Mitigate the encouragement to take risks so as not to devalue the praise. Rewarded behaviour is repeated behaviour. So, keep the recognition potent.

Talent Solutions Behaviour 5: Praise When Individuals
and Groups take Appropriate Risks—Example Three

What It Looks Like When Underutilized	What It Looks Like When Optimally Utilized	What It Looks Like When Overutilized
Your client's team members' growth and development as professionals is diminished because they do not explore new horizons.	The client encourages risk taking with recognition tempered with the acknowledgement that, while not all risk is good, the absence of risk is stagnation, which is deadly to organizations.	Risk versus reward is out of balance. The client describes risk as a reward in itself and encourages team members to push boundaries too far too fast.

Talent Solutions Behaviour 5:
Development Suggestions—Example Three

Underutilization	Optimal Utilization	Overutilization
Make it a priority to encourage team members to think outside the box by observing their risk-taking behaviour and offering recognition for appropriate risk.	Risk taking is a strategic behaviour and a strategic perspective must be maintained throughout when evaluating risk and interpreting it for team members in terms of organizational initiatives.	Explain to team members that risk is just what the word implies, uncertainty with a down as well as an upside. Risk is never a reward in itself when the organization's resources are at stake.

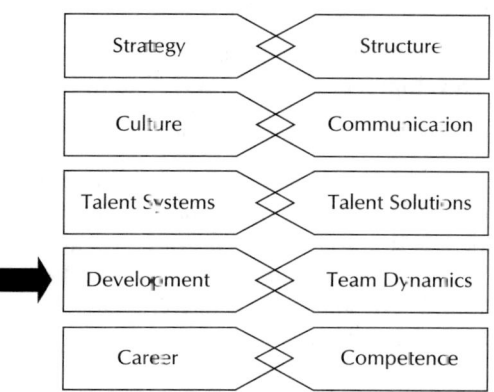

Development Behaviour 1:
Demonstrates Self-awareness—Example One

What It Looks Like When Underutilized	What It Looks Like When Optimally Utilized	What It Looks Like When Overutilized
Your clients operate in a manner oblivious to how words and actions are affecting others and the organization as a whole.	Everything your clients do demonstrates an appreciation for their role in the organization as well as its limits. There are no over-expectations or under-expectations in self or others.	Your clients think that everything done has a profound impact on everyone around else and beyond their immediate sphere of influence.

Development Behaviour 1:
Development Suggestions—Example One

Underutilization	Optimal Utilization	Overutilization
Help your clients seek input from others to understand perceptions of personal style and reflect openly on the content.	Help your clients remain aware that everything said and done affects somebody positively or negatively.	Help your clients develop a more realistic perspective on how much influence actions actually cause.

Development Behaviour 1:
Demonstrates Self-awareness—Example Two

What It Looks Like When Underutilized	What It Looks Like When Optimally Utilized	What It Looks Like When Overutilized
Your clients' lack of self-awareness can lead to confusion when one reaction from others is expected and another is received.	Knowing the realities of the role played in the organization leads your clients to create realistic expectations for themselves and others.	Your clients become too obsessed that others are not as tuned into their work as your clients believe they should or need to be.

Development Behaviour 1:
Development Suggestions—Example Two

Underutilization	Optimal Utilization	Overutilization
Enhance your clients' awareness of how words and actions are affecting co-workers and others.	Remaining clear about one's true influence in the organization will lead others to likewise remain clear.	Make check ins with cooperative and objective third parties as a part of a regular routine to remain objective.

Development Behaviour 1:
Demonstrates Self-awareness—Example Three

What It Looks Like When Underutilized	What It Looks Like When Optimally Utilized	What It Looks Like When Overutilized
Your clients do not receive the recognition or promotions thought to be deserved, and more senior executives express frustration that your clients 'don't get it'.	Having established realistic expectations, your clients appreciate why the organization rewards behaviour and the pathway is clear as to how they can be rewarded contributors.	Your clients do not feel they receive the recognition deserved because of constant thinking about recognition and promotions at the expense of focusing on the real work.

Development Behaviour 1:
Development Suggestions—Example Three

Underutilization	Optimal Utilization	Overutilization
Help your clients build new 'awareness seeking' behaviours into daily routines that solicit feedback to track with expectations others have and the kind of expectations your clients place on their colleagues and team members.	Nothing helps one learn more than teaching the skill one needs to improve on. Self-awareness grows and becomes more acute when helping team members to become more self-aware of how their own words and behaviours affect others.	Help your clients to establish plans that are tied to appropriate and predetermined recognition and promotion opportunities. This will help them keep things in perspective and set more realistic and appreciative expectations.

Development Behaviour 2:
Open to Feedback from Others—Example One

What It Looks Like When Underutilized	What It Looks Like When Optimally Utilized	What It Looks Like When Overutilized
Your clients either pay little attention to feedback that others try to provide or push back and argue when others try to share their observations.	When others give your clients feedback, your clients keep it in proper perspective and consider the source of the feedback and the diversity of agendas in various constituencies.	Your clients seek approval from others before doing anything. This behaviour can be immobilizing and can diminish other people's productivity when distracted by your clients' demands for feedback.

Development Behaviour 2:
Development Suggestions—Example One

Underutilization	Optimal Utilization	Overutilization
Help your clients pause before responding to critical feedback and reflect on the information. Encourage them to solicit feedback and not sit back and wait for it.	Self-awareness behaviours show up in a willingness to accept feedback from others. The value of feedback is more apparent as your clients become more visible in the organization.	Help your clients to incrementally reduce dependence on other people's approval by systematically extending your clients' independent behaviours a little bit every day.

Development Behaviour 2:
Open to Feedback from Others—Example Two

What It Looks Like When Underutilized	What It Looks Like When Optimally Utilized	What It Looks Like When Overutilized
People give up trying to communicate with your clients because of the resistance they encounter that blocks their attempts to communicate observations.	Your clients value feedback and an effort is made to learn new and effective ways to solicit it from people who are distracted, withholding or might be too busy to give feedback.	People at all levels of the organization avoid dealing with your clients because the demands for feedback are such an ongoing and predictable burden to them.

Development Behaviour 2:
Development Suggestions—Example Two

Underutilization	Optimal Utilization	Overutilization
Overcome feelings of being threatened. Be more receptive to feedback from others who make the effort to communicate it.	With a growing appreciation of how feedback helps with the learning process, your clients' openness to feedback also increases and reflects growth as a leader.	Help your clients determine the reasonable amount of feedback to expect and to solicit it from others in ways that do not apply undue pressure, leading to resentment.

Development Behaviour 2:
Open to Feedback from Others—Example Three

What It Looks Like When Underutilized	What It Looks Like When Optimally Utilized	What It Looks Like When Overutilized
If your clients receive critical feedback when feeling that the quality of the work should speak for itself, there is a tendency to be resentful and blame others for not understanding.	Your clients have an appreciation for the quality of their work both as an individual and the team as a whole. There is also recognition that others can give objective feedback, which will help to see beyond blind spots.	Your clients neither trust the quality of their work nor believe people when they give honest and positive feedback. Instead, your clients seek additional and continuous feedback to validate other feedback.

Development Behaviour 2:
Development Suggestions—Example Three

Underutilization	Optimal Utilization	Overutilization
Help your clients develop skills and habits around balancing new information with current knowledge, finding nonconflicting ways to express disagreement.	With increased openness to feedback, comes learning about ways to communicate feedback to others. It is important to focus on the organization's guiding principles and not on the personalities of those involved.	Begin to achieve balance between the actual quality of work and what needs to be challenged and improved by checking the work objectively against predetermined qualification criteria.

Development Behaviour 3:
Accepts Responsibility for Mistakes—Example One

What It Looks Like When Underutilized	What It Looks Like When Optimally Utilized	What It Looks Like When Overutilized
Credibility is seriously diminished as people observe the mistakes made, especially when your clients are oblivious to them or refuse to acknowledge them.	Your clients' willingness to accept responsibility for things that go wrong is a mark of suitability for increasingly responsible leadership roles.	Your clients can become a burden to team members, peers and managers by taking responsibility for every mistake ever made, anywhere.

Development Behaviour 3:
Development Suggestions—Example One

Underutilization	Optimal Utilization	Overutilization
Help your clients set up a network of trusted advisors who will provide regular objective feedback on performance.	Form an 'accountability corps' that monitors and provides growth and development advice to one another on matters of accepting responsibility.	Help your client establish some navigational beacons to guide how much or how little responsibility to accept for mistakes.

Development Behaviour 3:
Accepts Responsibility for Mistakes—Example Two

What It Looks Like When Underutilized	What It Looks Like When Optimally Utilized	What It Looks Like When Overutilized
Team members become less and less likely to accept responsibility for their actions as they experience your clients avoiding responsibility for mistakes.	Your clients are aware that willingness to accept responsibility for mistakes will have a positive impact on the team. The degree to which others take responsibility for mistakes is proportionate to the degree to which the leader accepts responsibility.	Team members become less and less likely to accept responsibility for their mistakes as they see your clients accepting responsibility on their behalf, even when the mistake had nothing to do with your clients.

Development Behaviour 3:
Development Suggestions—Example Two

Underutilization	Optimal Utilization	Overutilization
Help your clients learn the commandments of confronting problems, not people, and work with team members to increase accountability.	People can and will take advantage of a willingness to accept responsibility. Be vigilant to detect when people are shifting responsibility and placing blame where it does not belong.	Learning to coach others to accept responsibility for mistakes will help develop a much richer appreciation of why it is important to accept responsibility only when appropriate.

Development Behaviour 3:
Accepts Responsibility for Mistakes—Example Three

What It Looks Like When Underutilized	What It Looks Like When Optimally Utilized	What It Looks Like When Overutilized
The organization suffers from the expanding gap in accountability, and the erosion of confidence spreads to senior executives and customers.	Your clients consistently demonstrate willingness to accept responsibility for mistakes will be the foundation for an accountability code within the department.	The organization and those most responsible for career growth opportunities grow increasingly annoyed with your clients unreasonable hyper-responsibility.

Development Behaviour 3:
Development Suggestions—Example Three

Underutilization	Optimal Utilization	Overutilization
Help your clients set up a system of accountability and make it a cultural norm to accept responsibility.	With the growth of skills around accepting responsibility, it will become increasingly apparent that it is an organizational issue.	Nobody likes to work with a martyr, which is why it is important to demonstrate for team managers the growing ability to accept responsibility appropriately.

Development Behaviour 4: Seeks out Mentors and Key Advisors—Example One

What It Looks Like When Underutilized	What It Looks Like When Optimally Utilized	What It Looks Like When Overutilized
By avoiding advisors, your clients lack true growth and expansion in skill sets and capacity to embrace change and make the most out of professional opportunities.	Your clients engage people whose range of responsibilities includes providing strategic advice and counsel for their career development as a valued asset to the organization.	Your clients seek much too much advice and guidance from mentors and key advisors, placing far too little confidence in their own judgment and ability.

Development Behaviour 4: Development Suggestions—Example One

Underutilization	Optimal Utilization	Overutilization
Help your clients learn how to become comfortable with soliciting and receiving advice and mentoring from qualified people.	Help your clients learn to continue to appreciate that a dynamic system of trusted mentors and advisors is critical to individuals and the organization.	Help your clients learn to determine what the optimal balance of advice seeking should be and limit consumption accordingly.

Development Behaviour 4: Seeks out Mentors and Key Advisors—Example Two

What It Looks Like When Underutilized	What It Looks Like When Optimally Utilized	What It Looks Like When Overutilized
The stagnation in your clients' growth and development blocks their ability to be an effective mentor or key advisor to the team.	Your clients regularly seek out advice from key advisors to determine the appropriate level of counsel that should be provided for team members.	Your clients burden subordinates with excessive advice to the point that it immobilizes them and makes them reluctant to seek guidance.

Development Behaviour 4: Development Suggestions—Example Two

Underutilization	Optimal Utilization	Overutilization
As the benefit from mentors and advice begins to show, help your clients build a skill set to include providing mentoring and advisory assistance to others.	Remain open to the fact that some of the most reliable advisors can be team members. Many of them know the particulars of departmental challenges as well or better than their manager.	Help your clients learn to get skilled assistance to determine the proper amount of advice and feedback to give team members.

Development Behaviour 4: Seeks out Mentors
and Key Advisors—Example Three

What It Looks Like When Underutilized	What It Looks Like When Optimally Utilized	What It Looks Like When Overutilized
The people who know it is their organizational responsibility to mentor and advise are aware that your clients do not seek or respond to their assistance and begin to doubt your clients' growth potential.	A true partnership forms between those with knowledge, experience and organizational wisdom and emerging leaders. Up and coming employees with genuine loyalty and work ethic will eagerly seek the opportunity to accelerate their learning and advance their careers.	What appear to be authentic, sincere and genuine attitudes in emerging leaders can in fact be a more selfish agenda in seeking influence and advancement without earning it. Worse yet, some people might want their mentors and advisors to do their work for them out of laziness.

Development Behaviour 4: Development
Suggestions—Example Three

Underutilization	Optimal Utilization	Overutilization
Become strategically aware of how accepting the advice and mentoring of the correct people can be positioning to become more influential for the betterment of the organization.	Design and faithfully execute reward systems for those who take full advantage of mentoring and the strategic advice of experienced leaders. Make it visibly worthwhile to build and sustain relationships that share and pass forward valuable knowledge and skills. Make seeking knowledge and organizational wisdom a highly publicized and rewarded activity.	Design and implement accountability systems that require participants in mentoring and advising programs to demonstrate what they have learned on a regular basis. Schools test students to ensure learning is taking place. Organizations should do the same.

Development Behaviour 5: Commits to the Process of Growing and Developing—Example One

What It Looks Like When Underutilized	What It Looks Like When Optimally Utilized	What It Looks Like When Overutilized
Whatever bits and pieces of development your clients engage in are fragmented and produce little professional growth.	Your clients seek and maintain an appropriate balance between planning and action. Their growth and development are well planned and the plan is worked in perfect balance.	Your clients can invest far too much time and energy planning out a growth and development strategy without accomplishing any significant growth and development.

Development Behaviour 5: Development Suggestions—Example One

Underutilization	Optimal Utilization	Overutilization
Help your clients develop and follow a comprehensive learning and development plan that accounts for their ambitions and realities of their talent and capacity.	Tying growth and development to actual performance goals is a good idea. If it cannot be measured, it cannot be managed. Provide balanced management for development plans.	Help your clients tie this growth and development to actual work improvements that can be measured. Then measure, evaluate and revisit the plan accordingly.

Development Behaviour 5: Commits to the Process of Growing and Developing—Example Two

What It Looks Like When Underutilized	What It Looks Like When Optimally Utilized	What It Looks Like When Overutilized
Even if your clients encourage growth and development in team members, they will not take the work seriously knowing the limitations of their commitment.	Your clients' commitment to growth and development guides the growth and development of team members. As their role model, your clients demonstrate appropriate commitment.	Your clients are so consumed in growth and development that real-time work suffers. Their teams meander to and fro like a ship without a rudder.

Development Behaviour 5: Development Suggestions—Example Two

Underutilization	Optimal Utilization	Overutilization
Help your clients be the role model for their own team members to set the tone for them and to encourage their coordinated growth and development activities.	Adding measurable goals to the learning and development plan works for all team members. Setting an example will demonstrate to the team the value of measured performance.	To avoid plotting too strict a course of learning and development for the team and thereby limiting their natural development, consult with all of them on their learning plans.

Development Behaviour 5: Commits to the Process of Growing and Developing—Example Three

What It Looks Like When Underutilized	What It Looks Like When Optimally Utilized	What It Looks Like When Overutilized
More senior people who are responsible for organizational excellence will limit your clients' career potential in favour of others who are more committed to the growth and development of talent.	In an effort to model a true learning organization, your clients consult at all times with those above, below and beside them in the organization when developing and committing to learning and development plans.	Senior people who are responsible for organizational excellence will limit your clients' career in favour of those who can keep their desire to grow and develop in line with their execution of their responsibilities.

Development Behaviour 5: Development Suggestions—Example Three

Underutilization	Optimal Utilization	Overutilization
Help your clients include senior people in planning, or at least make them aware that all team members are participating in learning and development activities.	A big part of complete and balanced learning plans is the commitment to the larger learning organization. Take advantage of learning opportunities for the team and tell others about them.	Help your clients demonstrate (to those in senior positions) their ability to develop a strategic learning and development plan for themselves and their team members.

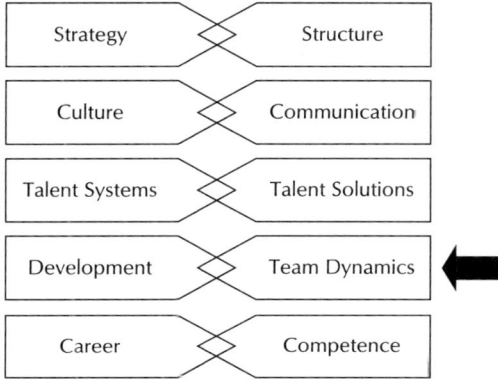

Team Dynamics Behaviour 1: Delegates
Appropriately—Example One

What It Looks Like When Underutilized	What It Looks Like When Optimally Utilized	What It Looks Like When Overutilized
Your client keeps all the work with little sharing of it, causing your client to become overwhelmed. Team members are underutilized and the team's effectiveness is reduced to the leader's capacity.	Everyone on your client's team is well aligned with his or her responsibilities, and the workload is distributed equitably, efficiently and effectively.	Your client loads the team members and peers down with work that is not their responsibility. The boundaries between your client's work and what belongs to others becomes blurred.

Team Dynamics Behaviour 1: Dynamics of a Team Suggestions—Example One

Underutilization	Optimal Utilization	Overutilization
Help your client break the habit of hoarding work and robbing everyone else of responsibility. Help your client begin distributing the workload appropriately.	Help your client overcome the temptation to hoard work and delegate work slowly and in small parcels to become increasingly aware and appreciative of how it is handled.	Consult with team members and peers while regularly revisiting roles and responsibilities to ensure equitable distribution of workload.

Team Dynamics Behaviour 1: Delegates Appropriately—Example Two

What It Looks Like When Underutilized	What It Looks Like When Optimally Utilized	What It Looks Like When Overutilized
Your client tends to inspect all departmental work for approval, supervision and scrutiny. This slows down the productivity of the whole department.	As a master delegator, your client is keenly aware that the more autonomy given to the team members, the more sense of ownership and pride they will invest in their work.	Your client does not appreciate the balance of workload or proper distribution of responsibility and confuses where one person's responsibility stops and another's begins, resulting in role confusion.

Team Dynamics Behaviour 1: Dynamics of a Team Suggestions—Example Two

Underutilization	Optimal Utilization	Overutilization
Help your client to get comfortable, loosening the tight grip and allowing people autonomy to do a complete job for the team.	Help your client make an effort to recognize the autonomy people need to feel properly invested and recognized for their efforts.	Help your client consult with team members and peers before assigning new responsibilities. This means ensuring there is clarity about everyone's responsibilities.

Team Dynamics Behaviour 1: Delegates Appropriately—Example Three

What It Looks Like When Underutilized	What It Looks Like When Optimally Utilized	What It Looks Like When Overutilized
Your client causes serious resentment and morale issues by taking on other people's work, especially if some of those duties belong to your client's own peers, manager and other executives.	Remaining vigilant about what is one's own work and what is someone else's is basic to your client's effectiveness as a delegator. It also provides an opportunity to reach out to others and form problem-solving partnerships.	Your client is so zealous at over-delegating that work is piled on the manager as well, which the manager doesn't appreciate—especially if he or she has difficulty pushing it back to in your client.

Team Dynamics Behaviour 1: Dynamics of a Team Suggestions—Example Three

Underutilization	Optimal Utilization	Overutilization
Help your client learn not to cross job responsibility boundaries without the expressed permission from the boundary owners. Therefore, engage boundary owners (above and below in the organization) when concerned about the work being done.	An increasing delegation skill set will pay dividends in reducing conflict as boundaries are honoured. In honouring boundaries, bridges are built between layers of leadership and partnerships in problem solving. Having a reputation for balancing workload will serve career ambitions well.	Help your client seek the manager's active involvement in workload distribution. This will ensure that the manager approves of the workload distribution between teams and will be supportive on the workload balance issues faced with the team.

Team Dynamics Behaviour 2: Celebrates Team Success—Example One

What It Looks Like When Underutilized	What It Looks Like When Optimally Utilized	What It Looks Like When Overutilized
Your client feels that when people succeed at reaching their goals they are simply 'doing what they're paid to do' and no further recognition is called for.	Your client engages the team members when discussing work projects to reach consensus up front regarding an appropriate way to celebrate achievement of team goals.	Your client is a party animal who over-celebrates, resulting in underwork. This tendency makes for popularity among some team members when they are allowed to overindulge at the expense of work.

Team Dynamics Behaviour 2: Dynamics of a Team Suggestions—Example One

Underutilization	Optimal Utilization	Overutilization
Help your client shift priorities to realize that motivating people is vastly different from being a demanding and exacting manager.	Your client establishes realistic benchmarks for seeing progress in a willingness to celebrate team success and then do not forget to celebrate personal professional success.	Help your client take the time to evaluate what type of celebration is appropriate. This should be predetermined before the team launches the initiative.

Team Dynamics Behaviour 2: Celebrates Team Success—Example Two

What It Looks Like When Underutilized	What It Looks Like When Optimally Utilized	What It Looks Like When Overutilized
When your client and team members succeed at reaching and exceeding their predetermined goals, your client rewards the team members by burdening them with even more punitive goals.	Because your client involved team members in the celebration planning for team achievements, they are candidates to examine how responsibilities should be distributed upon successful completion.	Your client's over-celebration can place a burden on the team members when it is time to catch up and make up for lost productivity. At that point, the team might feel resentful for letting the pressure build up on them.

Team Dynamics Behaviour 2: Dynamics of a
Team Suggestions—Example Two

Underutilization	Optimal Utilization	Overutilization
Rewarding appropriate behaviour ensures that it will be repeated. The team's success leads to better behaviour and broader responsibilities.	Workload distribution and success is dynamic. In the ever-changing marketplace, help your client consider what the optimal workload will be in light of the team's ultimate goals.	Celebrations require proper planning so as to not overdo it. Help your client plan the party so as to keep the ongoing workload in mind while celebrating current success.

Team Dynamics Behaviour 2: Celebrates Team
Success—Example Three

What It Looks Like When Underutilized	What It Looks Like When Optimally Utilized	What It Looks Like When Overutilized
Your client not only fails to provide recognition to the team members, but the senior management also notices that *they* are not being invited to any victory celebrations.	Your client is careful to include upper management when appropriate in the team's success celebrations. This shines a spotlight on the team members, and it makes people who are senior in the organization feel as if they were involved.	To the senior management your client's exuberance for celebration is charming at first, but becomes troublesome as the team's productivity begins to suffer over time.

Team Dynamics Behaviour 2: Dynamics of a Team Suggestions—Example Three

Underutilization	Optimal Utilization	Overutilization
Help your client take a lead from senior executives who have demonstrated talent and enthusiasm for celebrating team success. Ask for their help in developing this essential leadership skill. In the process, there will be positive recognition for this phase of professional development.	Celebration is a tiered activity. Even verbal recognition for good execution of activities should consider seemingly insignificant activities in light of how they move the team towards its goals. The tiered levels of significant behaviour should be aligned with appropriate levels of celebration to ensure consistency in expectations	One of the best dimensions of celebrations is to include the people senior in the organization. This is a way to (a) honour the team's accomplishments even more, (b) focus the attention of powerful people on what the team accomplished and (c) focus attention on individual accomplishment.

Team Dynamics Behaviour 3: Manages Team Meetings Effectively—Example One

What It Looks Like When Underutilized	What It Looks Like When Optimally Utilized	What It Looks Like When Overutilized
Your client does not hold meetings at all. This can be the poorest practice companion to not sharing workload with appropriate people. With no meetings, all opportunities that meetings provide are lost.	The ability to distinguish between when a meeting is needed and when it would be better to exchange information in another manner is a major indicator of your client's qualifications as a senior leader.	Meetings are so rigid and regimented that no one dares speak out about or challenge important issues for fear of disrupting the agenda and being berated for being out of order.

Team Dynamics Behaviour 3: Dynamics of a Team Suggestions—Example One

Underutilization	Optimal Utilization	Overutilization
Help your client study the fine art of becoming a meeting facilitator. Use your client's own experiences with good versus bad meetings to begin developing his or her own meeting facilitation skills.	Help your client to become a master meeting facilitator by learning new methods and techniques. Meetings are information forums, but they need to engage everyone.	Help your client recognize and even reward the efforts of people to speak truth to power. Invite team members to help draft the meeting agenda in advance and to frequently conduct the meetings themselves.

Team Dynamics Behaviour 3: Manages Team Meetings Effectively—Example Two

What It Looks Like When Underutilized	What It Looks Like When Optimally Utilized	What It Looks Like When Overutilized
The meetings your client does convene are chaotic and nothing gets accomplished. This produces confusion and uncertainty among the team members.	When a meeting is called for, your client can employ meeting procedures that include prior consultation with attendees on agenda and other ways that help ensure people will benefit.	By keeping a tight leash on team meetings, your client robs team members of the ability to learn and practise meeting facilitation skills.

Team Dynamics Behaviour 3: Dynamics of a Team Suggestions—Example Two

Underutilization	Optimal Utilization	Overutilization
Help your client develop an appreciation for the value of meetings— particularly when well structured and executed. He or she knows *good meeting* from *bad meeting*.	Help your client to become a skilled meeting facilitator by focusing on learning specific techniques like meeting process, preparation and follow up.	Help your client share leadership and facilitation of team meetings in order to build members' facilitation skills and to keep the entire team learning from one another.

Team Dynamics Behaviour 3: Manages Team Meetings Effectively—Example Three

What It Looks Like When Underutilized	What It Looks Like When Optimally Utilized	What It Looks Like When Overutilized
The meetings your client does convene do not promote or encourage creativity and innovation in any way. These meetings barely serve as forums for exchanging information and establishing working agendas.	Meetings are excellent opportunities for people to build on each other's ideas and opinions. They should be conducted to encourage creative thought and innovation more than merely as information exchanges.	Your client's highly structured meetings leave little space for creativity and innovation to take place. People do not come prepared to do anything but show up, sit down, and check out.

Team Dynamics Behaviour 3: Dynamics of a Team Suggestions—Example Three

Underutilization	Optimal Utilization	Overutilization
Help your client see the opportunity meetings present to stimulate creative thinking and innovation—building one idea upon the next to improve all processes, including how to set up a superior meeting.	Help your client consider meetings as wonderful opportunities to promote the immediate team's agenda and the organization's agenda—particularly as it applies to the manager's agenda.	Help your client make meetings celebrations of good ideas. To keep productive structure in meetings, invite team members' input on the agenda in advance and have people come prepared to share new ideas.

Team Dynamics Behaviour 4: Values the Ideas and Opinions of Others—Example One

What It Looks Like When Underutilized	What It Looks Like When Optimally Utilized	What It Looks Like When Overutilized
An inordinate amount of value and priority are placed on your client's own ideas with no value at all given to the ideas of others.	Your client recognizes and acknowledges that others have ideas and opinions and issues to be emphasized. In fact, their ideas can and often do support the agenda your client wishes to promote.	Your client fervently seeks out the ideas and opinions of others without offering up any original thinking in return, thereby potentially burning out a bearing in the organization's creativity and innovation engine.

Team Dynamics Behaviour 4: Dynamics of a Team Suggestions—Example One

Underutilization	Optimal Utilization	Overutilization
Help your client rearrange how to perceive the ideas and opinions of others. They must be transformed from threats to possible enhancements of or supplements to other positions.	Help your client to always search for consensus. While consensus is not always possible, collaborative working partnerships are based on respect for all ideas and opinions.	Teach team members how good ideas trigger more good ideas and build on one another. Individual ideas and opinions are springboards for better ideas and opinions.

Team Dynamics Behaviour 4: Values the Ideas and Opinions of Others—Example Two

What It Looks Like When Underutilized	What It Looks Like When Optimally Utilized	What It Looks Like When Overutilized
Your client takes the time to hear out the ideas and opinions of others on the team and even peers. However, their ideas are used as platforms from which to argue your client's own point of view.	Your client gives appropriate credit to people for sharing ideas and opinions, regardless of immediate value, because of a desire to create and sustain an environment where new thought is welcomed and encouraged.	Your client values the ideas and opinions of others to the point that team members feel as if they are doing your client's job and credit is being taken for their work.

Team Dynamics Behaviour 4: Dynamics of a
Team Suggestions—Example Two

Underutilization	Optimal Utilization	Overutilization
Help your client learn that ideas do not cancel each other out: Develop an appreciation for the ideas and opinions of others while still valuing one's own ideas and opinions.	Because the best ideas are composites of multiple good ideas, help your client express value for all ideas and opinions as they might help to refine other ideas and opinions.	The job might not be to generate new ideas. But, when facilitating the creative thinking of others, help your client give as much recognition as possible and to show appreciation.

Team Dynamics Behaviour 4: Values the Ideas
and Opinions of Others—Example Three

What It Looks Like When Underutilized	What It Looks Like When Optimally Utilized	What It Looks Like When Overutilized
Your client puts his or her career in serious jeopardy by treating the ideas and opinions of people superior in the organization as casually as the ideas and opinions of peers and team members.	Where an idea comes from is important. The higher the source of the idea on the organization chart, the more seriously it needs to be taken. Even if your client's ideas are similar, credit is given at the highest level.	Your client values the ideas and opinions of others to the extent that important people beside and above your client on the organization chart wonder when your client plans to start contributing ideas.

Team Dynamics Behaviour 4: Dynamics of a Team Suggestions—Example Three

Underutilization	Optimal Utilization	Overutilization
Help your client use the experience in appreciating the ideas and opinions of superiors as a model to appreciate the ideas and opinions of peers and team members.	Help your client remember that it takes a mixture of good ideas to produce a truly great idea, the better ideas may come from anywhere in the organization. Emphasize blending of valued ideas to produce good results.	Help your client be the visible champion of ideas and opinions. Also show value to the power brokers in the organization by becoming a master facilitator and champion of new and original ideas.

Team Dynamics Behaviour 5: Resolves Conflicts Between Colleagues—Example One

What It Looks Like When Underutilized	What It Looks Like When Optimally Utilized	What It Looks Like When Overutilized
Your client does not even acknowledge that colleagues have conflicts, much less make any effort to help resolve them. The oblivion might be intentional.	Your client is a person who accepts that conflicts exist and recognizes that they naturally occur among people with competing agendas. From conflict can come stronger ideas and relationships.	Your client spends a lot of time making sure colleagues do not disagree with one another about anything and leaves no room for new, original or innovative ideas.

Team Dynamics Behaviour 5:
Dynamics of a Team Suggestions—Example One

Underutilization	Optimal Utilization	Overutilization
Help your client study what conflicts are, what causes them and how they harm the organization. Then shift focus to learning techniques of alternative dispute resolution (aka conflict resolution).	With growing experience in resolving conflicts will also come the increased ability to identify common ground and common beliefs between conflicting parties. Help your client to practise identifying common ground.	Help your client tolerate differences of opinion, then skilfully manage disagreements, thus earning a reputation as a diplomat in the organization, especially if tension can be turned into profitable ideas.

Team Dynamics Behaviour 5: Resolves Conflicts
Between Colleagues—Example Two

What It Looks Like When Underutilized	What It Looks Like When Optimally Utilized	What It Looks Like When Overutilized
Your client is aware that conflicts exist but is uncomfortable with conflict in general and avoids dealing with them, even when colleagues ask for assistance.	Taking the perspective that conflicts are natural and can lead to better understanding and stronger relationships, your client develops ease handling and preventing them.	Your client makes mediation a primary work focus to a fault and becomes an ambulance chaser of sorts within the organization, manufacturing conflicts to mediate.

Team Dynamics Behaviour 5: Dynamics of a
Team Suggestions—Example Two

Underutilization	Optimal Utilization	Overutilization
Help your client discover why conflict is so uncomfortable on principle, and explore ways to begin dealing with conflicting opinions productively in non-frightening ways that emphasize win/win solutions that benefit everyone.	Your client understands what makes people uncomfortable with conflict and that make people avoid confrontation. Not being derailed by conflict, your client's conflict resolution work in the organization will release others to be less protective and more productive.	Help your client keep the mental radar sweeping to ensure that, if any conflicts arise, assistance can be sent to resolve them. Help your client become a champion of keeping the peace.

Team Dynamics Behaviour 5: Resolves
Conflicts Between Colleagues—Example Three

What It Looks Like When Underutilized	What It Looks Like When Optimally Utilized	What It Looks Like When Overutilized
Conflicts that your client does not help resolve, especially among his or her own team members, percolate upward and annoy superiors in the organization.	Your client's ability to calmly resolve conflicts draws positive attention from upper management. The ability to resolve conflicts will help your client's vertical mobility and pay big dividends for the organization.	Your client's focus is so consumed with dispute resolution that the powers that be in the organization begin to wonder if anything is being accomplished. Your client is not paid to be Judge Judy.

Team Dynamics Behaviour 5: Dynamics of a Team Suggestions—Example Three

Underutilization	Optimal Utilization	Overutilization
Help your client become aware that unresolved problems find their way up to higher levels where they can cause harm. Help your client learn conflict resolution skills and, in the process, also appreciate that superiors in the organization have conflicts of their own to deal with. Do not become one of them.	Help your client learn that the ability to anticipate conflict and prevent its occurrence is harder to recognize than resolving conflicts once they arise. That makes it incumbent on your client to let senior management know when potential conflicts have been anticipated, identified, dealt with and successfully avoided.	Help your client be the bearer of good news by reporting to upper management how many conflicts have been avoided or resolved quickly— putting people back to productive work sooner. In reporting how conflicts are being avoided, the powers that be learn how much time and money are being saved.

Team Dynamics Behaviour 6: Encourages Collaboration with Problem-solving Initiatives—Example One

What It Looks Like When Underutilized	What It Looks Like When Optimally Utilized	What It Looks Like When Overutilized
At its worst, underutilization of this behaviour will result in your client not engaging in problem solving, much less in bringing people together to form a collaborative approach.	As a well-balanced manager of people, your client is aware that the more input that can be generated towards solving a problem, the richer the solution is likely to be.	Your client tends to gather everyone possible together, regardless of the size of problem to be solved and turns everything into a catastrophe. Great theatre, but bad business.

Team Dynamics Behaviour 6: Dynamics of a
Team Suggestions—Example One

Underutilization	Optimal Utilization	Overutilization
Help your client understand the value and benefits to the organization and to individuals specifically in developing collaborative problem-solving skills.	Team members are encouraged and appropriately rewarded for collaboration, especially in tackling the most difficult threats to the organization and emerging with sustainable solutions. Policy makers give more institutional recognition and authority to those who consistently demonstrate collaborative behaviour.	Change existing policies and develop new ones that shift the focus from individual accomplishment and rewards to team rewards. Stop compensating and giving bonuses to employees based on individual productivity and profit performance. Rewarded behavior is repeated behavior. Be careful what you are rewarding.

Team Dynamics Behaviour 6: Encourages Collaboration
with Problem-solving Initiatives—Example Two

What It Looks Like When Underutilized	What It Looks Like When Optimally Utilized	What It Looks Like When Overutilized
Your client makes the desire known and even clearly articulates that individuals are expected to solve problems on their own and not to trouble anyone else in the process.	By building and sustaining a collaborative problem-solving approach, your client keeps more people in the game enthusiastic and invested in championing the solution.	Your client brings together team members to solve a problem but does not pay enough attention to what their problem-solving abilities are, thus allowing unqualified people struggle above their skill level.

Team Dynamics Behaviour 6: Dynamics of a Team Suggestions—Example Two

Underutilization	Optimal Utilization	Overutilization
Help your client learn to empower team members by facilitating problem solving rather than providing answers. Make sure everyone can join in the process.	Help your client learn to help others to learn problem-solving skills—creating opportunities for many people to enjoy more future success based on their problem-solving skills and abilities.	Help your client pay special attention to alignment between individual subject-matter expertise in problem solving and the subject matter of the problem itself.

Team Dynamics Behaviour 6: Encourages Collaboration with Problem-solving Initiatives—Example Three

What It Looks Like When Underutilized	What It Looks Like When Optimally Utilized	What It Looks Like When Overutilized
Your client not only encourages people to work out problems on their own, without collaborative effort, but also does not want problems brought forward or discussed with anyone else. This isolationist approach can really be denial that any problems exists.	Problems, like conflict, are better confronted early and often to keep them from growing larger. Not only does your client not deny the existence of problems, but also he or she looks upon them as opportunities for increased organizational collaboration.	Your client brings together people from throughout the organization to solve a problem but does not pay enough attention to their rank relative to the magnitude of the problem, sending a lion after a mouse the house cat could have caught.

Team Dynamics Behaviour 6: Dynamics of a Team Suggestions—Example Three

Underutilization	Optimal Utilization	Overutilization
Help your client understand that, without becoming someone in search of trouble, he or she can become much more aware of problems, both real and pending, and learn to build coalitions to address them as soon as possible.	Help your client to engage in coalition building, not just to solve problems, but to also enhance organizational structure and design to produce more scalable, durable and profitable outcomes in all phases of teamwork.	Help your client learn how people can work across disciplines easily enough, but that working across rank is a touchier subject in most cultures. Help him or her use the higher ranking players to add influence and institutional authority only when needed to accelerate the problem-solving process.

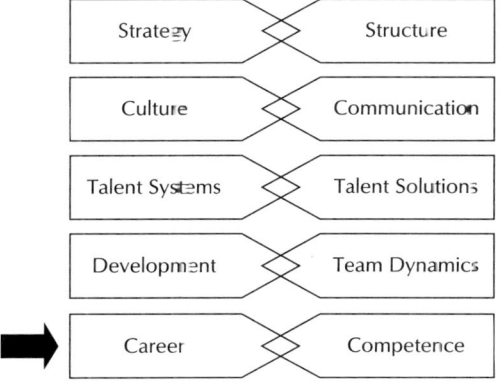

Career Behaviour 1: Demonstrates Life Balance—Example One

What It Looks Like When Underutilized	What It Looks Like When Optimally Utilized	What It Looks Like When Overutilized
Your clients work too much or avoid work. The former might be ingratiating to a demanding and un-empathetic manager. But living on either extreme diminishes effectiveness.	Your clients arrive at the office well rested, refreshed and ready to work because of finding relief and repose from working life in their personal lives. Your clients are able to focus on and derive benefit from hobbies, family and community life because work focus is left back at the office.	It is difficult to have too much life balance. The only possible downside is too much obsession with work–life balance in which your clients become immobilized by worrying about how to establish and maintain homeostasis.

Career Behaviour 1: Development Suggestions—Example One

Underutilization	Optimal Utilization	Overutilization
The problem might be objectivity when reflecting on their work–life balance. Help your clients get feedback from others to see their perspectives more clearly and demonstrate more appropriate and balanced behaviours.	Help your clients continue to study the ongoing benefits of a well-balanced work agenda and personal life. Although they can achieve a good balance, circumstances might shift causing a creeping imbalance that will adversely affect them.	Help your clients remain mindful that work–life balance issues can become too front and centre. You can coach them in techniques that will keep the correct perspective and preserve the balance once they achieve it.

Career Behaviour 1: Demonstrates
Life Balance—Example Two

What It Looks Like When Underutilized	What It Looks Like When Optimally Utilized	What It Looks Like When Overutilized
Your clients' lack of appreciation for life balance bleeds over into the way the team is managed and expectations are set for team members. Too much work or too much play adversely affects productivity and performance.	Your clients not only apply the principles of life balance to their own living and working issues but also help team members to achieve life balance. They understand that even one team member, living and working out of balance affects the system.	Your clients can become obsessed with team members' life balance issues to the degree that your clients' own issues are ignored or sacrificed. Your clients need to balance their self-interests with the interests of their teams.

Career Behaviour 1: Development
Suggestions—Example Two

Underutilization	Optimal Utilization	Overutilization
Help your clients learn to calibrate what constitutes appropriate expectations for team members in the way they balance work assignments and personal activities.	Help your clients remain vigilant to the tendencies that members of the team might have to lose life balance and deliberately, systematically and methodically engage team members in discussions on the topic.	Help your clients avoid over-monitoring the team members on their balance of life issues. It is hard for your clients to remain objective without the input from objective outside observers like you.

Career Behaviour 1: Demonstrates
Life Balance—Example Three

What It Looks Like When Underutilized	What It Looks Like When Optimally Utilized	What It Looks Like When Overutilized
The fact that your clients are not honouring life balance obligations to team members is causing ripples throughout the organization. Demanding overwork from team members is now considered to be harmful to the productivity of your client and the organization.	Your clients and team members are role models for how professionals should seek and achieve life balance. Moreover, they let senior management know the positive impact life balance has on the bottom line.	Your clients can become obsessed with their own life balance issues to the degree that other team members and their needs are ignored. This will produce friction and distract them from the team's mission and stated objectives over time. Among other things, motivation will suffer.

Career Behaviour 1: Development
Suggestions—Example Three

Underutilization	Optimal Utilization	Overutilization
Make sure to keep your clients current on creative ways through which the team is achieving life balance and point out the cost benefits. Involve your learning organization, if at all possible, to facilitate the learning activities and discussion.	To be better positioned as an advocate for life balance, encourage your clients to study the consequences and costs associated with people burning out or losing interest.	Help your clients consider the perspectives of others regarding their work–life balance vis-à-vis their own. Also help your clients to understand what a bad reputation they can potentially garner with upper management for not championing balance.

Career Behaviour 2: Offers Career Advice to Others—Example One

What It Looks Like When Underutilized	What It Looks Like When Optimally Utilized	What It Looks Like When Overutilized
Your clients' team members become convinced that your clients have no interest in their careers because these issues are never discussed with them.	Your clients regularly check in with team members and monitor how aware they are of the ways in which their current activities are preparing them for career growth.	Your clients talk to people about their career development to the point that they become anxious that their jobs are insecure. Without career growth savvy, such talk leaves some people feeling suspicious.

Career Behaviour 2: Development Suggestions—Example One

Underutilization	Optimal Utilization	Overutilization
Help your clients set up a regular schedule of conducting a career-building chat with each team member and holding them accountable for mapping a career path with the help of HR.	Help your clients look to systematize career management skills to ensure consistent application. Keep the conversation of career options alive for your clients and everyone within your clients' spheres of influence.	Help your clients to always emphasize how much their team members' contributions to the department are valued. Make sure the acknowledgements are specific, and not simply gratuitous.

Career Behaviour 2: Offers Career Advice to Others—Example Two

What It Looks Like When Underutilized	What It Looks Like When Optimally Utilized	What It Looks Like When Overutilized
Your clients' team members become convinced that their jobs are in jeopardy because your clients never discuss career issues with them, even when asked.	Your clients' discussion of career options with team members includes all dimensions of their work–life balance. The conversation also reinforces how career development helps the organization maintain a strong competitive advantage.	Your clients are so eager to assure team members of the stability and permanence of their jobs that they develop an unrealistic perspective of job permanence in general. Unrealistic expectations are the platform for disappointment.

Career Behaviour 2: Development Suggestions—Example Two

Underutilization	Optimal Utilization	Overutilization
Help your clients tie the career development discussions they hold with their team members to the level of proficiency they demonstrate in their current positions. Promotion for good work makes good sense to people.	Help team members look at what they do for the organization not as a job but as a set of responsibilities on a complete career spectrum. When employees see their jobs as value added to the organization they become less self-absorbed.	Help your clients remain realistic when discussing career options and career issues in general so team members have a clear idea of what sort of mobility they can reasonably expect from the organization.

Career Behaviour 2: Offers Career
Advice to Others—Example Three

What It Looks Like When Underutilized	What It Looks Like When Optimally Utilized	What It Looks Like When Overutilized
Without any career guidance from your clients, their direct reports might assume there are no career opportunities in the organization and start looking elsewhere.	The regularity and ease with which your clients discuss career options with their team members makes the team more relaxed and comfortable, hence they are able to do a better job.	Your client's team members are so busy scouting the rest of the organization for career-enhancing possibilities that management wonders why everybody wants to escape from your clients' department.

Career Behaviour 2: Development
Suggestions—Example Three

Underutilization	Optimal Utilization	Overutilization
Help your clients teach their team members how career rich the organization truly is. But keep it realistic and accurate as to where their best opportunities are found.	Help your clients understand that coaching their team members on career options is an affirming way to demonstrate how much they value their team members and their talents.	In spite of giving generous career advice, help your clients work hard to ensure that your clients' department is the best to work for in the whole organization.

Career Behaviour 3: Takes on Stretch Assignments—Example One

What It Looks Like When Underutilized	What It Looks Like When Optimally Utilized	What It Looks Like When Overutilized
Your clients refuse to stick so much as a toe outside the box and take their job descriptions much too literally. Collaboration suffers as everyone notices how little your clients extend themselves to help others with their assignments.	Your clients actively participate in meetings when their managers ask who will be willing to lead an experimental or difficult effort. Your clients acknowledge that the assignment must be important or the manager wouldn't have suggested it.	Your clients are so eager to take on new, exciting and even dangerous assignments that current work is neglected. They also forget to consider what the potential exposure is to the organization.

Career Behaviour 3: Development Suggestions—Example One

Underutilization	Optimal Utilization	Overutilization
Help your clients engage in systematic desensitization and practise stepping out of their comfort zones just a tiny bit farther each day. Encourage them to help others do the same thing.	Help your clients understand that accepting stretch assignments, even seeking them out, indicates that they are taking their own development seriously, with an eye towards career growth and expansion.	Help your clients impose reasonable limitations. Without an alternative arrangement to do the additional work, stretch assignments must be accepted and executed without neglecting normal day-to-day responsibilities and activities.

Career Behaviour 3: Takes on Stretch Assignments—Example Two

What It Looks Like When Underutilized	What It Looks Like When Optimally Utilized	What It Looks Like When Overutilized
Your clients' reluctance to venture forth and take risks can make for a cowardly or disinterested appearance, neither of which are desirable identities when positioning oneself for career opportunities.	Your clients share excitement about stretch challenges with team members. This conversation helps expand team members' horizons and gives them opportunities to join in the adventure, thus heightening awareness and willingness to stretch.	Your clients focus on the most adventurous assignments to be found, leaving the mundane elements of the job to subordinates to pick up. Unless your clients and their reports are test pilots, risk should be balanced in their work.

Career Behaviour 3: Development Suggestions—Example Two

Underutilization	Optimal Utilization	Overutilization
Help your clients integrate expanded experience through stretch assignments into conversations so people will be aware of how their professional boundaries are expanding.	By accepting and even seeking out stretch assignments, a signal is being sent to team members that a growth and development disposition is valued and respected in others. The willingness to take reasonable risk is a virtue in your organization.	Help your clients keep their managers and team members abreast of what is being done in stretch assignments so everyone can fully appreciate and also learn from the experience.

Career Behaviour 3: Takes on Stretch Assignments—Example Three

What It Looks Like When Underutilized	What It Looks Like When Optimally Utilized	What It Looks Like When Overutilized
The less your clients are willing to stretch current roles and responsibilities, the less commitment to the job is displayed. Senior management notices who is willing to take risks and who is not.	Your clients build a reputation for taking on the tough assignments and then presenting their teams, complete with new proposed organizational initiatives, at their managers' doorsteps, thus reinventing the jobs and the function of the department.	So eager are your clients to find adventure that their managers feel forced to find exciting assignments. The managers meanwhile wonder why your clients are so bored with their current jobs.

Career Behaviour 3: Development Suggestions—Example Three

Underutilization	Optimal Utilization	Overutilization
Help your clients understand that, by keeping their managers aware of how much stretching is going on, their commitment to the organization is also being communicated up the ladder.	It is important for your clients to discuss the stretch assignments being accepted with their managers. The managers need to know how current stretch assignments work into the learning plans and career growth maps that have been worked out.	Help your clients balance a willingness to take stretch assignments with a willingness to encourage their team members to do the same, all in the context of the organization's strategic agenda.

Career Behaviour 4: Proactively Communicates Career Goals—Example One

What It Looks Like When Underutilized	What It Looks Like When Optimally Utilized	What It Looks Like When Overutilized
Leaving career goals a secret becomes a self-fulfilling prophecy: By asking for no help, your clients receive no help. When they give no help to their reports and team members, the legacy is passed on.	Your clients make it clear to everyone who reports to them that a future with the organization is desirable. They go on to model for their team members and/or reports what a path for growth looks like and how it is discussed.	Your clients focus on nothing but the next career target at the expense of focusing on current demands. Under such a scenario, their obsession with their next career move might cost themselves a good shot at the target they desire so much.

Career Behaviour 4: Career Development Suggestions—Example One

Underutilization	Optimal Utilization	Overutilization
When your clients are unsure of how to discuss career development, line them up with an HR professional to become more familiar and comfortable with the career planning process.	Help your clients to adopt the adage: When in doubt, ask. Personal and professional growth begins where the comfort zone ends. Help your clients become willing to seek assistance when entering uncharted territory.	A future focus must be balanced with the realities of present position and the current roles the organization needs filled. Help your clients to take advantage of every objective guide they can find to keep career in perspective and in the context of the organization.

Career Behaviour 4: Proactively Communicates Career Goals—Example Two

What It Looks Like When Underutilized	What It Looks Like When Optimally Utilized	What It Looks Like When Overutilized
When prompted to discuss a development plan, your clients express little enthusiasm or desire to move into larger responsibilities.	The organization, through its HR function, is committed to growing and developing its talent. Your clients stake out a path to accepting increasingly greater organizational responsibility.	Your clients are so concerned about being on a fast track out of the current position that there is a lack of considering how important it is to gain experience and increase knowledge. This does not favourably impress HR.

Career Behaviour 4: Career Development Suggestions—Example Two

Underutilization	Optimal Utilization	Overutilization
As the career development process becomes more familiar and comfortable, help your clients take an increasingly proactive role in expressing a healthy curiosity about new and different positions.	Help your clients to freely express to their managers and HR professionals career goals for the next five years so the professionals can help with plans and preparations to get there.	Every statement made about how quickly and how far your clients and their reports want to move should be accompanied by a statement expressing their willingness to study, learn and develop new skill sets.

Career Behaviour 4: Proactively Communicates Career Goals—Example Three

What It Looks Like When Underutilized	What It Looks Like When Optimally Utilized	What It Looks Like When Overutilized
When offered career advancement opportunities, your clients turn them down in favour of staying in the safe space they currently occupy.	Your clients take full advantage of the career counselling available in order to make the type of career move decisions that make the most sense personally and for the organization.	By sending a premature message that they are after their manager's job, your clients give their managers the impression that there is a lack of understanding as to what the manager's job entails.

Career Behaviour 4: Career Development Suggestions—Example Three

Underutilization	Optimal Utilization	Overutilization
Help your clients to carefully consider how to make judicious choices about career opportunities that are offered and take advantage of your and/or an HR professional's learned assistance.	By acting as a role model for career growth, others are encouraged—including team members, direct reports and peers—to set themselves on career developments paths.	Help your client explore ways to let the manager and others superior in the organization know that there is an awareness that their jobs require enhanced skills and advanced knowledge to be successful.

Career Behaviour 5: Seeks out Situations that Promote Individual Growth—Example One

What It Looks Like When Underutilized	What It Looks Like When Optimally Utilized	What It Looks Like When Overutilized
Your clients hide from promotion opportunities like one of the organization's best-kept secrets. They then wonder why nobody offers them a promotion and become resentful.	Your clients pay attention to the growth and development needs of the organization and respond when human resources need to be multiplied and/or enhanced to move the organization forward.	Your clients raise their hands indiscriminately thinking only of how to get attention with the hopes that it will pay off in the long run. However, they have no plan or career map to follow, so they are not sure what to expect as a promotion offer.

Career Behaviour 5: Development Suggestions—Example One

Underutilization	Optimal Utilization	Overutilization
Help your clients seek multiple kinds of experiences to receive grooming for future roles. In the course of their practising, they will become increasingly familiar and comfortable in letting their work be known to others.	Since people are likely already aware of the strengths and weaknesses of others when functioning in a role, you can help your clients better appreciate how they can become more aware of their own strengths and weaknesses.	Help your clients make more informed decisions about when to step up and what kind of expanded responsibility is best suited personally and professionally in the context of the organization. Help your clients take a more proactive role in being noticed for current successes and accomplishments.

Career Behaviour 5: Seeks out Situations that Promote Individual Growth—Example Two

What It Looks Like When Underutilized	What It Looks Like When Optimally Utilized	What It Looks Like When Overutilized
Your clients play hide-and-seek when the manager or HR leader comes looking for someone to promote, hoping the manager and/or HR person will do the seeking out. This approach bears no risk for the employee.	Your clients become part of the dialogue that identifies the need to seek out volunteers to move the organization in new directions. As the conversation progresses, your clients will become part of the solution, often without noticing.	Your clients volunteer quickly in search of greener pastures and then try to escape the tasks involved with current projects. They want the glory without the grunt work. They want the success without the sacrifice.

Career Behaviour 5: Development Suggestions—Example Two

Underutilization	Optimal Utilization	Overutilization
Help your clients and their reports accept personal responsibility for career growth and development. The HR professional is an asset not necessarily an advocate. Help your clients understand that there is emotional risk involved in stepping forward to be counted.	As a coach or a manager who coaches, you can help your clients seek out stretch assignments that are challenging in new ways. To mitigate the sense of risk, you can slowly and incrementally help your clients get used to the idea.	Help your clients deal with what is troubling them in their current jobs. A move to another job should be for seeking more professional challenges, not fewer. The pursuit of opportunity should not be about escaping a bad or untenable situation but to grow and develop.

Career Behaviour 5: Seeks out Situations
that Promote Individual Growth—Example Three

What It Looks Like When Underutilized	What It Looks Like When Optimally Utilized	What It Looks Like When Overutilized
Your clients are genuinely not aware of how to recognize opportunities that will bring a career enhancement and, therefore, do not seek to be available when able to contribute.	Your clients not only volunteer for change leadership in the organization but also help spread the word that change will bring benefits. Your clients become champions of positive and planned change and invite others to participate and benefit.	Your clients volunteer not knowing what is being volunteered for, but assume the project must be (a) important or (b) better than what they are doing now. Others, including upper management notice and your clients can become known as volunteer junkies.

Career Behaviour 5:
Development Suggestions—Example Three

Underutilization	Optimal Utilization	Overutilization
Make it an active concern to contact HR and your clients' managers to explore what opportunities are available that will provide your clients with a platform to demonstrate increased interest and participation in the organization.	Teach your clients to check in not only to find out where the opportunities exist, but to step up and offer even more. Help them to be put first on the list to be notified and to stay on top of discussions of organizational change and transformation. Help your clients get their names on the short list for change leadership opportunities.	Help your clients make career decisions that are consistent with the career path you helped them map out. Encourage your clients to study opportunities hard before deciding about them. Ask questions of those who have volunteered before, conduct thorough research and form knowledgeable conclusions.

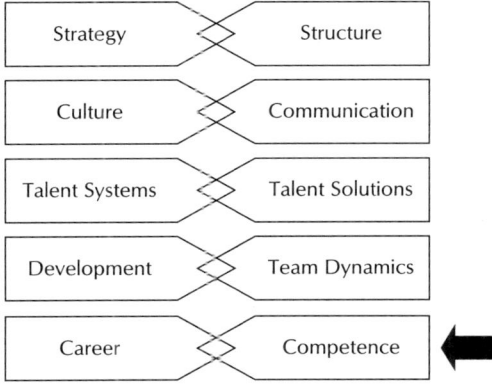

Competence Behaviour 1:
Manages Time Effectively—Example One

What It Looks Like When Underutilized	What It Looks Like When Optimally Utilized	What It Looks Like When Overutilized
Your clients are constantly behind and feeling overwhelmed by the time pressures to get work completed. Time demands seem unreasonable to your clients.	Your clients plan time well so that projects can be done in a reasonable amount of time with a reasonable amount of effort. Their skilled use of time is a good role model for their team members and direct reports.	Your clients feel so invincible that anything can be done at the speed of light. Far too much is taken on and this causes a failure to get it all done because the original time projection was too optimistic.

Competence Behaviour 1:
Development Suggestions—Example One

Underutilization	Optimal Utilization	Overutilization
Help your clients develop a healthier and more realistic notion of time. This will take time, some training and a lot of practice, guided by you, to gradually help your clients use time more efficiently and effectively.	Effective time management can be learned—and will be—once there is a commitment from your clients to develop new and improved behaviours. The time invested in learning time management skills is invested well.	Help your clients learn to look at the time available and the abilities needed to complete a project in a more realistic context. Delivering more than is promised in less time should be the goal you can deliver on more often than not.

Competence Behaviour 1:
Manages Time Effectively—Example Two

What It Looks Like When Underutilized	What It Looks Like When Optimally Utilized	What It Looks Like When Overutilized
Your client's team members impose on others for a bail out because they commit to much more than can be completed in the amount of time allotted. This is a habit. Directs and peers hate to see your clients coming.	Your clients invite others to participate in appropriate ways to share the burden and responsibility for projects, always allowing them sufficient notice to plan their time wisely. This responsibility sharing increases a sense of ownership.	Your clients panic and recruit everyone possible to join in on the crisis, even before it becomes a crisis. People eventually stop helping because these demands are unreasonable and annoying.

Competence Behaviour 1:
Development Suggestions—Example Two

Underutilization	Optimal Utilization	Overutilization
Study the tasks your clients agree to do, break them down into time segments and help your clients seek additional help for those tasks that call for assistance and do the rest on a schedule.	Help your clients learn how to look at tasks not only in terms of how long they will take to complete them but also in terms of how many people need to be involved. This is essential project management training.	Help your clients learn to set priorities so that every task does not appear to be of equal importance. In reality, few things are. Your clients will rest better when the most critical tasks go off their plates first.

Competence Behaviour 1:
Manages Time Effectively—Example Three

What It Looks Like When Underutilized	What It Looks Like When Optimally Utilized	What It Looks Like When Overutilized
Your clients may have had plenty of warning but still wait until the last minute to begin. When finishing on time is impossible, it feels as if there was not enough time allocated to begin with.	Your clients use reminders to check the progress of a project on a regular basis in order not to fall too far behind. Even short-term projects never become crises. Crises are often de-escalated to manageable problems.	Your clients work around the clock and have no life balance in order to get projects done sooner rather than later, thereby finishing early and then crash physically and emotionally, wasting the time that was saved.

Competence Behaviour 1:
Development Suggestions—Example Three

Underutilization	Optimal Utilization	Overutilization
Help your clients determine the reasons why operating in panic mode comes naturally to them. Discover why things need to be an emergency before attention is paid. This behaviour can be unlearned.	Help your clients work on the cognitive aspects of why time management is an issue and learn methods and techniques for setting priorities. What is learned will help teach others to recognize and deal with their issues of time management reluctance.	Help your clients to weave all successful behaviours into the same tapestry. The life balance referred to earlier is helpful in setting realistic priorities and keeping perspective in time commitments and time use.

Competence Behaviour 2: Adapts in Light of Future Trends—Example One

What It Looks Like When Underutilized	What It Looks Like When Optimally Utilized	What It Looks Like When Overutilized
Your clients refuse to grow and develop despite what everyone else accepts as a need to adapt with change and progress. The fear of the future is hard to budge.	The higher your clients rise in positions of leadership responsibility, the more comfortable they become around strategic thinking and the proper combination of operational, tactical and strategic (future) focus.	Your clients are so out in the future they look like they are enacting a Star Trek episode. There does not appear to be anything being done to address the needs of today.

Competence Behaviour 2: Development Suggestions—Example One

Underutilization	Optimal Utilization	Overutilization
Help your clients overcome being threatened by change and the need to adapt. Help your clients practise and become proficient at accepting small changes at first.	You help your clients overcome the tendency to resist change and future trends. This gain has a great deal to do with personal comfort zone and how growth begins where your clients' comfort zones end.	Help your clients seek professional help, if necessary, to balance their focus and attention between the realities of today and the anticipation that should be given to the future.

Competence Behaviour 2:
Adapts in Light of Future Trends—Example Two

What It Looks Like When Underutilized	What It Looks Like When Optimally Utilized	What It Looks Like When Overutilized
Your clients do not give their team members the opportunity to adapt due to your clients' insistence that their team members cling to the same outmoded policies and procedures that your clients refuse to give up.	Looking to the future as a leader is made a richer exercise for your clients by including the future considerations of their teams and how their team members' responsibilities will evolve over time. Your clients' growth and ability to adapt to future trends is the model for the team's adaptability.	Your clients lead their teams in preparedness for future trends to the point that team members must take care of current business needs on their own time. Keeping their teams that out of time management balance creates frustration and resentment from the team members.

Competence Behaviour 2:
Development Suggestions—Example Two

Underutilization	Optimal Utilization	Overutilization
Help your clients learn the skills needed to accept change and allow their team members to practise becoming comfortable with change.	When considering future trends, your clients think about the dynamics of their teams and what new demands and opportunities they will face as your clients develop new leadership skills.	Help your clients continue to develop leadership in team dynamics and help team members to use their time effectively. Teaching others helps clients learn.

Competence Behaviour 2: Adapts in Light of
Future Trends—Example Three

What It Looks Like When Underutilized	What It Looks Like When Optimally Utilized	What It Looks Like When Overutilized
Senior management loses confidence in your clients for not continuously adding value to the organization and for holding others back from adding value because they refuse to adapt.	Your clients fully appreciate the symbiotic relationship that exists with senior management. Your clients' adaptability in light of future trends is in large part informed by how much help senior management needs to move the organization along.	Senior management appreciates your clients' future focus but is troubled by their inability to deal with the needs of the present. They are aware that your clients are out of time balance and life balance and are expecting them to fix it.

Competence Behaviour 2:
Development Suggestions—Example Three

Underutilization	Optimal Utilization	Overutilization
Help your clients demonstrate through best practices their growing ability and willingness to adapt. Help them offer assistance when accepting change and passing the learning along to team members.	Your clients perceive that everything in one's personal and professional life ranges from solid to fluid, and that the relationship with the team, peers and senior management should be viewed as in a constant state of adaptation.	Your clients' success in balancing time techniques and procedures must be shared with senior management as well as with the entire team in order to receive the needed support, encouragement and guidance.

Competence Behaviour 3: Demonstrates Effective Problem Solving—Example One

What It Looks Like When Underutilized	What It Looks Like When Optimally Utilized	What It Looks Like When Overutilized
The thought of confronting a problem is frightening to your clients. Your clients' style is to ignore or avoid problems altogether. This means that problems are rarely solved unless they somehow resolve themselves.	Your clients are fast to acknowledge issues as they arise, but deliberate when arriving at a solution, properly assessing the urgency of the problem. Your clients understand the need to prioritize and apply the best and most effective remedy to the problem.	Your clients look at everything as a problem and do not distinguish or prioritize among problems that need urgent attention and those with less immediate down side. Truly important issues are given the same attention as merely interesting ones.

Competence Behaviour 3: Development Suggestions—Example One

Underutilization	Optimal Utilization	Overutilization
Help your clients work towards understanding the personal reasons why they avoid confronting problems. Is it a habitual avoidance? Do they lack the necessary skills? Are they simply engaged in the wrong activities?	Even though your clients are considered effective problem solvers, they continue to seek out objective feedback in order to avoid being tripped up in a blind spot. They remain alert at all time to the possibility that problems might arise.	Help your clients understand the need to distinguish between what is interesting versus what is truly important by determining priorities in the context of your client *and* the larger organization.

Competence Behaviour 3: Demonstrates
Effective Problem Solving—Example Two

What It Looks Like When Underutilized	What It Looks Like When Optimally Utilized	What It Looks Like When Overutilized
Your clients frustrate their team members who are eager to solve problems but are blocked by your clients' reluctance to provide them the necessary permission or resources to do so. Worse, your clients refuse to acknowledge that problems exist.	Your clients do not rely on personal opinions to arbitrarily arrive at solutions but consult with their teams, peers, senior executives and other key constituents. Consensus is not expected, but collaboration is always sought after for maximum buy-in.	Your clients hoard all the problems for themselves or insist that the entire team react to any size problem like a fire drill in an anthill. As a result, both your clients and their teams' problem-solving preparedness and effectiveness is severely diminished.

Competence Behaviour 3:
Development Suggestions—Example Two

Underutilization	Optimal Utilization	Overutilization
Help your clients focus on personal leadership development, especially in the field of team dynamics, as it will help with leading team members to become skilled problem solvers themselves.	Problem solving can be a science unto itself. Help your clients involve their team members in action-learning exercises designed to keep their problem-solving skills sharp, flexible and ready to be deployed at all times.	Help your clients learn that setting priorities is one of the most important skills to learn together with their teams. Help them learn to hold each other accountable while honing problem-solving skills.

Competence Behaviour 3: Demonstrates Effective Problem Solving—Example Three

What It Looks Like When Underutilized	What It Looks Like When Optimally Utilized	What It Looks Like When Overutilized
Your clients do not impress senior management with their continued failure to resolve issues senior management feels someone at your clients' level should be able to reconcile. Furthermore, your clients do not seem to feel senior management's approval is all that important or necessary.	From senior management's perspective, your clients form healthy coalitions among interdisciplinary teams that result in collaborative problem solving This effective problem-solving behaviour ranks your clients among the candidates for entry into senior management circles.	Senior management might be initially impressed that your clients can dispatch the troops to ferociously attack problems, but they will scratch their heads when they review overall financial and operational performance in your clients' departments.

Competence Behaviour 3:
Development Suggestions—Example Three

Underutilization	Optimal Utilization	Overutilization
Help your clients get real about the importance of senior management's opinions. Then help your clients learn how demonstrated problem-solving abilities—in organizational context—make senior management happy.	The ability to solve problems swiftly and effectively is not information to be kept as proprietary to the department or team. Help your clients learn to spread the good news and best practices around problem solving. Urge them to volunteer to promote and deliver problem-solving training.	Help your clients to do more than raise a cloud of dust, make a lot of noise and not much else. Senior management will be impressed when it can be demonstrated that their teams can anticipate and resolve complex problems quickly and sustain the solution over time.

Competence Behaviour 4: Shows Confidence
When Taking on Responsibilities—Example One

What It Looks Like When Underutilized	What It Looks Like When Optimally Utilized	What It Looks Like When Overutilized
Your clients avoid accepting any responsibilities other than those that are imposed and/or cannot be refused without the threat of job loss. When senior management asks for heroes to step forward, your clients close the doors to their offices and turn off the lights.	Your clients pay attention and know that confidence, or the ability to expect a certain outcome, is based on experience. That is why your clients show confidence when taking on new responsibilities. They have experience in consistently helping deliver the desired outcome.	Your clients are overly confident in taking on new responsibilities and take on more than they should, and/or take on new responsibilities that they are not qualified to handle, thereby blocking opportunities for peers, messing things up, and possibly overworking their teams.

Competence Behaviour 4:
Development Suggestions—Example One

Underutilization	Optimal Utilization	Overutilization
Help your clients make the transition from viewing change and new responsibility as burdens to looking upon change and new responsibility as opportunities to earn rewards and recognition.	You continuously help your clients understand and accept that some will always look upon new responsibilities and change as burdens, especially if they are not equitably distributed. Your clients commit to level the load.	Help your clients identify the underlying cause of their need to demonstrate overconfidence and bravado. Help them find a more appropriate and optimal balance of ability, competence and workload.

Competence Behaviour 4: Shows Confidence
When Taking on Responsibilities—Example Two

What It Looks Like When Underutilized	What It Looks Like When Optimally Utilized	What It Looks Like When Overutilized
Your clients erect a partition around their departments to fend off available responsibilities and/ or change opportunities— thereby not giving team members the opportunity to grow and develop. Neither your clients nor their team members do anything to impress senior management or each other.	Your clients' teams naturally look to your clients for signs of anxiety or concern when taking on new responsibilities. The hard-earned confidence your clients demonstrate is a positive sign to everyone. Your clients still make sure everyone receives the learning and development to fully understand the issue.	Your clients immediately hand off responsibilities to team members without discussion— not in an act of proper delegation or consideration for their time and abilities—but in an act of inappropriate urgency. There appears a desire to be quickly get rid of the threatening responsibilities as if they were hot potatoes.

Competence Behaviour 4: Development Suggestions—Example Two

Underutilization	Optimal Utilization	Overutilization
Help your clients learn that acceptance of additional responsibility is not a solitary activity. If their teams are firing on all cylinders, they will be in a good position to champion change and share new responsibilities.	Carrying workload and work distribution issues a step further, your clients understand that the equitability of responsibilities is a function of their leadership and subject to the beliefs and practices of organizational culture. Help them push cultural constraints outward if necessary.	Help your clients learn to engage the team in discussions about the implications of accepting responsibilities *before* committing to take on the additional load. Help your clients call for collaborative decision-making when it comes to accepting new responsibilities.

Competence Behaviour 4: Shows Confidence When Taking on Responsibilities—Example Three

What It Looks Like When Underutilized	What It Looks Like When Optimally Utilized	What It Looks Like When Overutilized
It is natural for senior management to give your clients additional responsibility as a sign of confidence in the ability to grow and develop. When your clients refuse to accept new responsibility time and again, senior management will pass them over.	Senior management develops more and more confidence in your clients as senior management observes, over time, acceptance of additional responsibilities—as needed by the organization—by your clients and their team members.	Your clients' exuberance and willingness to be overloaded as well as to overload their team members with additional responsibilities appears gratuitous to senior management who hoped to see better-balanced judgment.

Competence Behaviour 4:
Development Suggestions—Example Three

Underutilization	Optimal Utilization	Overutilization
Help your clients reflect on the value of demonstrating confidence in one's work. More importantly, help them to see how they are imploding their own career with their reluctance to take on new responsibility and champion change.	Avoid overstepping role boundaries when studying and commenting on organizational culture and workload. Help your clients be willing to graciously accept praise and recognition—and pass it forward to their team members—for willingness to shoulder more or simply work faster, smarter and cheaper.	Help your clients think of new responsibilities as good opportunities only if they can be balanced and appropriate in their distribution. Your clients must understand and accept that new responsibilities will not reflect favourably on them unless they can be delivered on time with an appropriate amount of effort.

Competence Behaviour 5: Exemplifies Leadership Behaviours Valued by the Company—Example One

What It Looks Like When Underutilized	What It Looks Like When Optimally Utilized	What It Looks Like When Overutilized
Your clients dismiss the ways that senior management defines leadership responsibilities. Your clients run a perpetual risk of alienating senior management by redefining the organization's leadership values and priorities.	The way your clients demonstrate leadership is seamless to the stated values, beliefs and behaviours of the organization. Your clients are walking, talking mission statements and vision statements for the organization.	Your clients take leadership issues to such an extreme that they become a caricature of the organizational culture and everything that goes with it. Others have trouble taking your clients' leadership seriously and they lose credibility.

Competence Behaviour 5: Development Suggestions—Example One

Underutilization	Optimal Utilization	Overutilization
Help your clients study and get to the bottom of the apparent appeal of resisting conformity and cooperation. Help them identify and quickly get past the reasons they push back against leadership values in the organization.	Your clients remain aware of barriers to the organization's cultural expectations around leadership. Your clients will clarify such misunderstandings and not allow resulting disconnects to derail their commitment to exercise leadership to support the organization's growth.	Provide guidance and direction as your clients seek objective assessments of their personal presentation styles by soliciting 360-degree feedback. Help your study and fill the gaps between how they want to be perceived and the way they are perceived by others.

Competence Behaviour 5: Exemplifies Leadership Behaviours Valued by the Company—Example Two

What It Looks Like When Underutilized	What It Looks Like When Optimally Utilized	What It Looks Like When Overutilized
Your clients do not encourage or support their team members or peers in striving for or adopting any of the leadership behaviours that will enhance their career opportunities within the organization.	Your clients accept the leadership challenge to be everything the organizational culture expects them to be and encourages others to accept as much leadership responsibility as they are competent to handle.	Your clients use company values and definitions of leadership inappropriately to justify nonproductive behaviour and inappropriately severe applications of organizational policies.

Competence Behaviour 5: Development Suggestions—Example Two

Underutilization	Optimal Utilization	Overutilization
Help your clients discover how helping others access leadership opportunities reflects well on them, and help them not to hold team members back from taking full advantage of advancement opportunities.	Your clients understand and work continuously to develop leadership abilities in themselves as well as the leadership potential of everyone on their teams. They know and teach others that the development of everyone helps the organization thrive.	Beware of a rules-driven approach that prohibits individuality, flexibility, adaptability and innovation. Help your clients learn that good leadership produces positive outcomes. It does not suffocate the positive energies and synergies in the organization.

Competence Behaviour 5: Exemplifies Leadership Behaviours Valued by the Company—Example Three

What It Looks Like When Underutilized	What It Looks Like When Optimally Utilized	What It Looks Like When Overutilized
Senior management is deeply concerned for your clients' futures with the organization because your clients can not seem to rise to the level and quality of individual and group leadership that justifies the organization's investment in them.	Your clients understand that organizational culture is the aggregate values and beliefs of everyone in the system. Furthermore, your clients lead in such a way as to reflect and sustain those organizational values and beliefs wherever possible.	Senior management is turned off by what appears to be gratuitous efforts on the part of your clients to fit into leadership ranks. For whatever reasons, they see your clients as over the top and not good ambassadors for the organization.

Competence Behaviour 5: Development Suggestions—Example Three

Underutilization	Optimal Utilization	Overutilization
Help your clients understand that their futures are at stake and there is no time to lose in turning around their questionable leadership situations. Help them take advantage of the organizational leaders' knowledge by asking how to fill the leadership gaps.	You help your clients understand that there is an interdependent relationship between them, their employees and their bosses that sustains their lifestyles and provides the major building blocks for their career aspirations. Sound leadership benefits everyone's interests.	You can help your clients connect the dots between the type of leadership that reflects and supports the organization's cultural values and what they are capable of and competent to provide. Then help them adopt those refined leadership behaviours and best practices.

Epilogue

This book began with a detailed treatise by ICF Global CEO, Magdalena Mook, extolling the virtues of coach accreditation. Her well-informed and well-researched argument is also a healthy dose of common sense. As long as the coaching industry remains unregulated, there will be no uniformly applied standards to ensure consistency, continuity and minimum standards of quality in the delivery of coaching services. As Magdalena explained, this is especially true when coaching leaders in organizations where much effort and investment are made to ensure consistent, enterprise-wide standards of excellence in leadership behaviour.

It is only fitting that this book closes with a peek into the future of coaching in enterprise environments as well as the craft of life coaching. That future is called *coach supervision* and it has arrived. Take the time to read the recent paper authored by J. Thomas Tkach and Joel A. DiGirolamo of ICF titled 'Coaching Supervision' (2018).[1] In this report, Tkach and DiGirolamo cite research conducted and opinions rendered by the European Mentoring and Coaching Council (EMCC), Association for Coaching (AC) and ICF.

Coaching supervision is not only widely practiced in Europe, it is mandatory for credentials from the EMCC and the AC. Coach supervision is, at its essence, a coach supervisor and a single coach or group of coaches working on the coach's work, that is to say, the craft of coaching. Tkach and DiGirolamo explain how coach supervision is distinctly different from coach mentoring.

---

[1] Available at: https://coachfederation.org/coaching-supervision-4/

When coaching enterprise-wide, the most efficient way to ensure coaching continuity and consistency in approach and quality of outcome—to ensure that coaching in every coaching engagement is aligning what the leaders do best with what organizations need the most—is to install coach supervision. How else will our enterprise-wide Ten Commandments be remembered, much less enforced?

About the Author

A former Walt Disney Company Marketing/Entertainment Division writer and line producer, and McGraw-Hill Divisional General Manager, Robert John Hoover has been active in leading the global contextual coaching and strategic talent management consulting practices at Partners in Human Resources International in New York City since 2006. John is a *New York Times*, *Wall Street Journal* and *Businessweek* bestselling author on leadership, organization development and organizational behaviour. John is certified by ICF as a Professional Certified Coach and is an adjunct faculty member at Fielding Graduate University where he teaches media psychology, organizational design and leadership, and at the American Management Association where he teaches communication skills, delegation, leadership and strategic thinking. He recently lectured at the University of Massachusetts at Amherst and coached MBA students at the Yale School of Management. In 2016, John began teaching Foundations and Theories of Coaching at NYU.

John created the curriculum for a new graduate certificate course at the City University of New York's Graduate School of Professional Studies. The new programme, Coaching in Organizational Context, integrates theory and practice of executive coaching with organization development and organizational change and transformation as outlined in John's co-authored 2009 book—*The Coaching Connection*. Besides lecturing at universities such as Columbia and Vanderbilt, John has been consulting and coaching clients in entertainment, media and publishing for over

20 years and has produced celebrity fundraising events in Los Angeles, Nashville, Phoenix and Washington, D.C. that have raised millions of dollars for Childhelp USA, March of Dimes, the Muscular Dystrophy Association, University of Southern California School of Fine Arts and the Alliance for the Arts in Thousand Oaks, California.

John is also the author of the bestselling book *How to Work for an Idiot: Survive & Thrive...Without Killing Your Boss*, which has sold over 200,000 copies worldwide in more than 24 languages and is available as an audiobook.